# PHANTOM TRAIL

To Geraint Jerkins,

Companion of the spirit.

Best wishes

Michael Vickers

# PHANTOM TRAIL

✦

## DISCOVERING ANCIENT AMERICA

*TRAVELS IN AMERICA'S "DISNEYLAND OF ANTIQUITY"*

*Michael Vickers*

iUniverse, Inc.
New York  Lincoln  Shanghai

# PHANTOM TRAIL
## DISCOVERING ANCIENT AMERICA

Copyright © 2005 by Michael Vickers

All rights reserved. No part of this book may be used or reproduced by any means, graphic, electronic, or mechanical, including photocopying, recording, taping or by any information storage retrieval system without the written permission of the publisher except in the case of brief quotations embodied in critical articles and reviews.

iUniverse books may be ordered through booksellers or by contacting:

iUniverse
2021 Pine Lake Road, Suite 100
Lincoln, NE 68512
www.iuniverse.com
1-800-Authors (1-800-288-4677)

ISBN-13: 978-0-595-34931-9 (pbk)
ISBN-13: 978-0-595-79645-8 (ebk)
ISBN-10: 0-595-34931-5 (pbk)
ISBN-10: 0-595-79645-1 (ebk)

Printed in the United States of America

# COVER ILLUSTRATION

*POVERTY POINT*—A principal centre of the Moundbuilder Culture, c.3800 BP (Before Present), on the western periphery of the Mississippi flood-plain, near Monroe, North-east Louisiana.
(Use of artwork image by permission of Jon L. Gibson*)*.

This book is respectfully dedicated to the
Phantoms of the Trail, and to those Americans
Who helped reveal them to me.

# *Contents*

*Introductory* . . . . . . . . . . . . . . . . . . . . . . . . . . . . . . . . xiii

Chapter 1   New York Plates—In the Deep South!? . . . . . . . . . 1

Chapter 2   Mammoths at Town Creek . . . . . . . . . . . . . . . . . . 5

Chapter 3   Thank You Mr. Roosevelt . . . . . . . . . . . . . . . . . . 10

Chapter 4   Cherokee Encounter . . . . . . . . . . . . . . . . . . . . . 15

Chapter 5   Spoiled for Choice . . . . . . . . . . . . . . . . . . . . . . . 23

Chapter 6   Georgia—An Official Welcome! . . . . . . . . . . . . . 27

Chapter 7   New Echota—A Shadow Descends . . . . . . . . . . . 30

Chapter 8   Etowah—A Living Presence . . . . . . . . . . . . . . . . 36

Chapter 9   Of General Sherman—and the Good Book . . . . 40

Chapter 10  Piedmont Country and the Crimson Tide . . . . . . 46

Chapter 11  "Alabama Pecan Mudslide"! . . . . . . . . . . . . . . . . 53

Chapter 12  Peaches and More! . . . . . . . . . . . . . . . . . . . . . . . 57

Chapter 13  Ghosts of the Confederacy . . . . . . . . . . . . . . . . . 62

Chapter 14  Luncheon Special . . . . . . . . . . . . . . . . . . . . . . . . 69

Chapter 15  The Edmund Pettus Bridge—Selma . . . . . . . . . . 72

Chapter 16  Old Selma and New . . . . . . . . . . . . . . . . . . . . . . 75

Chapter 17  Roots Deep in the Mounds . . . . . . . . . . . . . . . . . 82

| | | |
|---|---|---|
| Chapter 18 | Old Cahawba and the New South | 92 |
| Chapter 19 | Spirits of Moundville | 105 |
| Chapter 20 | Best-Kept Secret! | 112 |
| Chapter 21 | Chickasaw Homeland | 120 |
| Chapter 22 | Owl Creek and Sites South | 127 |
| Chapter 23 | The Golden Spire | 133 |
| Chapter 24 | America's "Hot Corner" | 139 |
| Chapter 25 | Grand Village and Natchez | 146 |
| Chapter 26 | The Heart of Ancient America | 152 |
| Chapter 27 | Mounds, Snakes and Mystery Treasure | 158 |
| Chapter 28 | Safeguarding Catahoula Heritage | 166 |
| Chapter 29 | The Ancients Are Present | 171 |
| Chapter 30 | Deep in the Delta | 177 |
| Chapter 31 | Poverty Point | 183 |
| Chapter 32 | The Golfing Ancients | 189 |
| Chapter 33 | Secrets of Ouachita | 197 |
| Chapter 34 | That Ole Alligator! | 211 |
| Chapter 35 | No Fishin'! | 218 |
| Chapter 36 | On to "Indian Territory"—Oklahoma | 227 |
| Chapter 37 | Cherokee "Green Country" | 232 |
| Chapter 38 | Wyandotte Encounter | 239 |
| Chapter 39 | The Miami Agency—At Last! | 244 |

| Chapter 40 | Route to "Brown Country" .................. 248 |
| Chapter 41 | Indians and the "High Rollers" .............. 256 |
| Chapter 42 | Raptors of the Plains ...................... 263 |
| Chapter 43 | High Plains Treasure ...................... 273 |
| Chapter 44 | Clovis Encounter ........................ 280 |
| Chapter 45 | Heart of the Sierras ....................... 287 |
| Chapter 46 | Trees of Real Antiquity .................... 293 |
| Chapter 47 | Sedona Surprise .......................... 304 |
| Chapter 48 | Sun City Finale .......................... 310 |

# *Introductory*

♦

## *The American Land—Echoes of Antiquity*

America is a big country. Its land possesses great beauty, enormous variety, immense vitality. These are things that most who have lived or travelled in America know.

What comes as a surprise to many, indeed to Americans themselves, is that there was a lot going on in this continent many millennia before the arrival of our European ancestors.

America's culture reaches down deep into the sub-soil of ancient civilisations. These were great civilisations, high cultures. In their antiquity, sophistication and accomplishments they rival Egypt and the Fertile Crescent, cradles of our Western culture. But these (pre-American) are very different civilisations, deriving from very different traditions and cultures. And it is these which define what in reality America is.

The advent of European interest, then occupation, of the past 400 years has added a modern layer to this antiquity. But little more. The roots of pre-American culture are buried deep. They have their own logic and momentum evolved over the past 20,000 years and more.

And this takes me to the reason for writing this book.

In the course of travelling and researching in America prior to writing *Phantom Ship*, a novel I recently completed, I learned for the first time about the antiquity of the continent. I was spell-bound and awe-struck. It was a revelation. The fact that I made contact with all this antiquity on the ground, beneath my feet in Ohio, West Virginia, Kentucky, Illinois, the Mississippi Valley, rendered the impact all the more powerful.

While my experience of some of these ancient cultures did come into the story of *Phantom Ship*, I was aware there was much more. These were the *real* roots of America. I was hooked. Hence this present book

*Phantom Trail* is a description, as well as a recount of my thoughts and feelings while visiting ancient, as well as many modern places, mainly in the American South.

And while my initial intention was to focus exclusively on "the ancient;" and to attempt to convey some of my own impressions on witnessing at first-hand these great monuments shrouded in the mists of time, in fact I found that a good deal of my attention became directed to the people and realities of historic, indeed current times.

As anyone who has travelled in the South knows well, there are two, not-unrelated subjects which above all others reside at the forefront of Southern consciousness—the Civil War (1860-65), and religion.

While at the beginning of my tour I felt a measure of frustration that these "modern" issues were seemingly intruding and obstructing my deeper quest; gradually I came to realise there was in fact no intrusion, no obstruction. Rather, ancient, historic and "modern" blended into a continuity; a continuity with clearly identifiable common elements. That said, however, I would confess that it was not really until I settled down to write that the pieces of this jig-saw started to fall into place.

As for the tour, it entailed a lengthy sweep of 5500 miles which started at Charlotte, North Carolina, and ended at Phoenix, Arizona. Most time was spent in the Mississippi Valley, the vast, powerful and mysterious heart-land of the ancient Moundbuilders. It is not without reason that one finds here place names with the ring of a familiar antiquity, including Alexandria, Cairo and Memphis. The Great Valley of the Mississippi is indeed "the Nile of the American continent."

As the reader will discover, I learned much. It was for me a journey of discovery. And the revelations did duly help towards recognition and understanding of links and "missing links"—indeed links between our European, Black African and Indian "presents"—with an antiquity which rises much closer to the surface of the American present than certainly I ever guessed or thought possible.

But enough said. The reader will judge for him or herself.

# 1

# _New York Plates—In the Deep South!?_

*Ellerbe Springs, North Carolina*—Five minutes out of Charlotte International, starting for Town Creek Mound, and the heavens opened. A monsoon descended. High winds, torrential rain hammered down. Two cars stalled on the main road, Route 74 running east out of Charlotte. I took refuge with some Black youths at a road-side Dairy Queen. They drew my attention to something I hadn't noticed. The Licence plates on my rental Chevy were *not* North Carolina. They were New York. The youths asked where I was headed. When I replied, "The Deep South," there was much merriment.

"They *love* Yankees down there!" I was assured the plates should guarantee a "*warm* welcome!"

The rain now eased. After 40 minutes it lifted.

After one or two false starts, I cleared Charlotte. Driving over good single-lane highways, through high hardwoods and rolling green meadowland, I made it to Mt. Gilead. The night was fast drawing in. A phone call from a Service Station failed to produce a bed at the B&B I had picked off the Internet. However, I was kindly referred to Ellerbe and this hostelry

(Ellerbe Springs Inn). I could hardly have done better. And Town Creek Mound, my first place of visitation, is just up the road. I think I can say I have very much landed on my feet.

There was a little difficulty with the Car Rental people when I arrived at Charlotte. My contact, Andy, was not about. Other sales people at the desk were baffled by his arrangements. I'll have to speak with him to clear matters. Still, I got a good 'un. Two-door, Chevy Monte Carlo; not showy or attention-attracting—with the exception of the plates—and white, which should reflect a bit of the heat. Huge wheels and big tyres guarantee a smooth ride, and also should ensure that I, and the car, will not disappear down any back-road pot-holes. The air conditioner is heaven!

So here I am. It's 9:30 pm. Very dark, very humid. Temperature about 85 degrees, with promise of 95 tomorrow. The Inn, screened by stately oaks, other hardwoods and a few Southern Pines, is set back about 100 yards from the main road.

This rambling old restoration Colonial homestead is a splendid place. It was the summer home of Colonel Ellerbe, an 1820s owner of several South Carolina plantations. The mineral springs, highly prized for their healing powers by the local Pee Dee Indians, were a valued feature. Then came the Civil War. Col.Ellerbe's sister suffered the indignity of her heritage being sold off on the nearby Rockingham Courthouse steps.

The property has had a varied existence in the intervening years. The present Inn was built in 1906. Several secluded cabins are settled round the sizeable property. The present owner has done much to bring new life to the old Inn.

Two women, one young and pretty, the other older, both gentle and courteous with pleasant light Southern accents, have seen to my needs. The Mancunian British Airways stewardess under whose *aegis* I travelled today could learn much about simple good manners and customer care from these two.

One is reminded that this is a country of over 270 million people. Even in this relatively remote village, the muffled roar and rumble of road-train traffic, not unlike in Ohio and the Mid-West, is more or less constant.

It is difficult to accept that eight hours ago I was looking down on the glacier-scaped barren grounds of Labrador and Northern Quebec. Mid-May and the ice and snow still had a firm grip on these rugged ancient lands extending to the horizon. Even the St. Lawrence in its lower reaches was bounded by ice on both sides. Yet here it's a sultry 85 degrees on a quiet Southern night, as settled in this big wicker rocker, I smoke my Hamlet cigar on Col. Ellerbe's front porch.

Certainly, Dame Fortune has smiled. A gracious, rambling house within its frame of white clapperboard and green shutters; casual, relaxed, not done-up, not fast-fooded. A pleasant stopping place with its hanging planters full of pink-blooming petunias.

About to retire, I feel a light brush against my trouser. I look down. A barred-ginger cat with big marmalade eyes looks up. She politely greets me. I scratch her back and ears. She is, I later learn, the Resident Cat. Her name is Gracie. Gracie's colleague, and Deputy-Resident Cat, George, a large dark tabby has also materialised. He accepts my homage while with pricked ears he maintains alert surveillance of his property. Large black winged beetles whiz about and smack into windows and shutters. George is off in hot pursuit.

In between the rumble of the road-trains I am tuning in to the silence and listening, feeling for the land.

I've ordered an early breakfast, 7:30. Then I'm off.

# 2

# *Mammoths at Town Creek*

*Town Creek, nr. Mt. Gilead, North Carolina*—Departure from Ellerbe Springs was difficult. Just the right kind of place for me. It was nearly 9:30 by the time I'd turned back onto the main road.

I back-tracked to Town Creek Indian Mound. The day was by then well hotted-up. Down a back road and there in a broad forest clearing it was. Rising to modest height, it was located at the back of the plaza within a wooden pallisade in the wider setting of green parkland. Within the modern, brick-built, air-conditioned single-level site building, gift shop and display areas were light, bright and immaculately kept.

There was an excellent video for a start, courtesy of University of North Carolina, Department of Anthropology. Then a look round the display area. Then a bus-load of school-children arrived. But, surprise, surprise; all were very well-behaved. Three lady teachers—one the spitting image of Helen Mirren—kept a tight rein.

Then a guide took us round the site. He was excellent. We were fascinated. And the children, all about 10 years of age, asked many very sensible questions. But best of all, he demonstrated. First, the use of spear against an imaginary Woolly Mammoth; then spear with flint point; then spear with atlatl (an ingenious spear-throwing device); and finally plain bow and arrow. The point of his demonstration was to show improvements in penetration, force of blow and killing distance. I took a quick look round. The solemn faces suggested we all fancied the chances of the Mammoth! Then as a special treat, he demonstrated use of a blow-pipe. Very accurate!

Even more fascinating was his account of life and death within the Town Creek pallisade some 1000 years ago. After clambering up the stepped slope of the Temple Mound and into the sacred space of the High Priest's Temple we found seats on the benches ranked against each of the Temple's four mud and wattle walls.

Our guide explained many things. How the gradual rotation of the sun's rays through the central vent above the sacred fire served to identify the seasons, the solstices, important tribal events and festivals. How it was very important for the Chief Priest to keep the sacred fire alight. How damaging for the people and dangerous for the Chief Priest it could be if the fire went out—for extinction of the fire, could mean extinction of life. How tribal life was organised on the clan principle—wolf, bear, beaver and deer. How tribal councils made decisions on the basis of prolonged discussion and clan consensus, rather than our modern adversarial way where there's always a loser—an excluded and aggrieved party. How women organised and controlled much of tribal life and family property. How Indians, understanding the basic principle of genetics, prohibited marriage between members of the same clan.

How the upbringing and training of children moved outside the authority of the nuclear family, and became the responsibility of the mother's brother, not the children's father—a provision which met with vocally expressed approval of many on the benches!

In the burial hut, initial mirth and chatter gave way to sombre, thoughtful silence. With life expectancy of 20-25 years, and high rates of infant and child mortality; with one of the displays showing a child being lowered by grieving parents into a shallow grave complete with grave goods thought necessary to meet life requirements in the next world, the penny dropped. "Had we lived at that time," observed one solemn girl, "that child could be me!" The other children eyed their classmate owlishly, then hurried to depart the darkness of the hut for the light of midday. A picnic lunch awaited them on shaded tables outside the pallisade.

Safe now in the familiar modern world of Cokes, Pepsis and carefully un-boxed KFCs (french fries and fried chicken), there were shrill squeals of delight, and no doubt relief, as they descended on the tables and tucked in with a will.

After saying thank you to our guide, then picking up a few craft items from the Gift Shop, I had a few final words with Site Manager, Archie Smith.

Did they have a "Friends of Town Creek," or the like, and could I join?

There was no such body, I was informed.

"But why?" I asked.

People locally, and often from a considerable distance, tended to come once, Archie explained. Often they came as children with a Primary School group—like this one today. They did not come again. There was no call for a "Friends Group." Support came from the State and the University of North Carolina.

It surprised and puzzled me that a site of such enormous cultural importance to the State and indeed the Nation could be subject to such public apathy. Here was a vital exposed root of the continent's culture. It was linked to other roots of the continent's culture. It was not just important, it was essential its significance be recognised. Was I really to accept that a culture capable of putting a man on the moon could blot out such stunning, such enriching realities? Surely there must be more. My tour, I was certain, would provide the insights and answers.

It was time to go. In mid-day heat, now well into the 90's, I departed for the west of the State, ancient homeland of the Cherokee people.

I made slow progress. In three hours I covered 50 miles as I now circuited Charlotte going west. This area was heavily populated by the mid-1700s. It still is. I was astonished at the densities. The car air conditioning helped raise my spirits and ease my frustration, as did a gallon bucket of ripe strawberries purchased for $5 at a road-side stand. Absolutely delicious.

Finally, about 6 pm, I cleared the traffic. At the same time I got my first glimpse of the Blue Ridge Mountains. In need of a bed I tried one or two recommended places. No luck. I decided therefore to keep pushing west and take my chances. With the light fading fast, I spotted a B&B sign. I followed the arrows. Fifteen minutes later, having negotiated a series of steep-pitched switchbacks I was deep in the mountains. Then quite suddenly on my right the B&B materialised. No ordinary B&B this. Fantastic, bright, modern house with lots of glass, light and soaring wooden beams.

And here I am. I had an excellent sleep. I have just consumed an equally excellent breakfast. I would have preferred less, but I got more. The home-made blueberry muffins I couldn't resist. This B&B is called, Inn at Mill Creek, which being beside an old mill pond and the bustling mountain stream which feeds it, is entirely appropriate. Brook Trout splash about in pursuit of hatching midges. Speckle, the resident dog, and I make a closer inspection. The trout, plump and frisky, vanish into the depths. I check my watch. Once again I want very much to stay. The peace and quiet, the green forested mountain, the bustling brook and this splendid house. I would be quite content to settle in. Do I really want to press on to ole Miss, and eventually Phoenix? Am I really going to manage the 5000+ miles of driving? Might I not best stop here?

Any doubts I might have are removed by my attentive host. "Sorry. No vacancies." Accommodation is filled for the next several days. With regrets, I therefore pack up, and by 9, the heat already building, am winding my way back up the switchbacks. There is, I console myself, one important benefit in departing now: conservation of cash! B&B in America, I am learning, is at the costly end of the accommodation market.

# 3

## *Thank You Mr. Roosevelt*

*Cruso, The Great Smokies, North Carolina*—I think I've arrived! The Pearly Gates have opened! "Unbelievable!" as our Margaret would exclaim. Once again, Dame Fortune has dealt me a superb card. After last night I didn't think I could do better. But I did.

I am deep in mountain wilderness. On both sides of this amazingly light and bright Frank-Lloyd-Wright-inspired "cabin" elevated high above the valley, cascading streams complement the silence with their steady, soothing rush and babble.

Hardly a cabin, but a small and magnificent house, this place is superb, absolutely perfect! And should I wish to explore Cold Mountain, all I have to do is follow the track beside the house up, and up, and more up!

I have already checked the lower stream for alleged Mountain Trout. Using childhood gear; willow stick, line, hook and worm, and scrambling over mossy boulders in the fading light, I searched a few tumbling pools. Nothing doing. Had I my fishing gear, there are rivers below, crystal clear, very cold, and begging to be tested with a fly. Such rivers! Proper trout rivers. Fast, shallow, rippled and bright! Ah well.

This morning, as I was setting out from Mill Creek, my host suggested that rather than return to Inter-State (IS) 40, I might like to try something more scenic. He directed me to the Blue Ridge Parkway. I am very glad he did. It is the most stunningly beautiful road I have ever been on. I was joining it at the tail end. In fact it runs 566 miles down the spine of the Appalachians from near Washington D.C. (including the 97-mile Skyline Drive) to the town of Cherokee near the State borders juncture of the Carolinas, Georgia and Tennessee. I traversed a mere 50 mile section. No trucks or rumbling road-trains! Commercial vehicles are prohibited! And no McDonald's signboards or any other commercial advertising. It too is banned. A few cars, a few motorcycles and bikes, and that was it. Maximum speed, 45 mph. A two-lane, excellently maintained road with gentle gradients, and wide, green, carefully mown verges. A magnificent stroll of a drive. The vistas and viewpoints provide a series of mountain, valley and river scenes of breathtaking beauty and great power.

Given the endless hills, steeps, secret places and valleys, what surprises me when one thinks of the 1830s "Trail of Tears" round-up of local Cherokees by the American Army (that is, when the remaining Indians in these their native homelands, were dislodged; and suffering *en route* heavy loss of life were marched off west, across the Mississippi to what then was called "Indian Territory" and now is called Oklahoma), is that it was possible to shift anyone—Indian or Whiteman—from this mountain country if he was bent on staying. And these military sorties and dragnets were carried out long before motorised transport and modern methods of access. It was all done by relentless foot-slogging, with horseback assistance where possible. Remarkable.

As for the Parkway, one can but utter a profound prayer of thanks to the spirit of Franklin Delano Roosevelt and the WPA (Works Progress Administration). Construction of the Parkway was undertaken and completed by one of its principal agencies, the CCC (Civilian Conservation Corps). Over the country as a whole, the CCC provided employment during the Great Depression of the 1930s for over four million people. Certainly, for the expenditure of 25 cents per worker, per day, the country got its money's worth. What was even more gratifying was to recognise not just here but with other CCC projects throughout the South, that the high quality of the original work has been sustained through maintenance of an equally high standard supported by continued funding from the Federal purse.

The young man, Charles, who owns and operates this "cabin" enterprise, is, like Jim from Mill Creek, another northerner. Jim came from Ohio; Charles is from New York State and is a Cornell grad. He's well settled in here; has about a half-dozen cabins—all modern-conveniences; but not excessive or fussy, just basic and sensible. Having been bitten by B&B prices my first two nights on tour, I was a bit wary. After a bit of negotiating I got a good price—albeit still on the pricey side for my budget—for the cabin rental. I may stay a second night if he doesn't chuck me out tomorrow.

Once again, I would be quite happy to settle in here. Forget my 5000-mile itinerary; forget the "Phantom Trail." It is a place where I could think, scribble, ponder, walk the hills and mountains, perhaps do a bit of trouting. It is my kind of heaven. This house, this mountain fastness, the whole feel of this place is set to the rhythmic energies and the powerful silence of solitary living and productive work.

I haven't yet made it to Cherokee. This afternoon I got as far as Waynesville in the valley. There was a massive traffic hold-up. So I did a bit of shopping instead. Tonight I treated myself to steak, a nice crispy green salad, marvellous beef-steak tomatoes cut in thick slices, awful lettuce, super-tender corn on the cob, alleged new potatoes that disintegrated into a grainy mush when boiled. What was good—steak, tomatoes and corn—was very, very good. What was bad—lettuce and potatoes—was awful. Orange sorbet popped into the food blender with the strawberry residue from my gallon bucket provided a tasty and refreshing dessert finale.

It has now cooled down. It did reach the high 90s today. But it was tolerable. The air conditioner in the car is very helpful. And the car, and I, have come through some rigorous tests. I was happy with this Chevy from the start. I am now coming to appreciate just how good it is. Coming down off the Parkway was a bit daunting. The drop down to the valley floor is a few thousand feet. I needn't have worried. The Chevy managed the ups and downs, the 180-degree switchbacks, the sudden swings and braking turns with no difficulty. It is a pleasure to drive—even if it *does* parade Yankee plates, always religiously observed I have noted. And this isn't even the Deep South. Indeed some might contend—misleadingly—that this isn't the South at all.

Enough of today's adventures. Tomorrow I shall visit Cherokee. Hopefully, I shall find some of my contacts. I'm looking forward to visiting Oconaluftee Village and the Cherokee Heritage Centre and its much-touted bookshop. Then if things turn out right I shall spend another night here in this superb Great Smokies wilderness retreat before moving on into Georgia. That is my plan!

# 4

# *Cherokee Encounter*

*Still Cruso, Great Smokies, North Carolina*—After all the sitting and driving of the past few days, I decided it was time for an early morning walk. Shake out some of the kinks. I had seen the trail beside the house. It seemed to offer the prospect of a bit of light exercise. Little did I know!

This "trail" in fact was hardly a track! No leisurely stroll this! I was in for a serious scramble! Starting off at a gentle gradient, the pitch increased sharply. The track then cut back and forth across a sizeable, cascading mountain stream strewn with slippery, moss-covered boulders. At times it went virtually straight up. I struggled on. Fantastic, magical rock waterslides dropped 80, perhaps 100 feet. I took frequent breathers. I reckoned my morning walks at home kept me in fairly fit condition. I was wrong.

About 2000 feet up, and with no end to the climb in sight, my lungs and banging heart told me enough was enough. I turned and looked down the track. It caused me to wonder how I'd got up! Across the valley, the sun was just lifting over the rim of the mountain. The feathery spring-greens of maple and sycamore were suddenly illuminated in this dappled, ethereal half-light. For a few moments I stood, and listened and watched. There was only the rush, splash and tumble of the stream. All else was still, silent.

Then overhead an early-patrolling crow spotted me. "Caw! Caw! Caw!", it shouted. A warning to all that an intruder was about. The spell was broken. I glanced at my watch. It was time to get back and get on.

After breakfast, I had a word with Charles. Would my cabin be available for another night? No, it wouldn't. However, if I was interested, another cabin was available. I had a look. Another splendid house, though this time of a traditional rustic log-cabin design. I said yes.

I decided on the Blue Ridge Parkway route to Cherokee. Charles said the scenery was even better along this final section. He was right. The road climbed even higher. The vistas over ripple upon ripple of blue mountain and winding green valley were breathtaking. It took me two hours—and another roll of film—to complete the 20 miles to Cherokee. I am not a picture-taker, I keep reminding myself!

Cherokee was a hive of activity. And it all seems to be about money. An entire separate development of riotous colour and flashing neon is devoted to casinos and gambling. Judging by the amount of traffic, trade is brisk even in mid-morning. Slowly, I made my way down this 'Corridor of Mammon.' Then I spotted the turn-off to Oconaluftee Village. Half-way up the winding approach road I turned into the Visitors Parking area. There were very few cars. Some young men and women were standing about near the Village entrance. I went over and had a word. The Village, I was informed, wasn't

*Cherokee Encounter* 17

open. Season Opening was Monday (this was Saturday). I should come back then.

If my main object on this tour had been to visit historic, rather than ancient/pre-historic sites, I would have been gravely disappointed. As it was I was only a bit put out. And there was a consolation prize. I met a very interesting man. His name is Davy. He is an artist, a lecturer, a writer, a businessman, an actor, amongst other things. He also is one of those in the vanguard battling hard to restore Cherokee tradition to modern Cherokee life.

"It is not an easy task," he declared. "But we are committed." The Oconaluftee Village is an important plank in what he sees as this progressive development. "Work at the Village is as important for the people working here—and these are mostly young people—as it is to the culturally appreciative visitor. Many Cherokee, like all other Indian tribes, or nations, have been progressively divorced from their roots."

He nodded towards the valley. "You have seen the cultural milieu in which the modern Cherokee is nurtured as you passed through town. The Whiteman's special gift. That is all that many know." He paused and glanced over at a stocky young man with a belligerent expression and a modified Mohican hair style who seemed to be leading group discussion. "So this is different. Working here for a while, puts them in touch. Starts the recognition and pride process; that there actually is more to life than a numbered bingo ball, and a one-armed bandit!"

I checked my watch. Time once again was getting on. I still had much to do. I asked Davy the location of the bookshop;

and did he perhaps know the whereabouts of Archie's contacts? Directions were provided. Finally, there was the "Trail of Tears" theatrical presentation. It was, I had been told, "a must." Where could I purchase a ticket? Davy shook his head. "No tickets, I'm afraid. Season doesn't start up till mid-June." He saw my disappointment. "However, if you want to have look at the Mountainside Theatre where it is performed, just carry on up this road to the top. Can't miss it....And you've heard of the Eternal Flame?"

I hadn't.

"Well it's the Cherokees' Sacred Fire. It was brought here from Oklahoma."

I was puzzled. "But isn't that back-to-front? Surely this is the Cherokee Homeland, not Oklahoma?"

"True," Davy nodded. "The situation is that the original Sacred Fire went West with our banished forbears in the 1830s. In 1951, Cherokee leaders from here trekked to Oklahoma and returned with coals from the Oklahoma fire. The fire was re-kindled here using these coals. You'll see it at the entrance to the Mountainside Theatre."

I thanked Davy, then following his guidance, pointed the Chevy up the hill.

The Mountainside Theatre—in fact it is an amphitheatre—was indeed impressive. As I looked down the sharp incline of rowed seats from my eyrie in the gods, I only regretted I would not be one of the 2800 to attend come mid-June. As for the Sacred Fire, the words of the inscription above it were certainly unambiguous. "This Fire will burn forever as a symbol of friendship eternal between the White man and the

Red man." I pondered this remarkable statement of trust. Were I a Cherokee, could I go along with it? Would the Whiteman one day dedicate such an inscription himself—and mean it?

Most of the rest of the afternoon was spent in the Museum of the Cherokee Indian bookshop. There was a tantalising collection. As at many other bookshops along the Trail, I had to choose. It was not easy. I settled on two Cherokee titles, plus four novels relating to Native American themes which it was impossible to acquire in England. I had discovered to my distress in Britain that "Books in Print" meant books in print from *British* publishers, or the British arm of an American publisher. Very little fiction relating to Native America, even by leading writers, and by British arms, was published in Britain. Thus it was a matter of seizing opportunities, and this one was golden. Together with my selections, I made a detailed list of other fiction offerings to retain for future reference.

By the time I left the Museum bookshop it was, at 98 degrees, very hot—at least it was for me; my internal thermostat was still adjusting. I then checked up on the people I sought. I wanted very much to visit the Cherokee Place of Emergence (Place of The Creation) and Sacred Lands which I knew to be in the mountains nearby. It was my hope that these persons might help. On two, Davy's directions drew a blank.

Eventually across the river from the main section of town I did locate the residence of Richard (Gee) Crow, revered Elder, and his remarkable wife Bernie, known State-wide and beyond for her traditional crafting skills. I rang the side doorbell. No reply. I thought I might try the front door. A furry black dog, about the size of a Norwegian Elkhound (I later learned it was a North Carolina Bearhound) occupied the "Welcome" mat. It opened an eye and surveyed me. It then curled a lip to display two rows of very white, very sharp-looking teeth and made some serious growling noises. Perhaps, like Cerberus, gate-keeper to the Greek nether world, it was guardian of the Cherokee sacred places? If so, it was doing a good job. I decided on discretion. The Cherokee sacred places were safe from my alien presence and prying eyes.

I returned to Cruso and my cabin via Waynesville and the valley route. Once again I was astounded at the density of the population and traffic. The roads were packed. Driving required close attention. There were many dips, bends and sudden turns.

My eye caught a road-side sign. "Fresh Bakery Shop". Tempted, I pulled in. Inside I looked for the "fresh bakery" goods and was distressed to find it was all "plastic" bread in cellophane wrappers. I squeezed a package of rolls. There was, I noted, no date stamp. I went to the counter. Where were the "fresh bakery goods," I asked? The assistant eyed me. Then in a casually dismissive tone which suggested that this foreigner might be forgiven for his ignorance, she informed me that this was a "Discount Bakery Shop." In other words, these were bakery products "fresh" from outlets where they had passed their sell-by dates. I thanked the assistant and departed.

Back now at Cruso and approaching the road leading to my cabin, I kept a sharp eye. That morning I'd seen—and dodged—a large rattlesnake at the side of the road. I looked carefully. No sign. I deduced it had either been having a snooze in the sun and had since removed itself, or that it was in the process of becoming someone's belt. Despite my dislike of snakes I hoped it was not the latter.

After grilling and consuming my remaining steak, again accompanied by corn on the cob and beef steak tomatoes—minus the self-destructing potatoes—I visited Charles at his office/cabin to pay up and say thanks. We got to talk a bit. Interesting man; thoughtful, perceptive, reserved; another escapee from the ethic of American middle-class, go-go, push-push materialist achievement. Yet also he's extracted the better values from this background of privilege—basic common sense, good grasp of reality, self-discipline, determination, stamina, attention to smaller as well as bigger details, ability to stand back, to assess.

Charles will do his own thing. It will bring light to the lives of many. Whether or not he is aware of it, Charles is in tune with the rhythms of this land; he is working towards the balance of lives long past, lives lived very close to this land. He will do well—that is, so long as he doesn't run afoul of the six-foot Black Snake that patrols his cabin. "He's harmless," Charles insists. "I often hear him at night in the loft. No problems with mice."

It's now Sunday morning. Once again it is very difficult to leave. I am so very comfortable here, in every sense. However, the car is now packed; I've taken a last look out over the valley and across at the green mountains still in the shadows. It's time to go. My eyes are giving me some trouble. Best that I don't push it today. Go easy. Perhaps stop over at Murphy and the River Hiwassee close to the juncture with the Georgia and Tennessee borders; maybe press on to my next Trail stop, Cartersville in Georgia and the nearby Etowah Mounds. Certainly, if I can manage it, I should try to clock up some miles. Phoenix is still a long way off.

# 5

## *Spoiled for Choice*

*Nantahala, North Carolina*—This being Sunday I decided I would attend church en route. As I drove the valley road from Cruso, back towards Cherokee and on to the Georgia border, I found myself spoiled for choice. There were churches large and small, and everybody was turned out in Sunday best. The Baptist faith—Full Gospel Baptist, Missionary Baptist, Reform Baptist, Pentecostal Baptist, Total Immersion Baptist, Evangelical Baptist, and others—was most fully represented, so it was a Baptist Service I chose to attend.

It was a large church in a small town. I was warmly greeted at the door by an elderly gentleman. He took me by the arm and delivered me to another very hospitable elderly gentleman. He started me up the aisle towards the front. But I suggested that as a visitor, might it not be best if I occupied a pew near the back? After all, I didn't want to occupy the seat of a regular. My guide smiled, nodded, duly turned me round, and near the back he signalled to some people who readily shifted over to make room. I thanked him and them kindly. We all smiled and expressed pleasantries.

I am not an expert on churches. Each, however, has for me a special feel. This church, with its sweeping balcony above, its ramped and flower-bedecked stage, its expanse of moss-green carpet, its light airiness, its off-white walls, felt like a theatre. Indeed, it was a theatre; a "Theatre of God." And a splendid performance it turned out to be.

After first being soothed by a Brahms violin and piano duet, we then were elevated by "Love Divine, All Loves Excelling." As a schoolboy, one thing I liked at Chapel was hymns. There were a number during this Service. I belted 'em out. Over the rest of the 11am to 1pm duration, the phalanx of robed clergy and elders on the dais presided over a Children's Service, which being Mother's Day was devoted to Mom, the unsung warrior in faithful service of the family; then we had a "Parent/Child Dedication" which saw proud parents lined up on the dais to have their infants-in-arms individually introduced to the congregation; finally we had the Pastor, a tall, slim, handsome man of early middle years and with a voice like silk, talk to us about "Jesus and the Love Bug"—an allusion to the Internet virus which that week had savaged computer systems world-wide. The gist of his sermon seemed to be that love was one virus that was very good for us, and that it was Jesus who could show us the way.

Before, during and after the service there were a great many messages and announcements; these providing an indication of the staggering range of activities fostered by the church and its parishioners. These ranged from traditional Notices of Birthdays, Marriages, Anniversaries and Deaths; to rousing messages for "Prayer Warriors", and Missionaries in the Field.

Finally, there was the weekly financial statement setting out in black and white the cost of doing God's business. This showed that the church and its ministry were continuing to maintain a small surplus on its $325,000 annual budget.

Altogether I was greatly impressed. This church, it seemed to me, was a very model of open, democratic accountability in all its manifold activities, and down to the very last cent. And when I shook the hand of the Pastor as we filed out after service, I told him so. He thanked me for my observation and confided that "this is the way the Lord likes us to do business."

Back on the road, the heat of early afternoon now pounding down, I was reflecting on the service, the Pastor, his congregation and the reassuring excellence of the example of community care they seemed to represent, when a thought suddenly occurred. The church was located in very much a mixed community. As I passed through town I'd seen plenty of black, brown and a few red faces. Yet at the service the only faces I had seen were white. Why then only white? Was it possible there was a flaw in this model of community excellence; that there might be limits to the inclusive Ordinances of the Almighty; indeed that the old "Southern (Baptist Convention) provisions" of Genesis, Chapter 9, Verse 25—"Cursed be Canaan (the son of Ham), a servant of servants shall he be to his brethren"—were perhaps here applicable? But maybe I'd got it wrong. Anyway, it was too late now to ask.

Having driven the stretch leading up to and on from Bryson City, I was relieved to enter a long corridor of cool and green. This was one of Western North Carolina's premier beauty spots, the Nantahala Valley. The river, wide, bright and clear ran its fast, winding course alongside the road. I pulled in at a shady park deep in the valley. Walking down to the river's edge I dipped my hand in the water. Very cold! Mmmm, I thought. Just as I reckoned. Superb trout waters. Then I heard a shout.

Looking up, one, then three, then a flotilla of a dozen or so canoes, their orange life-jacketed occupants shrill with excitement, came turning and sluicing down the rapids. No sooner had this company passed than another, then another and another came tumbling down through these rapids and on into the even faster waters below. I turned and went back to my car. So much for trouting! Perhaps at dark, or first light in the morning when the water had had a chance to settle from this intensive canoeing, there might be a chance. Certainly, any trout would be all too easily spooked.

But then, the up-side was that many of these people; very likely people new to the outdoors, and to the beauties of this magnificent area; these people would be adding their numbers to America's burgeoning army of concerned and active conservationists. Canoeists, just like fishermen, very quickly develop a strong attachment to favoured waters. And as I knew from experience, there are a lot more canoeists than trout fishermen. With canoeists involved, these mountains, this valley, these fast, clear-rippling waters have powerful allies. And when they shout, their numbers ensure politicians listen! Still, a pity about the trouting. But then the locals have probably got it all worked out. They usually have—the where, when, how and with what. Maybe next time.

# 6

# *Georgia—An Official Welcome!*

*Blue Ridge, Georgia*—Immediately on crossing the State line into Georgia, the light seemed suddenly brighter, the sun stronger and hotter. The land eased down, then flattened out. Driving became much easier. The road gradually widened; there were long straights. This was the famed Piedmont (foothills of the Appalachians) country. Huge expanses of rich, terra-cotta-coloured land extend to the horizon on both sides. The old cotton plantations are of course long gone. Where crops are planted, maize and some beans set out in thousands of neat rows are struggling hard for early growth in near-drought conditions. There has been no rain in this north-west sector of the State for nearly three months. Farmers are seriously worried. Despondent producers of the famed Georgia peaches find only small bullet-hard fruit in their wilting orchards. They are preparing for total crop failure.

I check the map. The old 1820s State Capital of the Cherokee Nation, New Echota, is not too far off the beaten track. I opt for a quick visit there before pushing on to Cartersville and the Etowah Mounds. At least with these lengthy straights I can finally make a little time. It's already 3 pm.

With the speedometer just touching a comfortable 75 mph and coming over a rise, I note a State Police car tucked off the road under a tree on the opposite carriageway. A few minutes later, I see a State Police car coming up behind me. Coincidence? I slow to let him pass. He does not pass. Rather he slows and flashes me to pull over. I pull into the shoulder; he pulls in behind me. In my rear-vision mirror I see him take a good look at my New York plate and grin broadly as he gathers up his notebook and steps out of his car.

Of packed, burly build and medium height, impeccably turned out in 'Smoky the Bear' hat, neatly pressed brown shirt and trousers and bright-polished badge, he appears. I lower my window. A waft of 95 degree heat negates the comfortable coolth of the air conditioning. He asks for my licence and car ownership. Fortunately my papers are all to hand. He examines them. I note a hint of disappointment. "You a visitor, then?" I reply in the affirmative. He regards me sternly, "You know the speed limit is 65?" I say I'm not sure. "You saw the 65 sign about a mile or two back?" I reply I've seen many signs with many different speeds the past hour since entering the State. "I clocked you at 78mph when you passed me back there." I don't argue, and try to look apologetic. "You're from England then?" I nod.

Fixing me with black, beady eyes, the Trooper tells me to stay where I am while he radios through from his car to check on my documents. I watch him in the rear-view mirror. He returns. I note he's relaxed a bit. He returns my documents.

"You'd best take *real* care. We take speed limits *very seriously* in this State." I apologise for exceeding the limit, but add that with all the different limits for local, state and Inter-State highways it is a bit confusing.

"Now let me give you a bit of advice. You want to watch your speed. This is your first and last warning. Lot of our boys out on the roads today. So you want to be sure you just ease back. *You hear?*" I said that I did hear and that I would proceed with care and attention to all speed limits. "Well," he said, "that's fine. You're free to go. And," he tapped his notebook on the roof of the Chevy, "I hope you enjoy your visit to our fine State of Georgia!"

# 7

# *New Echota—A Shadow Descends*

*Calhoun, Georgia*—Driving with some care, and now going cross-country on secondary roads, I arrived at the New Echota site with my watch showing 4:55. I prayed that 5 pm was *not* the closing time! My prayers were answered. Sunday closing I was informed by the site attendant was 5:30. Not ideal. Still I had a half-hour to have a quick look round.

From a site which had been levelled for plantation crops shortly after the resident Cherokees had been rounded up and driven off in the 1830s 'clearances,' the restoration achieved was remarkable. The sole remaining original building, Worcester House—family home and Mission House of Rev. Samuel Worcester—has been nicely spruced up and has a "feel"; though not a very pleasant one. Spirits remain restive here. The Supreme Courthouse, Print Shop, Council House and various residences are settled in building "footprints" as close to the original as possible. I view them all in their well-groomed parkland setting. I am perspiring freely. A large lady Site Attendant in a motorised golf cart is buzzing round locking up. I catch up with her. Would it be possible for me to have a little longer to look round? No it wouldn't. I point out that I've travelled all the way from England especially to visit sites like New Echota, and Etowah Mounds down the road.

"Sorry, but the gates are locked at 5:30. Nothing I can do. State ruling."

"Just like the Georgia State ruling to remove the Cherokees?" I reply.

She shifts her bulk on the buggy seat, looks at me sourly. "A State rule is a State rule."

Thinking I might try to make time in the morning, I ask when the site opens? "Closed Monday," she informs me. "All State sites closed Monday. And that includes the Etowah Mounds." Casting an anxious glance at her watch, she puts the buggy back in gear. "Gotta go now. You've got five minutes before we close." And off she buzzes.

This is not good news. I was counting on visiting Etowah Mounds tomorrow.

Departing the now-locked-up site, I loiter, reading and contemplating the writings on the mounted display boards. I note the 1836 words of leading Cherokee statesman Elias Boudinot. "The time will come when the few remnants of our once happy and improving Nation will be viewed by posterity with curious and gazing interest as relics of a brave and noble race,…perhaps only here and there a solitary being, walking, 'as a ghost over the ashes of his fathers,' to remind a stranger that such a race once existed."

I think of what *this* stranger sensed as he walked round the site. In fact I felt only a drawing down, a weariness and sadness; perhaps feelings not so different from those expressed by

John Ridge in 1826 as he faced up to what he rightly sensed was soon to come. "Solemn and gloomy is the thought that all the Indian Nations who once occupied America are nearly gone....In the lapse of half a century, Cherokee blood, if not destroyed, will wind its courses in beings of fair complexions, who will read that their ancestors, under the stars of adversity and the curses of their enemies, became a civilised Nation."

What, I wonder, would Ridge and Boudinot make of New Echota and the Cherokees today? Would they too sense the lingering lament for what has been lost, destroyed? Would they sense the anger, the shame, the outrage I feel right now at the betrayal, the treachery, the all-consuming greed of my racial forbears—treachery and betrayal which duly were to cost Ridge and Boudinot and thousands of their countrymen their lives?

The Whiteman by then had control of most of the Georgia land. Why could he not leave the so-called "Five Civilised Tribes" (Creek, Cherokee, Choctaw, Chickasaw, Seminole) who had accommodated to his customs and institutions, to get on with their own lives, on those lands remaining to them? What demon drove him to grab *all* the Indian lands; to drive the Civilised Indians, his friends, out? Did he not perceive the fatal symbolism, the terrible whirlwind which his actions shortly would reap? And did he not realise the shadow this would cast over the soul of all White America; an ever-darkening shadow which persists to the present day?

As I started up the Chevy, turned up the air conditioner and headed for nearby Cartersville and the Etowah Mounds, I was aware that a mood and an atmosphere was lowering down over my mind and my feelings. It was a mood and atmosphere that was to stay with me throughout the Deep South; one that was only slightly to lift as I made my way through Oklahoma, Texas, New Mexico and Arizona.

Yet while my White ancestors had brought disgrace on my race by their collective behaviour over the past three centuries, I was aware that harsh, cruel and unjust actions were nothing new to the peoples of these lands. Over the 1000 years or so preceding the arrival of the Whiteman, the old Mississippian leaders who dominated through priestly/political authority, ruled with an authoritarian, often bloody hand. Perhaps as in Ancient Egypt at the time of the Pyramids, so in Ancient America at the time of the Mounds? What is it in the lands of both which invokes this harshness, this severity, this authoritarian and feudal behaviour? In land so beautiful, so vast, so strong and powerful in its own right, one capable of fostering high cultures, it seems a contradiction.

Or is it?

The immense richness, the fertility of these lands stretching across the South and on both sides of the Mississippi invite intensive cultivation. And intensive cultivation of crops means deployment of mass labour if maximum productivity is to be secured—or it did until the start of labour-saving mechanisation some 150 years ago. It could be said that just as the Pharaohs ran the show in Ancient Egypt, and did amazing things; so the Mississippian Priest/Political leaders, the Great Suns, and indeed moundbuilding cultures before them, achieved equally great things when they ran the show in Ancient America.

Taken in this context, it might be suggested that the Whitemen who ran the show in Georgia and the South for the "Golden Century" (1750-1850), were simply following an established tradition. The mood may not be nice, the atmosphere may be oppressive, but the system was very efficient, evolved a high culture, and at its height, was enormously productive. It might even be suggested that it was only the inhibitions and prohibitions of a Democratic Constitution which served to hamstring, then destroy this engine of national wealth-generation; to hasten the decline of these fertile lands and those who ruled them.

Perhaps it is simply that modern America has been confronted with the decay and deterioration of a system which refuses to die. And yet, and yet. Is there not something in the very soil of these lands which gives rise to these passions, this stubborn-ness, this determination to persevere? At the same time is there not equally something in the soil of these lands which draws great cultures up only for them to decline and sharply to fall? Is not this what the archaeaolgical record, and the very few historic glimpses of America's Ancient Civilisations and cultures, show?

Perhaps in the end there is an even simpler, more basic perspective. Was not and is not the intrusion of the Whiteman in America akin to the Roman takeover of much of the ancient Mediterranean and Western world as it then was? While the Romans held imperial sway, the peoples of these lands found ways of accommodating. But once the alien Roman rulers had gone—driven out or simply departed—the local residents breathed a long sigh of relief and got on with life as *they* preferred to live it. Here in Georgia, as indeed in all of White-conquered America, it is as though the Romans came; that in the short period of their occupation they have left a profoundly alien imprint on the land and its peoples; and that they have not yet departed.

# 8

## *Etowah—A Living Presence*

*Cartersville, Georgia*—It was past seven by the time I reached Cartersville. The Etowah Mounds site is on the southern outskirts of town. I checked the gate. Locked. Everyone was long gone. And sure enough, the Opening Times sign showed that the site would be closed tomorrow (Monday). Having parked the car, I followed the security fence perimeter for about 200 yards. At this point there was a dip in the six-foot-high wire mesh. And behind the dip were two sizeable mounds, one large, the other smaller. I could feel their pull.

Would the Mississippians be offended if I paid them an after-hours visit? These mounds, the pallisaded town and the surrounding settlements, home to many thousands of people some 800-900 years ago, would have been busy day and night. Travellers and visitors, except during certain times of religious and ritual observance, were always welcome. I cast another eye over the mounds. I extended my sensors. No question; the vibrations were favourable. So over the fence I went.

Immediately there was a feeling. Not a vibrant buzz as at Chillicothe, or a tingle at Marietta by the steamy Ohio, but rather a sense of movement, vigour, of purposeful activity. It was still hot, but the evening sun now cast long shadows. As I passed beneath the Temple Mound, all 63 feet of looming height, spreading three acres at the base, I was aware of life all round me. This indeed had been a centre of importance, a Regional Capital perhaps vying with its sister metropolis Ocmulgee, 120 miles to the south-east, and Moundville, about the same distance to the South-west? Moving through the central plaza space towards what had been the main burial mound, standing at perhaps half this height, then past another principal mound and three lesser platform mounds, "residences for revered Village leaders" according to the literature, the sense of the place came through with force and certainty.

This was a minor Cahokia. Though there was not the chilling force of oppressive presence, nevertheless a feeling of watchfulness, of lurking apprehension was induced. Moving on to the river bank which bounded the town on one side, I looked out on fish traps exposed by severe low-water. And as I watched and pondered, suddenly busy brown bodies flash up; there is the happy clamour of women and children at work. A big carp-like fish is brought thashing and twisting to a bankside basket. Another, frantically seeking escape, careers over the shallows throwing up drenching jets of spray. It evades but briefly its animated, shouting pursuers. They pounce and two grinning youths manhandle it to the bank and into the big reed basket.

A little further down-stream, dugout canoes, some huge, are pulled up on the bank. Crew-men, their powerful copper-brown bodies gleaming from the sweat of their recent exertions, loiter, laugh and jest. Their masters proudly display to grave tall men in short-feathered head-dresses ornaments of flashing copper fire, great black translucent stones, bright coral, fine fluted silver and other rare and precious items.

I look back at the Temple Mound. In front of the Temple building on high, a man in bright-coloured garb signals gravely to the traders to approach. They quickly restore the displayed items to the baskets. At a barked order, two crewmen hastily approach and lift the baskets. The traders, still talking earnestly and gesticulating, make their way through the thronged open plaza towards the broad, terraced steps of the Temple Mound.

Suddenly I hear the blast of a car horn. I turn and glimpse a rising spume of dust beyond the boundary fence. There is another horn blast and another spiralling spume as a second car rockets past.

It is, I realise, time to go. My Etowah Mississippian friends have their busy lives, their challenging duties to attend to. As for me, a good "Knight's" sleep after what has turned out to be rather more than the rest-day I had planned, will be very welcome.

Post Script—Strange. Having had a restful "Knight" (at the local Knight's Inn) and a good sleep, I look out on this modern strip of garish neon. Even in these early hours Taco Bell, Burger King, omnipresent McDonald's are pulsing out their messages of mass consumption. There is much traffic and activity. I reflect. Busy though to my eye it all may seem, this I realise is but a faint glimmer, a subdued provincial bustle compared to great festivals, celebratory imperial events on these very lands beneath my feet some 800 years ago. These great events, these seasonal religious gatherings which drew added thousands from afar—perhaps like those traders I saw arriving last night—concerned triumphs and solemn observances bearing not only on the fortunes of the Great Sun of Etowah and these his subjects, vassals and devotees, but on all of Ancient America.

# 9

# _Of General Sherman—and the Good Book_

*Nr. Cartersville, Georgia*—Today, I think I can say I was properly introduced to the South. A few miles out of Cartersville, the Chevy slowed to pass through a small town which looked like it had been lifted directly from a Hollywood Western movie set. The town's main street corridor of squat, tin-roofed, grey-weathered clapboard buildings, the morning heat shimmering off road and roof conjured images of John Wayne, of Gary Cooper and "High Noon." Towards the far end of the corridor I spotted a gift shop. There was a large sign planted in front. "C'mon In And Have a Coffee on Us!" And so I did.

It was cool inside. Two big overhead fans, quietly whip-whipping round kept the air nicely stirring. The coffee was fresh, hot and welcome. I had a good look round. It wasn't crowded. I was the sole customer. There were a number of prints and paintings on display. A painting of the Etowah Mounds appealed to me; also two prints of an old house "in land," so to speak. I found the prints very compelling, but at the same time very disturbing. The feeling they evoked was one that first had been triggered at New Echota; that hovering sombre aura, that lowering, painful sense of loss.

"Do you know this house?" I asked the woman who ran the shop; her name was Jeanne.

"Just outside of town," she replied.

"It's got a very powerful message for me," I said. "The yellow house, the dark green leafy trees, the burning sky at sunset. I don't quite understand it. But it's telling me something."

She smiled, a small wry smile. "No doubt it is. It was one of the very few houses Sherman didn't burn when he and his army came through here."

"...Sherman?"

"Perhaps you've heard of him?" She cocked a bright eye up at me. "General William Tecumseh Sherman, Commander of the Union Forces in these parts?" Jeanne paused and slipped one of the prints into a bag. "This town was levelled, pillaged, burnt and destroyed in that 60-mile-wide swath he drove east to Savannah and the sea. Crops, animals, buildings, not to say people; all that was left was a smouldering ruin!"

Unwittingly I had touched a very live nerve. After a few moments of embarrassed silence and trying to turn the conversation onto a less sensitive subject, I asked if she had lived here long.

"About 15 years," she laughed. "Bit of a newcomer."

"And where did you come from?"

"Down on the Gulf. Mobile."

"It takes a bit of time to settle in with these people, then?"

Again, the wry smile. "You could say that. Folks are very close round these parts. Keep themselves to themselves; to their own kind."

"Their own kind?"

She sighed. "Well, when folk move into this area, the first thing that other folk ask is: 'What church do you belong to?' And upon the response of the newcomer much rests."

She saw my puzzled dismay. "For instance, if the newcomer says 'Methodist,' the response may be 'Hmmmph!'; if it's 'Presbyterian,' maybe 'Hmmmm'; if it's 'Baptist,' there may be a variety of responses, depending on what kind. Baptist is definitely the best thing to be round here."

"And what if you're Catholic, or maybe Episcopalian (Anglican)?"

She laughed. "Papists are highly suspect. And the same, more or less goes for Episcopalians."

I ventured further. "And what of followers of the Jewish, Moslem, or perhaps Hindu faiths?"

She paused. "Well, people aren't disrespectful. They don't call 'em names; at least not to their faces. It's just like they don't exist."

Having gone this far down the road, I took the final step. "And what if the newcomer says he doesn't belong to any church? What then?"

Jeanne looked up at me; still the wry smile. "Well then, that newcomer might just as well turn right round and leave town!"

And this was not the end of it. Alice, a colleague of Jeanne's who had come in from the back and who had been following our conversation, spoke up. She recounted the experience of her son. He had been invited to attend a "Fundamentalist" service. "Why," exclaimed Alice, "when he discovered this was a group indulging in snake worship, I can tell you he didn't stay long! He made for the door real quick!"

There is, I later learned, a considerable Fundamentalist following of snake worship throughout the South. "And it's all right here in the Good Book!" I was reminded by a fervent, and very-much-alive devotee I later encountered in southern Mississippi. My attention was directed to Genesis, the Garden of Eden, Adam and Eve, and the Serpent, and also to the New Testament Gospel of St. Mark (Ch16, v.18). So long as you "believe," the snakes—rattlers, the deadly copperhead, cottonmouths—are your friend. If not, they know! People regularly get bitten and die. Satan, it is believed, has "taken their spirit."

I thanked Jeanne for sharing her thoughts with me. It had, I said, helped me to come to terms with uncomfortable, disquieting feelings I was experiencing.

"And if I may ask," she inquired, "what is the purpose of your visit?'

I told her it was principally to visit sites throughout the South of the ancient Moundbuilders.

"And where are you heading?"

I said that the focus of my attention was the lands of Mississippi Delta in its middle and lower reaches. I mentioned I was particularly looking forward to the celebrated site at Poverty Point in Louisiana; that I had read and thought much about the high culture it had fostered some 3000 years ago.

"And what town is it near?"

I said it was in the heart of the Deep South near Monroe.

"That's not the Deep South!" she spat out. "That's *Yankee country!*"

"So where does the Deep South start in Louisiana?" I asked.

Her reply indicated that for this one had to experience New Orleans. There was a further hint that this culture might still extend to certain coastal areas, and perhaps as far up as the city of Alexandria in mid-Louisiana.

I checked my watch. It was already nearly mid-day. I was getting behind again. I thanked Jeanne and Alice. Not only was I pleased with my purchases, but I said that what she had discussed with me had provided much room for thought.

"Well," said Jeanne as she opened the door for me, allowing a blast of heat to enter, "Southern folk are hospitable, courteous and kindly." She flashed another one of her wry smiles up at me. "You'll get along with 'em just fine." Then she paused; I could see she was carefully weighing her words. "But just bear in mind that they all love their Bible. They just love the Good Book. As for that ole Civil War; well Sherman and his rag-tag army, why they just came through here yesterday," she fingered the door-handle, "or maybe the day before."

The Chevy was parked in front of the shop. I opened the trunk to stow my treasures.

Jeanne noted the New York plates. Like the Black youths in Charlotte, she laughed. "You want to be careful when you're down in ole Miss, and one or two other places. Down there, New York means only one thing. *Yankee!*"

I thanked her for the reminder.

"And one other thing. Some people may think your English accent's cute. But not all. A lot of people down there are descended from French, Spanish, Irish and German stock. They don't have pleasant memories of the English."

"But surely," I objected, "that was a long time ago?"

Again that wry smile. "As I've already indicated to you, folk down here have long memories. And they've had lots of time to let their thoughts fester. For many, there's not been much else to do. They don't forget! My own great-grand daddy was Irish. Came out at the time of the famine—you know, when all your nice English gentlemen landowners put profit ahead of their starving Irish tenants. Well my great-grand daddy had a bit of the Celtic language. Only words I learned from him in Celtic were swear words. They all referred to the English!" She laughed. "Wouldn't do you no harm to broaden that accent just a tad!"

# 10

## *Piedmont Country and the Crimson Tide*

*Mt. Cheaha, Alabama*—As I headed south, still staying off the beaten track, and keeping an eye on the speedometer—I had not yet mastered the Cruise Control system—the Chevy making easy work of these long straights, I reflected not only on what Jeanne had told me, the advice she had provided, but also on what I had seen—or not seen.

So far in Georgia I had seen very few Black people. Indeed, until I got to Cartersville, it was as though this was a White-only country. In Cartersville too, it was not until I drove through one down-town section that I saw any Black faces at all. And in that section, much of which looked like the wreckage left in the wake of an IRA bombing campaign, the Black presence was total.

It was evening and many people were out and about. I asked two youths standing casually in the road for directions. They took a good look at me, the car, the plates and were slow to respond. As one of them rolled a toothpick in his mouth and looked me over, it was easy enough to see what he was thinking: 'Who is this Whiteman? He a straight? Maybe an undercover drugs officer? FBI agent? Why has he come in here? What is he after?' There was tension in the air. Others were silently watching. Finally I got my directions, thanked the youths and drove on.

And now as I passed through this flat, rich land with its fine red soil, its huge expanses of hard-struggling maize and bean crops, I again saw no Black faces, and only the occasional White face, and this mostly behind the wheels of ancient, battered pick-up trucks. Vehicles, it seems, live long down here.

Half way down another long straight, I saw one of these vehicles coming towards me. It then pulled across the road, and in a cloud of dust stopped in front of a ram-shackle store with a big, rusty Coca Cola sign in front. A cold Coke would be welcome. I too pulled in.

Squat and broad, the store was cool and dark inside. There was no sign of the man from the truck. I found the old-style cooler, lifted the hinged metal cover, and removed a bottle of Coke nestled deep in a binful of crushed ice. It was very cold. I snapped off the lid and took a swig. Heaven!

"Nothing like a nice ice-cold Coke on a day like today! No sir!" A stout Whitewoman in a cotton-print dress that had seen better days, shambled in from the back. I agreed that a cold Coke was very welcome. We went on to talk about the weather, the three-month drought, the fears of the farmers, the threatened failure of the peach crop. Then a phone rang in the back. Nobody answered. I paid up and thanked her. "Y'all have a nice day, now," she called out as, with the phone still ringing, she shambled back out of view at slightly increased pace.

Another lengthy straight, then passing through the town of New Georgia, and suddenly I found myself rolling up a gently arced ramp and onto Inter-State 20 heading west. The traffic was heavy and fast. I put my foot down, pulled into the outside lane, set the Cruise Control (which finally I had mastered) at 73mph, and let 'er roll.

Hardly had I got myself and the Chevy settled into serious driving than we were over the border and into Alabama. I stopped at the Welcome Center. It was cool and spacious inside. I gathered a few brochures. There was not much about Alabama's Ancient Civilisations, its Moundbuilders, or indeed its most recent Native American inhabitants. But there was much about "The Crimson Tide." This, I discovered, was the State's most treasured icon of popular culture, The University of Alabama football team.

Assisted at the desk by a coolly civil young-ish man, I checked routes and sites. It was not till the end that I realised that the maps and brochures he was deftly opening for me was all being done with only one hand. The other was a neatly pressed sleeve casually tucked into his jacket pocket. As I stepped out into the furnace of mid-afternoon, I pondered. Was not this a meaningful metaphor for the South, as I was coming to feel it?

Before departing the tidily maintained Rest Area I took a brief look round. Flower beds were bright with red, pink, yellow and orange blooms. How, I wondered, did they manage it in this blistering heat? Orville, one of the gardeners, revealed the secret: *underground* watering controlled by time-switches on the tapped supply. And while Orville went on to inform me about the flora here in the Rest Area and in the Talledaga Hill Country beyond, I found I was not so much taking in what he said, but how he said it. It was his voice.

For the first time I was hearing a heavy Southern accent. I was entranced. It was just like cascading syrup; delicious, smooth; and with great lyricism, abundant gentle humour in the expression. There was an astonishing range of remarkable sounds when he got to talking about the weather, the need of rain to "plump up the peaches." Lovely!

Back on the Inter-State, the Chevy was hardly up to speed when the turn-off to the Talledaga Forest Parkway came up. Once again FDR's Civilian Conservation Corps (CCC) had done its stuff, albeit a mere 25 miles in this instance. It was a superb piece of single carriageway, clear of all commercial traffic, gently winding, dipping and rising along the spine of this lower-lumbar section of the Appalachian foothills. I was heading for Mt. Cheaha, which at 2400 feet is the highest point in Alabama. Deep in Creek (Indian) country, it is believed to have lain within the sovereign domain of the Great Suns of Etowah in the early years of the last millennium, and before this of the ancient Moundbuilding peoples who penetrated and first settled these lands up to 10,000 years ago.

I stopped at a hill-top lay-by.

Here was a very different kind of beauty to that of the Blue Ridge and Great Smokies. These mountains were in reality substantial well-wooded hills. Here was intense heat, open, dry land beneath high Southern Pine and hardwood; a heady scent of pine-needles rising from the red earth. I looked up. A pair of Turkey Vultures, wing-fingers extended, soared and circled, riding the up-draughts overhead.

A few miles further and the car was climbing sharply. Another two minutes and I was on the heights of Mt. Cheaha (Cheaha in Creek, means "high place"). Whether viewing from the breathtaking panoramic vista of Cheaha Restaurant, or the Summit Tower of the CCC-built edifice at Cheaha's peak, the spreading heat-hazed scene was one of deep green hills, parched brown uplands and winding emerald valleys. It was easy to see why the Creek peoples and those who preceded them in earlier millennia, placed such value on this land. Pleasing to the spirits of both the Upper and Lower worlds, it also afforded unparalleled opportunity for surveillance of life and movement ranging 25 miles in every direction.

Elated and awe-struck by the beauty and power of this great land-scape stretching out before me, and with my mind and spirit settling into life here as it may have been when the Great Suns of Etowah held sway here 800 years ago, I felt a tap on my arm. I turned to find a bearded Whiteman in Alabama State Park uniform standing beside me.

He nodded towards the distant hills shimmering in the heat. "Fine sight. But not so clear today." Josiah—for this, he informed me, was his name—paused, took a deep breath and sighed. "I bless the Lord each day for the privilege of working here." He chuckled. "And I also pray to the Lord each day that my bosses won't move me on!"

Josiah had worked here many years as a Ranger. To him Cheaha State Park was as close to Heaven on Earth as you can get. I offered my surmise that no doubt people who had lived here over the past several thousand years had felt much the same way, though perhaps with a particular appreciation of its strategic advantages.

Josiah fixed me with a measuring eye. "It's coming, you know. Coming soon!"

"It's coming?" I inquired cautiously

"Right there in black and white in the Good Book. Are you ready?"

There followed an impassioned, biblically erudite dissertation from Josiah on the "cess" into which America currently was plunged; on the portents of the Second Coming of Jesus Christ; of the need for Repentance; of the imperative "to be one with Christ" if Salvation was to be secured. "He that believeth and is baptised shall be *saved*," declaimed Josiah, "but he that believeth *not* shall be damned; Mark 16, verse 16."

This was not quite what I was expecting here on the heights of Mt. Cheaha. Scanning the roll and ripple of the distant skyline, I thought on all the ardent devotional exercises, the immensely complex cosmologies that Mississippians had evolved to link man in spirit and flesh to his worldly circumstance; of the specific, diverse beliefs of Creek, Choctaw, Chickasaw and Cherokee peoples; of the powerful observances that had served over 3500 years ago to bring order, security and the commitment of devotional labour on a massive scale to effect construction of the great, precision-engineered Earthen Mounds of the Mississippi Delta. And now another faith, one of world-range and great power was rolling across and rising from these rich Southern lands.

There was a sudden "Bleep! Bleep!" It was Josiah's mobile phone. He answered. His presence was required back at the office.

"Michael," he said, reaching over and grasping my hand firmly, "it's been a pleasure to meet you. Sorry, I've got to go now." He laughed. "But then that's always the way, isn't it? The important things being forced into second place!"

I replied that perhaps the time would come when we all got our priorities right; when "the last would become first." Josiah laughed, patted me on the shoulder, then turned and was gone.

# 11

## *"Alabama Pecan Mudslide"!*

*Calera, Alabama*—As I guided the Chevy down from Mt. Cheaha, then along narrow, winding pine-forested roads, I realised that time again was closing in. Already it was 5:30. Selma, well to the south, was my destination. I stopped and checked the map. It was too far to make it before dark. And I didn't want to push hard anyway. This after all was the heart of Phantom territory. This was the reason I was here. I wanted to give myself a full chance to see this rich and responsive land; to sense the power; to feel for the messages, the rhythms rising from it. Best therefore to drive on for an hour or so, then see what accommodation I could find.

About to head off cross-country again on dusty dirt roads, I spotted a Dairy Queen. I was parched and hungry. I pulled in. When I am travelling, I prefer to eat light. My stomach is a bit uncertain. But one thing it can manage is Ice Cream Milk Shakes. And in the absence of real dairy ice cream, Dairy Queen, in my view, provides a very good second-best, and at reasonable cost.

Checking the Menu List, I was about to opt for my standard "Chocolate Thick Shake," when my eye was arrested by an item on the Specials Board above the counter. "Don't Miss it! Today's Special: *Hot Double-Chocolate-Fudge Alabama Pecan Mudslide*!" I didn't even try to resist! Back in the coolth of the car, Mudslide in hand, I ladled with a spoon, then slurped with a straw. The fudge, the chopped pecans (a much-favoured nut in the South), the thick chocolate chunks peeled off the inside of the container, the thick ice cream itself; it all went down a treat. Superb. A meal in itself—which in fact was just as well, for as it turned out I wasn't going to eat again till morning.

An hour's driving in the fading light through great expanses of flat, sparsely-populated back-country, took me south of Birmingham and west to Calera, a small town straddling the Birmingham-Montgomery motorway. I saw a motel, but decided to press on to the next town, Montevallo, in hopes of finding something which might offer a little peace and quiet.

It was dark by the time I got there. Driving slowly up and down Montevallo's few residential streets I watched anxiously for B&B or Guest House signs. Nothing. Not even a motel on the outskirts. Things were beginning to look serious. I resorted to an approach I'd used successfully elsewhere when accommodation seemed non-existent and the hour was late. I pulled into a gas station. "Where is the Montevallo Police Station?" I inquired. The attendant, looking somewhat alarmed, very hastily told me.

It wasn't hard to find. After explaining my predicament, the Desk Sergeant, having first consulted two immaculately uniformed young officers—one White, the other Black; the first Black official of any sort I had seen since departing Charlotte—informed me there was neither Guest House nor motel in the town; that all private accommodation was occupied by students from Montevallo University. He advised me there was a very good motel in a nearby town. "Calera," he said, "is your closest possibility." It seemed to me in a town this size, there must surely be a spare room or two available. But there was no point in arguing. I'd best take myself, my New York plates and English accent, double back, and give Calera a try.

And that's what I did.

And here I am. Still at Calera.

I might add that breakfast measured up to its advance aroma. Hot, fresh-ground coffee, as many cups as I wanted; real fresh-squeezed Florida orange juice; a big plate of scrambled eggs, bacon, tomato, and sausage; lots of toast with real butter and raspberry jam; a few hot "biscuits," a Southern speciality akin to what I call a scone or a tea-biscuit, very tasty with butter generously applied; also a dish of grits. I'd always wondered what grits are. Now I know. A sort of translucent porridge made from coarse ground maize (corn), usually served with a generous dollop of butter. I tried them out. Not for me; at least not just yet. An acquired taste perhaps. And all of this for $3.50. Very nice indeed.

A point of interest. This restaurant/truckers' cafe is attached to the motel. Most of these "attached restaurants," I have learned, are operated separately from the motels. The reason? Apparently the Indian (from India) people who have got into the American motel business in a very big way, and who lease or own the motel facility, like all good Hindus, do not eat meat. And as most Americans do, the restaurants are subleased, or owned/operated by Americans, often locals. I can only say that if all the linked restaurants rustle up food of this quality, the arrangement has worked!

It's now nearly 9:30. The temperature is creeping up towards 95. It is very sticky. I was aiming to continue my back-road, cross-country travels to Selma. But I've decided on a short detour.

I was informed by my breakfast companions, John and Virginia, that I must try for some Clanton peaches. "They've got 'em. They're in! It's just down the road."

As I am very keen to taste a succulent Southern peach about which I have heard much, I have decided to head first for Clanton. "You can go cross-country to Selma from there. No problem," John told me.

So Clanton it is.

# 12

## *Peaches and More!*

*Clanton, Alabama*—A half-hour south from Calera on the Birmingham-Montgomery Motorway and there was the sign. "Clanton—Peach Capital of the South! Turn Off Next Exit." I duly turned. With visions of fat, juicy peaches dancing in my head, I pulled in at the first big road-side Fruit and Veg Market Store. "Fresh Peaches! Fresh-Picked Peaches!" shouted the sign.

There were other mid-morning customers nosing about. I checked the stands of Fresh Produce. Big heads of crispy lettuce, bunches of fat, red radishes, huge beefsteak tomatoes, lots of cucumbers, and red and green peppers (not the hot kind!), then a variety of greens, and potatoes, big or small, and loose or in 50 lb. bags. Finally I came to the fruit section. Lustrous purple grapes, seedless green grapes, huge pink grapefruits, Florida oranges, apples, lemons, kiwi fruit, a few baskets of strawberries, of cherries. It was nice to see all these high quality fresh fruits and vegetables. But where were the peaches?

A "Produce Assistant" was busily re-arranging the display of purple grapes. I tapped her on the shoulder. "Excuse me, I wonder if you can help me?"

The Produce Assistant, a large, smiling woman wearing a voluminous, loose-fitting T-shirt with "The World's Biggest Peaches" emblazoned across two huge technicolor peaches on the front, replied that she'd be happy to try. I pointed to the "Biggest Peaches" on her T-shirt. "That's what I'm after."

For a moment the sunny smile departed. Then she laughed. "Oh, Peaches? Yes, yes." I followed her back to the front counter. She pointed to a half-dozen small plastic boxes, each containing eight yellow-ish-skinned fruits about the size of a large plum. "These are what you're after. Fresh-picked this morning. Our speciality!"

I reached over and carefully squeezed the fruit. Bullet hard.

"Do you have anything bigger? Perhaps a little riper?"

She looked up at me. There was the hint of imminent injury in her manner.

"You see," I explained, "I'm travelling. Looking forward to a juicy peach or two for my lunch."

The smile returned. "Well, these peaches are a bit toothsome. But that's how a lot of folk like 'em. More vitamins and nourishment this way than when they're big and fat." She picked up a box, then another. "Seein' as how you're a visitor, I'm gonna give you a special price. I'm givin' you three of these for the price of two!" She laughed and juggled the boxes. "You've got plenty here for lunch, breakfast *and* dinner, and for a few days to come!"

I wasn't really interested in purchasing any of these peaches. But I didn't have the heart to say no. And they could be ripened. Still before paying up, I put a few questions to this woman, whose name I had now learned was Lula. What did she make of the shortage of rain, the delay of the season, of the threat of crop failure worrying Georgia peach farmers?

"Well," said Lula, "those Georgia boys are spoiled! We here in Alabama always make do with the weather God gives us. And He gives us, year on year, these lovely peaches. Sometimes they're big and fat. Sometimes they're small and firm. And sometimes there's a bit of one and a bit of the other." She laughed and put the boxes along with the bag of beefsteak tomatoes and two oranges I'd also bought into a bigger plastic box. "Just like all our chilluns," she fussed the oranges into place. "We love 'em all the same!"

I handed over the cash. She rang it up and gave me the change and a receipt. "So you're from the North?" she declared more than asked.

Taken off guard, I looked for a moment into those alert blue eyes. "And why do you think that?"

She nodded towards the Chevy parked outside the door. "Those plates."

I explained I was from England and that I was touring round the South looking at some of the old Moundbuilder sites. I'd started from Charlotte, I told her, and the plates were on the Chevy when I rented it.

"They knew you were headin' South?"

I said they did. But that in fact I'd picked out the car myself.

"Hmmm." She ran a thoughtful finger round her mouth. "Well, between you and them, you didn't do yourself no favors."

"Why's that?"

She laughed. "Well a lot of folk down here have strong feelings about Northerners. It's about a little quarrel we had with 'em about a hundred and fifty years ago. I expect you in England may have heard about it. It's called the Civil War." She checked over the items in the box and paused over one of the baskets of peaches. "You don't have to take them peaches if you don't want 'em."

I said that while they weren't quite what I was expecting, they were alright. I'd let 'em ripen up a bit.

She shrugged. "Well, that's fine then. You might just remember that folk down here do, errr, like to do our Yankee friends a favor when the opportunity arises, if you take my meaning."

I said I'd remember.

I was picking up my box of fruit and veg when Lula asked where I was now heading. Selma, I told her. "Can I make a suggestion?" she asked. I said I'd welcome any suggestion.

"Well, you'll be going south. Just a bit down the road you'll see a sign to the Confederate War Memorial. Now I know you're here to look up them ole Indian sites, or Moundbuilders, or whatever. But if you've got a few minutes, a visit there might give you just a tiny feel for why folk down here feel as they do." She touched my arm and smiled. "And I think you might feel somethin' too.…Anyway, I've done enough talkin' to keep me goin' a week—and I dare say, you too!"

Lula paused by the door, pensive in her "World's Biggest Peaches" T-shirt. "You know, us Southern folk ain't half as bad as some folk make us out to be." She cast a quick glance up at me. "You might care to bear that in mind when you're visiting Selma." She saw me out the door. "And you have a good day now."

# 13
## *Ghosts of the Confederacy*

*Marbury, Alabama*—I checked my watch. Only 10:30. I could manage it. It's true the Civil War was not on my agenda. And yet it was. And not just because it was so close to the surface of basic Southern feeling. But also because it might help me to start to get a grip, to gain some understanding of the immense power of this awesomely fecund land; of its strangely seductive mystery and menace; of the passions it engenders today, just as it did 150, 1000, 3500 years ago.

The sign to the Memorial—it is in fact called the Confederate Memorial Park—directed me off the highway and onto a dirt road. A mile or two, and I was at the entrance. Inside the Park along the loop-road, settled beneath tall Southern Pines, were several period buildings, a church, a Post Office and a timber-frame Museum & Gift Shop. I pulled into the Museum parking area. It was my turn to note the licence plates. Most were Alabama, a few were Georgia, and the same for Mississippi, Louisiana and Tennessee. In a covered open-air pavilion beside the Museum a considerable crowd of mostly elderly people were chatting and drinking coffee.

Lunch was already on the barbecues. Burgers and sausages gave off an appetising aroma.

One of the picnickers offered me a coffee. She then saw the sweat on my brow and the soaked front of my shirt. "Maybe you'd prefer something nice and cold?" I said I'd be most grateful. She duly produced an ice-cold Sprite. I thanked her. "My name's Georgia Pickens. But you can call me Miz Georgia. Most folk do."

From Miz Georgia, I learned that most of these visitors had come to pay their respects to Confederate Veteran relations buried in the Confederate Home cemeteries. They did it several times a year. Some of the men were members of the United Sons of Confederate Veterans; most of the women were Daughters of the Confederacy. Both these bodies, it was explained, continued to do much to ensure the names of the Confederate fallen were remembered and honoured; that the cause for which they had fought was not forgotten. This was the Alabama Branch.

The Home here at Marbury, 35 miles north of Montgomery the State Capital, had been set up some 35 years after the Civil War to provide for the care and living requirements of needy, and by then aging, Alabama Confederate Veterans. Only Veterans of the Union cause were granted Federal pensions. And as Alabama, like all States of the Confederacy, had been devastated by war and then systematically stripped and plundered in the post-War years, it could do desperately little for those who had suffered greatly for the cause and were in dire need.

A private initiative in the early 1900s resulted in donation of the property and construction of the Home. Two years later when the State of Alabama agreed to take on the administration and funding, the Home blossomed into an impressive 22-building complex. Residency reached a peak of 104 Veterans and wives during the World War I years. At least in their declining years, said Miz Georgia, these Veterans, many never fully recovered from terrible battlefield wounds and disablements, were afforded a measure of comfort, security and respect. "It was an opportunity for us to honour our own. My grand-daddy," she pointed to a cemetery across the open space, "lies in his grave over there." I could see tears were starting to run. "And I just love to come and visit with him. And he likes me to visit." She dabbed her eyes with a lace-embroidered hankie. "A person knows these things."

Miz Georgia shook her head and laughed. "Now don't you pay me no mind. I'm just a sentimental old woman. Never even met my grand-daddy, you know. He died before I was born. But it's a funny thing. I know all about him. And it's been no trouble knowing him just in the spirit." She snuffled and wiped again. "Maybe a bit like our Blessed Lord. We only know Jesus our Saviour in the spirit and we love him just fine."

Miz Georgia pointed now to the Museum. "That's the place you want to see. A chance to get to know a little bit about our boys on their home ground, you might say. I do believe you'll find it most interesting." I thanked Miz Georgia for talking with me, for sharing her thoughts, and wished her well with her picnic. I asked also that she send my best wishes to her grand-daddy; that she should tell him that an English visitor was thinking about him. She said she would.

Miz Georgia was quite right. The Museum was more than interesting. A brief tour provided the answer to my feelings, so far as the weight of recent history was concerned. By the time I'd finished I felt both privileged and humbled. It was now my turn for tears. In an under-stated, poignant way, the facts of the Southern cause spoke for themselves. There were the Confederate gray uniforms, the flags of Dixie, of Alabama, the rifles, the sabres, the knives and bayonets, the Battle Colours of the Alabama Regiments, the stark photos of soldiers in the field, the graven images of Old Comrades. And then there were the letters home from the front.

Finally there was the Farewell Address of General Robert E. Lee to his men of 10 April, 1865. Lee commended them for their efforts, their valour and their constancy. But then came the death blow. He informed them that the Southern cause was lost. The contents of this letter, in a few moving sentences, conveyed very powerfully the terrible wrenching sense of loss, not just of the War, but of an entire way of life. It was the death of the body of the South. But the spirit, as only a week or so travelling over this land and soil, rich, powerful and constant over the millennia, had conveyed to me, was very much alive.

About to depart the Museum, I noted two hand-written items, framed and mounted, in a dark corner. I read one, then the other. They completed and confirmed in this modern day, what General Lee in 1865, in the final despair and shock of defeat, had conveyed in those terse but deeply moving words to his men. These written items were brief poems. They were written by Sgt. Benjamin R. Gormley; the first in 1988, the second in 1992. I quote them in their entirety.

## *The Southern Dead Are Sleeping*

> The Southern Dead are sleeping,
> In a thousand Southern Glens,
> The moss and willows beckon,
> With the breath of Southern winds.
>
> Though the blood-stained Cross of St. Andrew
> Is tattered now and furled,
> They bore it high on every field,
> And o'er every ocean of the world.
>
> It wasn't through their failing
> That the gleaming turned to rust,
> And the dreaming of a Nation
> Is enshrined within their dust.
> Some would have their deeds forgot,
> Their monuments swept away,
> But while Southern blood flows in our veins
> Those knaves shall never see the day.
>
> Teach your children of their story,
> Of battles lost and won,

They must keep memory's light a'burning
Till Southern rivers cease to run.

The Southern dead are sleeping.

The second poem is entitled simply,

## *Confederate Veterans, 1937.*

Those ancient men are passing,
To a far and distant shore,
Where their comrades wait from long ago,
Beyond the battle's roar.

They once clasped hands with Destiny,
And gave away their youth,
For the dreaming of a Nation,
And simple Southern truth.

They sit before the fireside
In the dwindling Soldier's Home,
And speak of long-gone glories,
Of the haunted fields they roamed.

They bore their tattered battle flags
To the very gates of Hell,
And split the forest solitude
With their piercing Rebel yell.

Now they feebly totter
In their Memorial Parade,
Each year the ranks grow thinner,
And more graves beneath the shade.

When the last Gray Cavalier
Rides off to meet his God,
When the final flag-draped coffin
Has slipped beneath the sod,
When the final notes of Dixie
Have echoed down the wind,
'Twill be left to us, their Southern sons,
Their memories to tend.

# 14

## *Luncheon Special*

*Autaugaville, Alabama*—Back in the Chevy, driving over heat-shimmering, arrow-straight, terra-cotta dirt roads, the miles clocked up quickly. Again, these vast fertile lands, most in unkempt fallow, the rest under bean cultivation, extended to the horizon on both sides. All signs now pointed to Selma. With about 20 miles to go, I passed another sign. "Sarah's Diner," it announced; and in red letters below, "Luncheon Specials!" I checked my watch. It was lunchtime.

Sarah's was on the far outskirts of the village. A number of pick-ups of the traditional variety, and a few of more modern manufacture were parked under the tall pines at front. There was space close to the entrance. I eased the Chevy in.

Inside was a very full house. But finding an empty booth down the side, I slid in, poured myself a tall glass of ice-water from a big plastic jug chinking with ice cubes—a most welcome provision in all Southern eating establishments, I was to learn—and consulted the menu. I decided on "Sarah's Pork Chops Special;" this to include "Pork Chops Southern Style, cabbage, home fries and gravy, corn bread and grits," followed by a "Big Slice of Sarah's Home-Made Pumpkin Pie."

Sarah, a trim, quick, quietly spoken White woman came to take my order. "The Pork Chops Special," I requested, "without the grits, please."

The instant I spoke a sudden silence descended at the other tables. The all-white, all-male clientele, most in bib-and-braces overalls, concentrated on consumption of food. Only gradually did the low buzz of laconic Southern drawls resume.

Though a bit well done for my taste, the "Pork Chops Southern Style"—which turned out to be pork chops fried to a crispy frizzle—provided good protein bulk. As for the vegs, they were fine; I skipped the grits; and the large chunk of Pumpkin Pie was moist, tasty and altogether excellent. And all for the price of $3.00.

As I smoked a post-lunch Hamlet—a pleasant change from the terrorist non-smoking regimes operated by nearly all establishments I was to visit during my tour—and let my meal settle, I looked round. Interesting. Here I was, 20 miles from Selma, city of the big Civil Rights break-through of 1965. But where were the Black people? The only Black presence I had spotted here at Sarah's was through the serving hatch to the back kitchen. There, to the accompaniment of clattering crockery, two, large, heavily perspiring Black women could be glimpsed tending to the frying and cooking. Intermittently a black hand banged another laden plate onto the hatch counter. For the rest, it was a White-only exercise. White proprietor/waitress, White clientele, and now a White visitor—and, it was to be noted, all seemingly getting on with their respective businesses very nicely.

By the time I was ready to go, all but one of my fellow diners had departed. Each as he left, I noted, had taken a good long look at the New York plates. The remaining diner, Caleb was his name, noted what I was noting. "We don't get too many New York plates down this way," he observed.

I watched him for a moment. He worked a toothpick round his molars.

"You were round in the 60s" I asked?

He nodded.

"And those plates. They bring back memories then?"

He smiled, loosened one of his braces and shrugged. "Mmmm. Some."

I explained I was from England; that the car was a rental; that I was visiting the ancient mounds.

He looked across at me. "Well," said Caleb, slowly measuring his words. "No need to fuss. Them days of serious ill-feeling are long gone." He lifted his forage cap and scratched his scalp. "Besides, the weather's a bit too hot right now to work up any nastiness!" And with that he was up and gone, the screen door banging behind him.

# 15

## *The Edmund Pettus Bridge—Selma*

*Selma, Alabama*—It was past two by the time I reached Selma. First contact was with the customary fast-food/light industry belt, all soul-less blare and aimless hustle over pot-holed roads. Then came the desolate scatter of dense, semi-derelict shanty-town sprawl. Finally, moving into the core of the city, the streets suddenly widened into magnificent, broad, green corridors, bordered at leisurely intervals by huge white-columned ante-bellum houses of statuesque proportion and breathtaking beauty.

It was the sudden-ness of it all, the jolt of the contrast. I took a deep breath. I felt my heart lift. And if I hadn't grasped the point before, I did now. This said it all. This is what the Old South was fighting for. Indeed it is the ghostly presence which still stirs, which hangs heavy over these sultry Southern soils.

Coming up to a major street bordering this central section, I made a right turn. It was a wide, busy road flanked by shops and buildings in what was obviously the old business district. A few blocks on I pulled up for a stop-light. In the distance I

*The Edmund Pettus Bridge—Selma*

saw the outline of what looked like a bridge. Could it be? Another two blocks, another light, and I looked again. It was indeed a bridge, and in broad black letters on the overhead cross-beam were the words, "Edmund Pettus Bridge."

The sight of this bridge stirred strong emotions. I had only seen Martin Luther King in person once. That was in June 1963 at a mass "March to Freedom" in Detroit. However, along with everybody else in this world of modern mass communications, I had seen the Edmund Pettus Bridge many times. It's image, what had happened here, and the significance of these events were branded deep in my consciousness. And here it was in the flesh, so to speak. It was an important moment.

Parking close to the bridge, I made my way up and onto the walk-way beneath the arched grey beams. The mid-afternoon sun was blazing hot, the humidity very heavy. The Alabama is a very big, very wide river, something TV and film footage never conveyed. This was not a short crossing. Pick-ups and cars drove slowly past. Occupants cast quizzical eyes in my direction. I was the only person on foot.

Coming to the end, there was a metal post at the road-side. On it were mounted two signs. One was a large poster announcing "La Rouche—Democrat—For President." A smaller metal sign above it stated that this road was the "Selma to Montgomery March Byway."

That was it. I pondered this sign for a few moments, the sweat streaming. This was the precise site of arguably America's land-mark event of the past century. And this was how the Authorities chose to represent it.

Doubling back, I reflected on these signs, this bridge and what it all meant. To the successors of those who had lived and flourished in those magnificent ante-bellum Plantation Town houses I'd seen here in Selma, and indeed throughout the South, the Edmund Pettus Bridge could not be other than a bitterly resented provocation, a deeply painful reminder of all that had once been theirs, and that now had been lost.

But to those in the Old South who did not share this heritage and this view, people of both Black and White skins, and indeed to most of the modern world beyond, Edmund Pettus Bridge represented something very different. The reality was the symbol: a bridge to a new future, to new hope, to a new freedom, a new humanity.

Back now on the Selma side, I noted a modest plaque at the bridge exit. It gave brief details of "The Selma Movement," those actions bearing on the support and ultimate approval of the Federal Voting Rights Act of August 6, 1965. A bit further on, pulling back a dense, leafy overhang I discovered a second sign. It gave directions to the "National Voting Rights Museum." I never did find this Museum.

# 16

## *Old Selma and New*

*Selma, Alabama*—Heading back to the car in the shade of old river-front warehouses and industrial buildings, most restored to new life as gift shops, fashionable boutiques and cafes, my eye was arrested by a handsomely engraved sign. "Skills Assessment Center," it said. What, I wondered, was this all about?

Blissfully cool inside, the spacious Reception lounge was done up in tastefully subdued modern decor. I learned from a neat, blonde, most articulate young woman, that this Center was a spin-off of The Selma Movement. Federally funded, the Center provided skills assessment, and where necessary, guidance for local people seeking to improve their abilities, particularly in the use of modern computer technology. It was a superb facility. There was an impressive array of resources, interview/work rooms, high and low-tech equipment. The women running it—two White, and one Black, who was the receptionist—were very efficient, helpful and informative. There was one thing, however, I could not help but observe. Not a single person was being assessed!

I thanked the women and stepped out once more into the draining heat of the Selma afternoon. Splendid facility, no doubt. But I couldn't help feeling that it was perhaps geared to expectations which, for the majority of local clients, were a bit beyond their current reach.

Further along, and much in need of a cooling drink, I came to one of Selma's oldest establishments—so the brochure informed me—the St. James Hotel. Inside it was not only cool, but very modern, very expensively restored. I inquired if I might have a nice, cold Fresh Lemonade. My request was greeted with an odd look. I was offered a beer or a coke. I declined. Could I, however, have a look round, I asked? "Please do," said the stout, neatly suited young White lady manager.

High-ceilinged, with a maze of carpeted corridors giving onto a restaurant, a large dining room, various sitting and conference rooms, I came at last to a secluded, red-tiled courtyard. I stepped cautiously out. Suddenly, wondrously there was this luminous, green-shaded open space, silent except for the cooling babble of the circular, palm-surrounded water feature. Tier upon graceful white-railinged tier, the quadrangle reached up one, two, three levels. I lingered, absorbed in wonder and admiration.

About to depart this oasis, I saw advancing a stout man of middling height and years. His crumpled white linen suit had seen better days. Taking out a big blue handkerchief and mopping his florid brow and face, he gestured at the courtyard. "Nice bit of work, sir?"

I agreed.

"You a visitor to our fair city, then?"

I replied in the affirmative.

He looked me up and down, then mopped again. "You interested in the old Selma or the new?"

I explained that I was from England and that I was visiting ancient mound sites.

"Not many of them round here!" he snapped back.

There was, I said, a lot of antiquity throughout the Deep South, Selma included. Perhaps, I added, he might have suggestions.

He glanced at me again. "Well sir, if anyone can give you any suggestions, that person is me. The name is Horatio Beauregard Duke." He extended a white podgy hand. The handshake was remarkably firm. "To most people round here I'm known as Beau." He gestured to a table on the palazzo. "I'm about to have my favoured afternoon libation. A nice, long, cool Gin Collins." He leaned forward, "Of course, not quite the same thing as our traditional Mint Julep, a favoured drink which has 'gone missing' from many a Southern establishment. Still, a very fine substitute. Highly recommended. I wonder, sir, if you'd do me the honour of joining me?"

In the course of the next hour I learned a good deal about Selma, and much else pertaining to the Old South in general. Beneath this very courtyard, Beau informed me, slaves fresh off galleys transporting them up the Alabama from Mobile and the Gulf, were "stored" in holding rooms prior to auction or distribution to Plantation owners, slave traders and whoever else might be interested in these precious goods.

Old Selma, said Beau, was at the very heart of the cotton economy. The surrounding lands were enormously productive, the wealth they generated fabulous. Selma was "the

Queen of the South." At its height in the years before the Civil War, he went on, there were many magnificent Plantation Town houses, owners competing to create and construct the most opulent and imposing residence. It was a time of high culture, high fashion and high living. It provided, declared Beau, a "high-water mark" of civil culture challenging the great houses of New Orleans and in the "King Cotton strongholds up and down the Mississippi."

"Our forefathers provided this young Nation with an example; an example of what levels of wealth, what standards of refinement, of achievement could be attained." Beau mopped his brow. "My great-grand-daddy used to say that when those Northern traders and businessmen came here to Selma, their eyes bulged, they were green with envy, they became consumed with jealousy." He laughed. "You see, they had nothing that even came close to matching us."

And then came the Civil War. Beau paused and called over the Black waiter. Two more Gin Collins' were quickly to hand. "Sherman had one or two tries at Selma. But it wasn't until the final days of the War that the Yankees got through." He explained that Selma was the "engine room" of the Confederacy, a major producer of arms and munitions; and for that reason the Union had long been anxious to shut Selma down.

The defence under renowned Confederate General Nathan Bedford Forrest—later to become first Grand Wizard of the Ku Klux Klan—had been spirited and fierce. However, heavily out-manned and out-gunned, and virtually on their last legs, the Confederates swiftly succumbed and the Union forces took Selma. There followed the customary rape, pillage and arson, though some of the great houses, said Beau, once they had been thoroughly ransacked, had been spared the torch. These were the fine houses I had earlier seen; albeit, he added, much restored the past 40 years with the aid of public and private funding.

Beau gave his Collins a delicate stir, then took a long pull on the straw. "Now some people say the Old South still lives. I say the Old South died in April 1865. The Civil War killed it stone dead. It was 'Gone with the Wind.' It was not coming back. And it wasn't just the War. Things had changed. The price of cotton had dropped. Mechanisation was coming in. Our overseas customers—Britain, France, Germany, Holland—were tapping other suppliers. And then our Northern friends were pressing the Washington Government hard and successfully to restrict our competitive position and freedom of trade."

He laughed. "You could say the writing was on the wall by the early 1850s. But we chose not to read that writing." He vigorously mopped his face. "There was, as they say today, 'a window of opportunity,' a period when we could have adapted, diversified, re-structured, made some hard compromises. But we didn't."

Beau ran his finger down the side of the frosty glass. "Maybe my great-grand-daddy and his friends had grown over-confident. Maybe it was just 'pride cometh before a fall.' I don't know, Maybe it wouldn't have made any difference anyway—those green-eyed Northern boys were bent on destroying us. Who can say."

As for the past 130 years, Beau had strong views. "The War," he said, "meant not only destruction, obliteration of our economy, the devastation of our beautiful and productive lands. It meant obliteration of our natural leaders—something, I believe, your English people learned in the aftermath of WW1. It was a terminal blow. Those that weren't killed were mostly destroyed economically, or driven into exile. And those that took over down here were of an inferior grade."

Beau wearily shook his head. "Some of these people still think that such barbaric institutions of monumental ignorance and provocation as the Ku Klux Klan can serve effective rearguard functions; that by twisting and turning biblical interpretations that Black folk can be held down and White dominance maintained; that by battling blindly against the combined tidal waves of all these modern tides, that 'the South will rise again'."

Beau absently poked the ice cubes with his straw. "It is the counsel of fools and ignorant people." He poked again. "And thanks to the contribution of our Northern friends, that's all we got left. The dregs of the barrel."

Beau took one last pull and placed his glass back on the table. "One thing in the Bible you never hear these folk quote: 'He who is last, will one day be first'." He got up, ran a hand over the front of his crumpled jacket and buttoned it. "And that's exactly what's happened round here, give or take a bit. Black Mayor—first time in Selma—many Black officials, professionals—accountants, doctors, lawyers, judges. And of course lots of White fellow-travellers catching a ride on their coat-tails."

He laughed and gesticulated to the silent courtyard galleries, perhaps to spirits, to robust presences not so long departed. "I wish 'em all good luck. And in time we'll get things going again. Signs of it now. New people, new ideas, promising new developments."

Beau accompanied me to the door. The heat had eased a bit. "But that's the New South. And, in time, it'll throw off all the vicious nonsense of the 'Old Guard' ignorant."

He took a deep breath and gave his brow a final mop. "But as for the Old South, the fine manners, the great houses, the great passions, the great people with the fire, the vision, the consuming energy, the talent; the people who forged and ran this society in those days; that's dead and long gone."

There was an edge of irony in his laugh. "But there's one thing no army, no jealous and vengeful person, not even Sherman can take away. And that is a man's memory!"

# 17

## *Roots Deep in the Mounds*

*Selma, Alabama*—Beau mopped his brow. "If you don't mind my asking, where are you heading now?"

I said I'd heard there was an Archaeological Park south of Selma at Old Cahawba; that there were sites dating back to 2000 BC, and indeed that Old Cahawba itself was of interest."

Beau smiled and shot me a glance. "I did make a boast, didn't I? About me being the sole possessor of local wisdom; of making any suggestion worth making?"

Any suggestions, I replied, would be most welcome.

For a moment he mopped and pondered. He checked his watch. "Now it's getting on a bit. There's one or two places I've got in mind, but we need more time Do you have plans for tonight?"

I said I didn't.

"Well, there's a place I know. Very nice. Fix you up fine. You could stop over tonight, then I could take you on a grand tour—well, a mini-tour anyway—a few sites that might interest you. What do you think?"

It was an opportunity and I seized it.

Beau made a call on the hotel phone. I then followed him in his car to a quiet, green street in the not-quite-old section of Selma. He stopped in front of a modern, white, frame-built house set well back on a lush green lawn bordered by bright, neatly-tended flower beds and shrubs. Beau hopped out of his battered old Buick, hustled up the path and knocked at the door.

I was surprised to see the door opened by a Black woman. Beau made polite conversation, then introduced me, "a traveller from England" to Mrs. Marva Sanders. After a bit more lively chit-chat—I could see there was mutual regard between these two—Beau told me he'd be by to collect me at 8:30 sharp in the morning. With that he bade farewell, hopped back into the Buick and rumbled off.

Marva, I quickly learned, was a very busy person. Along with tending to the needs of the occasional visitor, she looked after her Accountant husband, Leon and their two boys, worked as an Operating Theatre nurse, was active with various local groups concerned with needs of handicapped children, single mothers, the blind, the elderly; and on the lighter side sang in the local Pentecostal Church choir, was a keen bird watcher, folk dancer, gardener and amateur archaeologist. A Selma native—as was her husband—Marva had trained in the North at the Massachusetts General Hospital in Boston.

An extra place was set for me at the family table. At 6 pm we ate. Being baseball season, the boys, Jerrold and Aaron, keen athletes both, provided up-dates on the day's practice. Their father quizzed them on tactics for their weekend game. Then there was school-lessons talk, and another interrogation.

Then it was office talk from Leon, and hospital talk from Marva. Finally conversation turned to me. What, Marva asked, caused me to come all the way from England to visit Selma and the Old South? I told them of my interest in American antiquity; that there were mounds and sites all through this area; that it was perhaps interesting to consider that White and Black residents of the past 300 years added only the most recent "surfacing" to a 3000-7000 year-old "mound" of basic Southern culture.

For a moment there was silence. Marva turned to me. "Perhaps you've heard of Old Cahawba?"

I said Beau was planning to take me there tomorrow.

"Well," she said, "it's surely worth a visit. We've spent a bit of time there, pokin' and proddin' with our local Project Archaeology group. All kinds of stuff, from recent to way back, as you say. The boys," she gestured to Jerrold and Aaron, "are great hunters and collectors."

I said I'd heard the land round there was "loaded."

"Loaded," said Leon, "is the correct term." He straightened his knife on the white tablecloth. "Our forefathers learned this for fact. There was hardly an inch of the 5000 acres of Rosalie Plantation land that my grand-father, his predecessors and the 250 other slaves who cultivated and carefully tended that land, did not know intimately. They recovered an enormous amount of material, much of it just thrown away because they did not appreciate its significance and importance." He got up, disappeared and returned. "You may recognise this implement." He hefted a sizeable chunk of polished, satin-smooth granite, blunt at one end, narrow at the other. "It's called a celt; used to chip flints and create other stone tools." He passed it to me. It was a magnificent piece, about six pounds. The last celt of this size and perfected quality I had seen was in another "family collection" I encountered in south-east Ohio.

There were places on Rosalie, Leon stated, where field hands dug out old spear points and stone chippings by the bucketful. "In some places, I heard it said that these stone remnants were a downright nuisance to men tryin' their best to do a nice, clean bit of ploughin'. Held 'em up. Damaged the plough-share."

Leon now reached over and carefully handed me two small items.

I looked. My heart skipped a beat. One was a bird effigy stone pipe, identical in size and stylised form to Hopewell pipes I'd seen in Ohio; the other a finely-worked shell gorget with a center-engraved water spider, the spitting image of an artifact I'd seen in a Mississippian collection at Cahokia. Leon then produced some small shell beads and an animal stone effigy which almost certainly were of Poverty Point period culture.

The Sanders family watched in silence as I ran my fingers over these items, turning one, then another, examining the gorget, hefting that magnificent celt. I couldn't believe what had been laid out in front of me. In a sense, I need go no further. Here was the proof of the age-layered antiquity I was seeking. And it was all contained in the lands of a single local plantation. Here was life in the outreach of the Great Valley from perhaps 10,000 BC, through the recognised base periods of Poverty Point, then Hopewell, and on to "modern times" of Cahokia and the Mississippians only 800 years ago. I sat back dazed but enormously excited.

On putting a few careful questions to Leon I learned that while all these items had come from Rosalie Plantation where his kin had worked the better part of 200 years, first as slaves then after the Civil War as freemen and share-croppers, the exact locations of the specific finds were not known. "My grand-daddy had 'em in a couple of shoe-boxes under his bed in the family cabin. He was doin' some cleanin' up and was about to throw 'em out. Everybody, he said, had some of these bits and pieces; didn't amount to anythin'. But I'd seen 'em many a time. To me they were beautiful, precious, just like family. I couldn't bear to see them go out like so much trash. So I asked my grand-daddy if he'd give 'em to me. And he did."

Leon went on to say that he, Marva and the boys had spent much time in recent years checking over particular sections of the old Rosalie land. They'd found two or three palaeo "fall-out" sections along the creek (areas where bank erosion had revealed new artifact deposits); another site three feet down in mid-field with pottery fragments, stone implements, spear heads and some stone beads; and throughout the entire area at depths up to three feet they continued to find small sites dense with flint and stone chippings, and the occasional cache of arrow points.

'The first few times through with the plough on these lands—it was the same on all these big estates—must have been very hard going," said Leon. "If all these items are still sprinkled round today—as they are—they must have been packed in pretty heavy back then."

I told the Sanders' that what so greatly impressed me about what I had been shown was that it spanned the full spectrum of known American pre-history, and all within the land-frame of a single plantation. Leon laughed. "Well, I liked 'em. You can't help it; these things are so finely crafted, so neat, so beautiful. But if it hadn't been for Marva, they'd probably have stayed in the shoe-boxes. I'd have gone no further."

"When I was at Mass General," Marva cut in, "Leon was at Harvard. I was a bit curious about these things. My folks had a few of their own. So I persuaded Leon to take a course in American Archaeology. He did. And we both learned. And things just sort of went on from there." She laughed. "Leon ended up taking every Archaeology course they offered. So that's how we learned about ole Miss, the 'River Nile' of this great continent, the cradle of American civilisation—many thousands of years before it was 'American'! It was through those courses we learned also about Poverty Point, the Adena, and the amazing—and amazingly widespread—Hopewell culture, the rise and fall of Cahokia and the Mississippians, our nearest ancestors, and a lot more."

Leon was playing absently with his dinner knife, his features sharp in outline. "You said something earlier; something about the Whiteman, the Blackman and their kin being only the most recent 'surfacing' on the ancient mound of Southern culture." He fiddled again. "Would it surprise you if I said our kin go right down to the base of that mound?" He looked up at me. "Down as deep, maybe deeper than most English people extend their roots in native English soil?"

I said that I felt roots were very important. And it had, I added, greatly interested me to hear Marva refer to her "Mississippian ancestors."

Leon explained that both he and Marva had part Indian ancestry—he Creek, Marva, Choctaw; both tribes deriving from the ancient peoples who first came to these Southern lands. "Following the conquest of America by the Whiteman, then the importation of Black Africans to work these lands, there was a gradual mixing of Black with Indian blood. Many Blacks were captured in Indian raids; some escaped to Indian communities as runaways." And Indians captured by Whites during the many White-Indian Wars, Leon pointed out, were themselves often enslaved. Thus over the generations there was much integration within the slave community. He and Marva, he added, had come by their ancestry by this route. And by the time of Emancipation, the Indian/Black mixed-blood element was prominent throughout the South. "And if during your tour of these regions, you take note, particularly of the facial features of Black people you meet, you'll see," he laughed quietly, "just as with all of us Sanders' here, that the Indian presence remains strong today!"

He paused; then turned to me. His black eyes had a mischievous glint. "And if you have a *very* discernin' eye, and care to look, you may recognise that more than a tad of Indian blood runs in the veins of many folk down here who would be mortally offended if you were to suggest they were anythin' other than very pure White!"

Marva spooned out fruit salad into bowls and handed them round. "So you see," she said, "us folk here are pretty local. We go back a good bit. Our roots reach right down into the Stone Age of that mound of yours. We've got a share in all those great civilisations and cultures—and yes, in their failures and horrors, as well as their triumphs and great achievements—that have come and gone over past millennia."

"As for those trinkets and baubles," she flourished her serving spoon at the items I had neatly laid out, "well, I think you'll understand they're much, much more than baubles to us. When we, when the boys, touch them, we're touching our heritage. Jerrold here," she pointed her spoon at the smaller boy, "he believes that's how our ancestors keep tuned into us, and vice versa. Isn't that so Jerrold?" The boy turned a bright pink round the ears.

Silence reigned while the fruit salad, with lots of fresh orange and mango bits, was consumed. It didn't take long.

"I hope all this talk hasn't given you indigestion," said Leon.

"Quite the contrary." I said that my understanding had been much-expanded; my appetite for Selma and Southern culture much sharpened.

"Maybe we've at least been able to give you an idea of what applies to a lot of folk round here. A lot of Black, and so-called Black folk like us, have deep roots in these Southern soils." He laughed. "And many of us have our 'heritage collections.' We know and sense things about this beautiful, enormously powerful land, that most White people are totally ignorant of. With a very few exceptions, none of them have 'heritage collections'," absently, he traced a finger over the tablecloth, "partly because they of course don't have the heritage, but also because they've never had any close, any intimate contact with the soil of this land. Our people worked and re-worked this land, generation on generation; they knew every inch by the touch of their hands, by the feel of their un-shod feet. They were in close touch with the rhythms of Mother Nature, her Seasons and her needs. It is all this, and as we have indicated, much more, going much deeper, that our ancestors have passed to us. It is a rich inheritance. And we are grateful."

Leon had stressed that "with very few exceptions," White people had had no intimate association with the soil of these lands. I wondered about Beau. Could he be one of these exceptions? I asked the Sanders' how they'd come to know Beau.

Both Leon and Marva laughed. "Mr. Beauregard," said Marva, "is part of Old Selma. But he is part of the Old Selma that has always been a bit different. His folk were owners of the old Grovewood Plantation. Its pride was one of the finest neo-classical houses in the South. They had a few hundred slaves. Mr. Beauregard's people knew that soil just as well as any one of them, and better than most. They didn't draw lines too sharp. Slaves didn't run away from Grovewood. But many ran *to* it! Everybody wanted to live and work there. And those that were there took care to ensure they remained."

"Yes," added Leon, "Mr. Beauregard, his people, they have been one of the very few exceptions; exceptional people, exceptional man." He caught Marva's nodded gesture towards the artifacts, and laughed. "And yes; he's got his 'collection'.

And there are some who say it's a *true* 'heritage collection'—just like ours!"

Jerrold and Aaron disappeared to baseball practice. Marva and Leon chatted a bit more with me. Then it was to bed. It had been a very long and arduous day for my head, and it was clamouring for rest. Under the "whip, whip, whip" of the ceiling fan blades, the air stirring gently, the heat now eased, I quickly dropped off.

# 18

## *Old Cahawba and the New South*

*Selma, Alabama*—At precisely 8.30 next morning the doorbell rang. It was Beau in his white linen suit. He was perspiring and mopping, and announced he would conduct the tour using his Buick. Marva said I could leave my car, which I'd already packed, out front. I thanked her for the Sanders family's hospitality. She smiled, then took my hand. "You pay attention to Mr. Beauregard, now. And I hope you enjoy your tour."

In the Buick I found we had company. There were two Black men in the back seat. As the Buick growled and rumbled into action, Beau performed the introductions.

"Michael, I'd like you to meet my friend, James Arthur Davis." He gestured to the smaller man, sharp of feature, burnished brown of skin. "He's a man who knows a thing or two about our ancient forbears and antiquities round here." Beau mopped vigorously. The only air conditioning in this car was what came in the windows. "…He also practices a little law, when time permits." There was a chuckle from both men.

"And the man beside him, well I've asked him to come along just to ensure we all stay on the right side of the Lord!" Another subdued chortle. "Please meet the Reverend Jesse Greer, Pastor of the New Life Evangelical Church, Inc. Rev. Jesse is a man of many parts; businessman, entrepreneur, community activist, as well as a Minister of the Gospel. And he also knows a bit about the life that some say still goes on beneath our very feet!"

It was a short run west on the main road out of Selma to the Old Cahawba turn-off. From there it was a stately progress for several miles along a straight road hemmed in by forest green. The only signs of life were a pair of white-tailed deer and a flock of crows. The deer, their flags aloft, rocked over a fence and vanished into the forest. The crows turned out not to be crows. "Wild turkeys!" exclaimed Beau. "They're a bit relaxed right now. Out of season—'cept for poachers!"

It was Beau who proceeded to fill me in on the recent history of Old Cahawba. It had been Alabama's State Capital in the early days, 1820-26, and was thought to be an ideal location. Being close to the center of the State, and with the Cahaba and Alabama Rivers and their tributaries giving access to most of the principal cotton-producing and slave-consuming areas, the site seemed ideal.

City fathers, however, had not taken sufficient notice of one important factor: flooding. It proved a recurrent problem—much over-played by some, Beau maintained. Thus by 1826 the decision was taken to abandon Old Cahawba for higher and drier ground up-stream at Tuscaloosa. Still, said Beau, the attractiveness of Old Cahawba to traders, businessmen and others remained. Gradually the town was re-inhabited. By the 1850's it was going strong. In 1859, construction of a railway line further increased its commercial prospects and triggered a building boom.

With the Civil War, however, came the start of the second and terminal decline of the town. The Confederate Government tore up the new rail-lines for urgent use elsewhere; 3000 Union prisoners were crammed into a make-shift, water-logged, lice-infested camp in the center of the town. Trade on the river came to a stand-still. And then, said Beau, came the *'coup de grace'*: the devastating flood of 1865. "It didn't do those Union boys a whole lot of good;" and with the destruction of river commerce, and defeat of the South imminent, "people just packed up and left."

It was, declared Beau, a tragedy. "The beautiful buildings, the fine residences were mostly reduced to rubble. And yet with the advantage of hindsight, we can now see that Old Cahawba's *raison d'etre* had passed. The days of huge and valuable cargoes, of fabulous profits; these high days had gone. Trade in slaves and cotton was in sharp decline. And this decline became terminal. By 1875, Old Cahawba here was a ghost town. And today," said Beau, "that's what it remains. Yet another reminder of the high days, the lavish achievements of a way of life that was brought to its final demise by the events of the War and those developments that followed—not all of these the products of Northern spite!"

"I guess you could say," growled Beau, as he now stopped and we all got out of the car, "what happened here was symbolic of the bigger picture. Old Cahawba was the Old South.

It boomed while Cotton was King; and when King Cotton and all that went with it came crashing down, then, just like the Old South, so did Old Cahawba." He cast a slow, sad eye round. "The only people who now tread these abandoned streets, who view these moss-covered ruins are hunters, fishermen, a few visitors curious about our past, and," he grinned and laid one arm on James, the other on Rev. Jesse, "a few other folk whose interest and curiosity probes deeper!"

The great Live-Oaks, the hanging drifts of Spanish Moss provided some protection from the morning sun. The humidity was stifling. Walking along the bluff facing onto the Alabama, I could see there was the remnant of a landing platform. James Davis noted my glance. "Bit of a pier where fishermen can get in and out. But not always that." He slapped a mosquito on his arm. "Modern development." I asked what had been its original purpose. I was startled by the force of the rhetorical flood that was triggered.

Up this bank from that pier in 1824, stated James, came the great American ally and Revolutionary War hero, the Marquis de Lafayette and his retinue. On a Memorial Tour of America, this renowned French General who had rendered such vital assistance during and after the War of Independence, was here at Old Cahawba, on this very green, greeted and feted at a great reception and feast.

Moving along this promontory where Cahaba met Alabama, the waters wide and light-chocolaty, James pointed to a moat. It was a deep cutting which ran inland along one side. Here I learned that digs down into and along the side of this bank had been productive. Once the undergrowth tangle had been cleared, and the very angry resident Water Moccasins and other deadly poisonous snakes displaced, artifact hunters had made some great finds. These included pottery fragments, stone implements and varied decorative stone artifacts.

"You see," said James, "not only the slave traders and cotton dealers, and 800 years before them the great Mississippian leaders, but also over the past 5000 to 10,000 years, maybe longer, these items show that man recognised the strategic value of this particular site." Throughout the entire area, declared James, as we slowly made our way round the site and now back towards the car, stone, pottery, flint—arrowheads, spearheads, and the customary masses of chippings—confirmed the importance of this Old Cahawba locale.

Rev. Jesse had said little during our Old Cahawba explorations. But on the return drive he reminded us of the deeper dimension of what we had seen, what collectors and archaeologists had found.

"Maybe it's my training, my trade in spiritual dealings which has sharpened my perceptions, my responses." He laid a hand on James' arm. "Maybe it's the blood of the ancients which both James and I share—we descend through Creek lines. But whatever it is, I feel a life vibration not just from the fine artifacts I've uncovered myself; I feel it rising from the very ground beneath our feet. Some places it's strong, like a buzz, pure electricity; like in old places of concentrated living like Old Cahawba. Other places it's just a gentle, warm vibration, like a reminder to let us know that our ancestors, though departed, remain close.

"You see," said Rev. Jesse, settling back in his seat, "this in fact is a big part of our message at the Life Church. Us folks, whether of Black/Indian blood, plain Black, plain Indian, or plain White—or any of the crosses in blood that may exist—have our Saviour in Jesus Christ."

"Amen!" chorused James and Beau.

"…But beneath Jesus, infusing his body, his spirit, his meaning for us today; beneath Jesus is the well-spring from which he draws, from which we are all refreshed; and that is the sweet waters, the everlasting messages of the ancients. It is these which bring us strength and unity, which bring us continuity and security in Christ." Jesse paused. "You see, we are all one; the ancients, us, in the spirit of Christ. He reaches down and holds us all!"

"Oh yes!" called out Beau, "Aaamen!"

For a few minutes as we all let the message of Rev. Jesse settle, the only sound was the rumble and growl of the trusty Buick. Crossing the Cahaba as we now approached Selma, Rev. Jesse was stirred once again.

"You know, we got us a gold mine here!"

He pointed up-river. We all turned and looked.

"Yessir! A gold mine! I can see it all now!" He waved his hand grandly. "An Internationally-acclaimed 18-hole golf course! Designed by Tiger Woods! Fine double-decker clubhouse. Then a little further along," he pointed again, "up that way, an 'Adventure Recreation World'. All kinds of outdoor games for young and old; and beyond it again, a testing woodland course for bikers—the pedal variety—and a whole cluster of 'Woodland and Nature Walks'." He was getting really warmed up now. "And lots of food places. Nice places. Open places. Picnic benches. And none of that nasty fast-food. No sir! Nothing but the best of our fine Southern cooking!"

"And a dispensary for Gin Collins'and Mint Juleps?" inquired Beau?

"Yes sir! Mint Juleps! Gin Collins'! All kinds of nice, long, ice-cold drinks. And for those who want 'em, hot too!"

Rev. Jesse reached over the seat and put his hand on my shoulder. "And here's the really great idea. You see, us folk—all sinners, each and every one of us—we're never satisfied are we? Of course, we've got somethin' to look forward to—if and when we finally get through them pearly gates! But in the meantime, we would truly like a little pleasurin', in fact a whole lot of pleasurin' in the here and now!…So you just imagine," he gestured up-river again, "a nice wide arc of a bridge over the river at that point." He smiled broadly. "That bridge, my friends, is the 'Path to Paradise'. You just follow that path and all your wishes'll be fulfilled; all your dreams come true!"

He leaned back, wiped his brow with his shirt sleeve, then gestured emphatically with both arms. "The whole she-bang! The whole concept! The whole thing! I've called it 'The Selma Experience'! Now what do you think of that?"

More silence. Then James spoke up. "Well Jesse, that's a powerful concept." There was just the hint of mockery in his voice. "I expect you've got the designers at work. When are we going to see the draft plans?" There was a chuckle from Beau.

For a moment Jesse simmered. Then he flared.

"The trouble with folk round here is they've got no vision! I can *see* 'The Selma Experience' clear as a bell. Can't you?"

'It's not that we can't see it, Jesse," countered James. "It's just that, I guess, we're wondering what flesh you've got on the bones?"

Jesse lowered his voice. His words now came slowly. "We've got us God's Little Acre. It's right here in our beautiful Selma and this fine countryside around. But we ain't never gonna get out of our drab little post-Civil War back-water mentality if we don't let go a bit; if we don't let our imaginations soar; if we don't seize on opportunity; if we don't have the sense of adventure, the confidence to invest our faith in those things that are within close reach of the man who's got the push, the courage to reach out and grasp them!"

Jesse lapsed into silence. The rest of us observed the scenery, then the string of fast-food and mini-mall establishments as we entered Selma's outskirts.

Passing through the now-familiar shantytown, I noticed a substantial single-storey, white clap-board building with a modest silver cross mounted above the double front doors. "Church of Everlasting Life" it said in large black letters across the boarding.

I said to Jesse that this looked to me like a "real community church." Did he know anything about it?

This raised a cackle of mirth from my companions. "You see, Michael," it was James. "Jesse here not only knows about that church, he *owns* it! Just like the six…"

"*Seven*, now!" corrected Jesse.

"Right. Seven others in Selma and district."

Jesse smiled. "Yessir! I do God's business. And in his benevolent way he's done business with me." He laughed. "We have a very generous Creator. Never let me down." Rev. Jesse, I later learned, also owned most of the Convenience Stores in the locality. All were well patronised. Credit terms were generous.

"So the people who live round here," I gestured towards a few littered yards fronting frame houses in seeming danger of imminent collapse, "they're your parishioners?"

Jesse followed my eyes. "You reckon this is all just one big pig heap? That's what you think, don't you?"

I didn't know what to think, I lied.

"Well let me tell you. Most folk who live in those houses, they're happy people. You go inside. You'll feel the happiness, the love. Those are good people. God fearin' folk."

He pondered for a moment. "You see, what White folk never can understand, and…" directing a meaningful glance at James, "what some of our White-educated brothers choose to forget, is that the Black man, the Indian; they have always lived different from the Whiteman. You see, the Whiteman, he just settles down, he makes his home his little castle—sometimes big castle. But for the Indian, and to a large extent the Black man, all the land and the forest, the trees, the waters; all of these are his home. His house is where he dreams his great castles of imagining. But for the rest, his house is for him just a temporary staging post; where he stops for now before he moves on. And he *will move on*!"

Jesse carried on in the same vein. He made clear to me what I should have known, but didn't. I thanked him. He laughed and clapped me on the shoulder again. "It's alright Michael. You White folk may be ignorant. But you can learn; just like the rest of us!"

We were now on the streets of downtown Selma. Beau pulled up and dropped off James and Rev. Jesse near the Pettus Bridge. I thanked both for their assistance; for their help in filling in many gaps for this White visitor. Having wished me well on my tour and bade farewell to Beau, they set off down the street. Jesse was still worked up. He was gesturing and shouting. James, small, neat, walked with quick, steady gait beside him.

By the time Beau pulled in behind my Chevy back at the Sanders', it was past two. He asked if I'd like to join him for a Collins and a sandwich at the St. James. I declined. Once again time was pressing. I had ambitions of visiting Moundville—site of the South's largest Mound complex—before the day was out. And that was another 70 miles or so cross-country.

"Well," said Beau, "I hope we've been able to give you just a glimpse behind the curtain of what too often passes for the Deep South." He laughed. "It's true there's much darkness in all this bright light; in this sultry climate. Just part of our geographic fate, I often say. This fine, rich, immensely productive soil has caused man to do some damn fool things over time—and we're not the first! But it also has fostered some great thoughts, great passions, great aspirations; some great creations, great achievements." He laughed again. "Man at his best, and his worst, you might say. The Devil and the Angels live close, side by side, in every Southern soul. And colour, in that sense, makes no difference at all!"

He then spoke of Rev. Jesse. "You saw, and you heard Rev. Jesse. Very simply, through all the fire and contradiction, Rev. Jesse, and many more like him, are the heart and the spirit of the New South; that New South that's just about ready to break fully from cover." He paused. "You see, our people were not inclined to tune in to what the ancestors, the kin of Rev. Jesse and his people had to say. They have always had important messages. But it's one thing to listen; and quite another to hear." Beau mopped his beaded brow. "Out of that great jumble of ideals, aspirations, obsessions; out of all that, and down at the root, is the energy, the will, the drive, and in fact the practicality in modern terms—difficult though it may often be for us to see it—that will carry us forward.

"What Rev. Jesse needs is the patient support, the friendship, the encouragement and gentle guidance of those who understand through their backgrounds, the difficult, often treacherous ways of big business and finance. It is such people, mainly Southern Whites, who need to steady and guide the plans and ambitions of the likes of Rev. Jesse." Beau shifted himself in the car seat. "After all, in that great surge of energy, that bucaneering spirit, he's not so different from the Whitemen who made the last great impact on this land and this country."

Beau mopped again and laughed. "Of course, it did take a power of persuading to convince Rev. Jesse after he'd been to New York City and seen the skating rink at Rockefeller Center, that novel and adventurous though it might be, an outdoor ice-rink in temperatures of 80-95 degrees just would not work! That was one of his more recent schemes. He did not take its rejection in good grace! We all got a good lambasting!"

Beau then touched on James Davis. "Now James may seem like your 'Black Whiteman'. Many of his own people think this." He wagged his head. "You'd be mistaken. In his own way, James is as fiery, as ardent as Rev. Jesse. It's just that he's followed another route. James has made a lot of money; does a lot of work for some of the big Northern and Global corporations with forestry and chemical interests down here.

"But were you to drop by his office, you'd see a scattering of all kinds and conditions of local folk. You see James has this old-fashioned belief that every man is entitled to a fair trial. And a fair trail means a good defence. And Black, Indian, White; the man may not have the readies to pay. But James will fight hard for each. And I can assure you there's no shortage of cord-wood for his fire, or prime venison and catfish in his freezer!"

It was time to go.

I thanked Beau for his time and all his efforts on my behalf.

"As I said," laughed Beau, "there's light in the darkness. And there's a gap in the curtain. I've just tried to give you a little feel for the force, the spirit behind that light. We have a lot to be proud of in Selma. Just a pity it's taken so long to recognise. Anyway, good luck with your Mounds. I truly hope you find what you're seeking."

As I headed north-west out of Selma, over yet more magnificent stretches of rich Southern flatland, I reckoned that perhaps the person of whom Selma should be most proud, and indeed grateful, was Horatio Beauregard Duke. I hoped there were a few more like him. Everything needs its catalyst, its facilitator. Beau was that person.

And reflecting on this, I felt the weight of darkness lift slightly. I laughed to myself. I had been looking for ways to ease this burden. Yet perhaps the secret was that this burden, this weight of darkness was a reality. Always had been. Southerners through the millennia had learned to live with it, to draw strength and inspiration from it, to create their own forms of light within it. So, I now recognised, should I.

Another two hours to cover 30 miles—serious road re-surfacing was underway—and it was evident that Moundville was going to be out of visiting reach today. Best therefore to find a place to stop over and make a day of it tomorrow. However, a stop-over place in these back-country parts was not easy to locate. Finally, at Greensboro, some 20 miles south of Moundville, I found a motel. It was somewhat battered, but very comfortable; and again run by Indian (from India) people. A restaurant is attached; this one run by the Indians themselves.

# 19

## *Spirits of Moundville*

*Greensboro, Alabama*—Departing Greensboro next morning, the experience was not unlike entering Selma, albeit on a smaller scale. The fast-food strip, then the run-down business and shantytown sections, finally an Old Greensboro district almost as stately and beautiful as Old Selma; they were all there. I stopped at the Post Office, then at a gas station. Very few people were about, and those that were weren't hurrying. The temperature was already 95 degrees.

It was 9:30 when I turned into the approach road to Moundville Archaeological Park. This was it! I had been waiting a long time for this moment. After a stop at the Orientation Building, a viewing of the orientation video, and an informative chat with two very helpful women Attendants, it was back into the car to start my tour of the "Moundville Circuit."

Very quickly I was aware that reality was far exceeding even my high expectations. It was an awesome sight. The road roughly followed the perimeter of the vast, 300-acre ancient plaza. Twenty-six earthen mounds were set at intervals of 200-300 yards along the margin. Along one side was a 60-foot bluff facing onto the Black Warrior River, a vital artery giving connected access to the Mississippi on the west, and the Alabama and ultimately the Gulf of Mexico to the south.

Parking near the 60-foot Temple Mound, I climbed to the top. The sun was high overhead, the heat fierce. What a view! From this spot, the Great Sun of Moundville was indeed Lord of all he surveyed.

800 years ago, this was a booming metropolis, seat of the Moundville City State and its imperial extensions. Inside the distant surrounding timber palisade lived 4000 leading citizens, Masters, Chieftains, Priests and Specialists. And on a May day just like today, this number would be swollen by many of the 10,000 to 15,000 residents and workers who lived in villages and small towns beyond the city walls. I could see and sense it all, even smell the acrid wood smoke from the many fires.

Round a distant platform mound on the far side of the plaza, plumes of blue smoke were rising. Here the distinctive Moundville pottery, shaped and etched with distinctive stylised designs, was being prepared for firing. Further on, copper workers were carefully crafting delicately embossed designs into this soft, richly-gleaming metal. And from the group of hut-stalls directly below and a short distance from the base of this Temple Mound came the continuous staccato "clack-click, clack-clack!" Flint-knappers were hard at it.

Ordinary flint items for functional use—knives, scrapers, drills, arrowheads of many kinds and designs—were being produced by a large number of apprentices and journeymen. A little apart, a few senior craftsmen and Masters were working on quality pieces destined for ceremonial use, for elite trade and export markets. In fact, there was today a degree of urgency in their activity. The arrival of eagerly awaited Trader Chiefs from the "Copper Country" to the far north was imminent. Special pieces, including several effigy pipes and a ceremonial mask were being crafted to mark this important occasion.

And there was another community event anticipated with even greater interest, indeed concern. Victorious War Captains soon would be returning with many captives. This was timely. The Spirits of Fire and Earth were growing impatient. There had been signs. They must be placated. Second plantings were due shortly to begin.

As the priests had so often warned; all must be in proper alignment, in harmony with the spirits of the Fiery Orb, with the Bright Elements in the evening sky, with the dark and powerful deities of the Earthly Firmament, and with the explicit demands and requirements of the ancestors. There would be great relief as well as great joy when the needed sacrifices were duly made.

For the rest all, it seemed, was in order. The usual noisy crowds were jostling round the bases of the ceremonial mounds. There was much to-ing and fro-ing at the hut-stalls. Weighty baskets of beans, roots and greens; the carcasses of a dozen freshly killed deer were being lugged into the central section of the plaza. Intermittent waves of cheering came from the direction of the Ball Courts.

Stepping back past his two watchful bodyguards and into the shade of the Temple building, the Great Sun now prepared for the Report of his Civic Engineers. They had been supervising construction of a ceremonial mound in a nearby village on what had turned out not to be dry ground, but an elevated section of sub-surface swamp. Huge amounts of fill material were required. And to shift this fill, the labour of several hundred strong men was needed.

The Great Sun summoned one of his Temple officials. There was a surplus of warriors. Many had been idle for the whole of the past year. The Warrior Chieftains would select suitable men. And while warriors considered manual labour beneath their dignity, they could not refuse a Royal Command. Bowing gravely, the official, ducking his short-feathered head-dress below the door lintel, trotted off to do his Master's bidding.

The sun was now directly overhead, the heat approaching 105 degrees, the humidity stifling. Departing the presence of the Great Sun, I descended the Temple Mound and crossed the Circuit Road into the plaza. It was huge and dead flat. Mounds dimpled the perimeter. Atop a platform mound of some 20 feet, I scanned the plaza again, then sat down.

At first it was just me, the sun, the heat and the silence. Then gradually, the power of this enclosed ancient place, the buzz, started to come through. Faint at first, then just as had been my experience when visiting Hopewell sites in the Ohio Valley, it increased. Walking now through the central open space I could feel the vibrancy, the surge of life all round me. But at the same time I sensed something unsettling, something threatening. I felt the need to watch my back as well as my front.

Back in the car, the air conditioning on full, I contemplated the power of this place, its huge expanse, its presence. At Etowah I had experienced brief contact, but nothing like this. Was there a message here for me? The ancients of Ohio, of Grave Creek in West Virginia, of Cahokia had in years past made themselves known to me. Their presence and power was strong. But I had discovered no message.

I laughed. Perhaps I should stop asking questions, stop trying to analyse, don't force things, just let 'em happen. After all, man in these earlier times relied on intuition, trusted his instincts. Perhaps I should do the same.

The Moundville Museum and Bookshop was not only a blessed cool retreat, but an Aladdin's Cave. There were a number of marvellous displays, but the high point was the Bookshop. It provided the most varied and appetising collection yet. Once again it was a matter of agonising over which few to purchase, and which to add to my reference list.

I was not alone in my book snooping. Also perusing the volumes was another visitor. His name was Alan. We exchanged a few words. A native Alabamian, he, it turns out, has been a keen archaeo-hunter since childhood, with a particular passion for the palaeo-peoples. He has a biggish collection and is very proud of it. We talk about various sites. He speaks of Florence, a city in north-west Alabama situated on the banks of the Tennessee River. There is a large number of palaeo sites in the area. He speaks of 134—I believe this was the number—separate town and village/settlement sites he and his colleagues uncovered in just the five-square-mile area round Florence.

Alan speaks with feeling about the restrictions that the Tennessee Authorities have placed on the archaeo-quest for artifacts. It is all, he says, very sad. For on the Tennessee River, amongst many other streams and rivers, erosion cuts into the bank, and as the banks are "peeled back," new strata of prehistory are constantly being revealed. With the ban on collecting, however, the items duly released by erosion simply tumble into the river and settle into the silt of the river bed. "Gone forever," laments Alan.

Alan is first and foremost a palaeo-man. 10,000 to 8,000 BC is his period. And he feels these people close. Like Beau's friends, he takes the view that man of palaeo times, is man of today—separated by a few years. An Auburn (University) graduate, Alan took a degree in Engneering and currently works for a big electronics firm in Baltimore.

"Did you not consider archaeology as a career option?" I inquired.

"Not many jobs going in archaeology," he replied. "And a man's got to eat!" So Engineering is Alan's job. Archaeology and palaeo-hunting is his passion.

"And what about you?" he asked. "What's your interest?"

I thought for a minute. What was my interest? "I guess you could say I'm a collector of cultures. Who these people were, how they lived, what kind of feelings they had about themselves and the world round them."

Alan nodded. "If you can, you want to get up to Florence. Bit off the beaten path. Up in the north-west corner near the Mississippi State border. Fine big mound right by the river. And a great little museum. Fantastic palaeo points. That

*Spirits of Moundville*

museum, that collection, brilliant! Best-kept secret in the world of American archaeology!"

Back in the car I checked the map. Florence was indeed off the beaten track—about 200 miles. Too far. And time was pressing. So with regrets and misgivings I headed west into ole Miss.

By early evening I was in fast-food alley on the outskirts of Columbus. I found a Days Inn Motel. Very nice, bright, clean room. And with Air conditioning. I then located a Dairy Queen. This time no Mississippi equivalent of that splendid "Alabama Pecan Mudslide." Just a plain chocolate thick shake which the counter girl, mobile phone glued to her ear, swiftly prepared. Refreshed and fed I returned to the air conditioning and bed.

# 20

## *Best-Kept Secret!*

*Columbus, Mississippi*——Handle, site of the legendary "place of emergence" of *Nanih Waya*, ancestral deity of the Choctaw and Creek peoples; and Philadelphia, where I am keen to visit the Choctaw Reservation, are within close reach. Further, the map indicates I can readily move south and west, towards Jackson, Vicksburg and various ancient sites bordering the Mississippi River.

However, I am still thinking about Florence. I check my assortment of Mississippi materials. I discover a brochure and detailed map of the Natchez Trace Parkway. The Parkway, I find, runs diagonally from the north-east corner of Mississippi close to Florence, on a line to Natchez in the very south-west of the State. I check the distance. About 310 miles. I note also a succession of marked pre-historic mound sites along the route. I read that the Parkway is another of the FDR and WPA/CCC projects of the Great Depression years. I am greatly encouraged. My experience so far of FDR and the WPA/CCC has been excellent. I change my plan. Florence and the Natchez Trace Parkway it is.

Driving north from Columbus, it clouds over. At Tupelo where I hit the road to Florence, the heavens open. Rain! And it's torrential! The first drop I've seen since that deluge at Charlotte. I wonder about the Georgia and Alabama peach growers. Has their plight been eased? (Later TV weather maps show that the rain failed to reach these drought areas.) Another 100 miles and I am approaching the bridge over the Tennessee to Florence.

At the neat, trim chocolate-box-type "Colbert County and Muscle Shoals" Tourism Office I am given explicit directions to "The Florence Indian Mound and Museum" by a very helpful and highly efficient woman Attendant. She even provides me with a local map with the route highlighted. I am grateful. I can't miss. Or can I? I drive a five-mile circuit. I am not pleased to find I'm back where I started.

However, second-time lucky. Having taken further directional advice, finally I locate the un-marked side street near the river. I make another turn through high, wire-mesh gates, and there it is. Or rather there they are—the towering mound with the snug little museum at the base beside it.

I can hardly wait to see this little treasure trove. Alan has sharpened my appetite for contact with the "living artifacts" of palaeo life. I try the door to the museum. It does not open. I check my watch. Just 4 pm. And it's not Monday—a Closed Day for many sites. I try again. No luck.

On this tour I have managed to persuade myself that if the ancients want me to see, I will see. If they don't, I won't. Disappointed but appeased by my policy of acceptance, I climb the mound. It is steep. When I get to the top—it is about half the size of a football field—there are benches, and these are shaded by the leafy reaching arms of sizeable hardwoods.

Consulting my brochures I find one on "Florence Mound…the Largest Domiciliary Mound in the Tennessee Valley." It is 42 feet in height. I read on. It is another of the colossal engineering achievements of the Mississippians. And as at Moundville, Etowah and Cahokia it is located close to the river. I further learn that in earlier times there were numerous other mounds close by; and that all were enclosed within a massive earthen wall, 15 feet high and 40 feet in width. The rich, alluvial flood plain stretched for miles. It was, it seems, another Moundville in both scale and sophistication.

Contemplating all this, I hear a shout from below. "You've got to leave now. We're locking the gates!"

I pick my way down the precipitous steps. The man is one of the Museum Attendants. Clearly he is anxious to shut up. I explain my plight—that I didn't know about the museum's 4 o'clock closing; that I've heard exciting reports about the museum's collection; that I'd be very grateful if he'd let me have just a peek.

He is not impressed. He glances impatiently at his watch. I am informed it is already 15 minutes past closing. Rules are rules. He revs the engine of his car.

I hear a door close and look round. Departing the museum is a woman. She is heading for her car. She too looks in a hurry.

Nothing ventured, nothing gained. I hasten over to her. "Excuse me!" I repeat my story. She fusses, then listens.

"Alright. Ten minùtes!" She tells her colleague she will lock up. He departs in haste.

Inside she keys off the security system and turns on the lights. She guides me round the principal displays. I am stunned. The grouped palaeo points, fanned out on royal blue velvet backing are breathtaking, exquisite. Wafer-thin, finely flaked and shaped, they clearly are ceremonial pieces, epitomes of the craft of the master-knapper who created them. And there is more. Another display case. More fine points, though these bear the marks of use. These were turned up during 1930s TVA (Tennessee Valley Authority) excavations.

I ponder and smile. It is the paradox. It took the Great Depression of the 1930s to uncover for the Nation not only it's real spiritual wealth, but the depth and richness of its cultural heritage. Once again the CCC has made an enormous and lasting contribution. And once again I say a prayer of thanks to Mr. Roosevelt and the WPA.

Another display case shows notched points of wide variety in size, and in colours from grey, to pink, to butterscotch-ripple-white. Finally the case containing beautifully smooth, finely perfected stone axe heads, mauls and celts catches my eye—the celts about half the size of the one in the Sanders' "family collection."

I take a last close look at those elongated points in the blue velvet case. Each is perfectly shaped, perfectly balanced, each a masterpiece of bi-facial multiple flaking technique. I shake my head. Fantastic, unbelievable. And, I am informed, all were discovered in a single bundle by a local woman digging her garden! "Best kept secret in the world of American Archaeology," said Alan. I agree!

It is time to go. The kind woman—her name is Lavetta—locks up and switches the security system back on. We exchange farewells. She smiles. I think she is aware that these extra ten minutes were appreciated.

It is past five by the time I cross back over the Tennessee. The motels I see in fast-food alley do not impress me. Costly, drab and noisy. Besides it's still early. I decide to push on. By the time I reach the town of Cherokee and the access to the Natchez Trace Parkway it's already seven. I decide to push on further. This is tourism country. There'll be no trouble picking up accommodation along the way.

The Parkway is superb. It's fully up to the standard of its Blue Ridge relation. Same wide green verges, single roadway, no commercial traffic, 50 mph limit. Is there no end to these magnificent benefactions of FDR and the CCC? Marvellous. This is to be my motoring stroll for the next 320 miles. I can relax—"But keep a very sharp eye on your speed!" Lavetta warned. "One or two mph over the limit and they may get you. Five or ten, and you're definitely for it! It's all too easy to edge past the limit. Take care. And set your Cruise Control." I have set it.

A short distance on through rolling country of green meadows and light woodland I pull into my first Parkway site, Bear Creek Mound. Everything—descriptive display board, manicured mound, neatly mown expanse of grass—is superbly set out. Certainly things would not have been this neat and tidy when the first people camped here—a transit hunting settlement—some 10,000 years ago. As for the mound itself, this I discover is a relatively recent addition. A modest, gently-rounded construction, it was built somewhere around the time of the birth of Christ. Having walked slowly round the site, I climb the mound, then sit down for a few minutes. I cast my being back in time. Slowly the power of this now-silent place starts to rise. Clearly the ancients are about. I feel the gentle pulse. I now remember that one set of those wafer-thin, exquisitely crafted spear points on display at the Florence Museum were recovered from this area.

The sun is slipping fast towards the horizon. Where am I going to sleep? There's no point in leaving the Trace Parkway unless I have to. I check the map. I note a campsite at Tishomingo State Park. It appears to be just a few more miles down the road. I decide to take a quick look.

Back in the car, and a few hundred yards on, I see some crows in a field about 100 yards from the road-side. For a moment I carry on. Then the penny drops. I hit the brakes, turn round and go back. I pull over and look again. Noting my presence, the crows take off in quick bursting flight.

They are, of course, not crows at all, but Wild Turkeys! My first sighting since travelling with Beau and his companions along that Old Cahawba road. Never mind. At least this time I spotted 'em!

Turning to resume my route, lo and behold, right on the verge, pecking nonchalantly is an exquisite large bird. I roll quietly to a halt, lower the window and observe. It does not run away; just lifts its head and observes me. It then with slow dignity climbs to the top of the verge, and while still watching me, nestles down. I realise now this is a hen turkey. And she is very beautiful; nothing like the grey and white, red-wattled domestic gobbler. Beneath vanilla markings on her head and throat she has glossy, warm brown plumage. Worked into this plumage are luminous purples, blues, bright oranges and yellows. She is a magnificent bird. I cluck a little to her. She clucks quietly back. She remains nestled in the grass as I now slowly move off. I curse my stupidity in running out of film. What a photo that bird would have made!

It is getting seriously dark when I reach the Tishomingo Park turn-off. Passing down a narrow, winding road through high pines I eventually come to a lake. On the far side I see camper-van sites. I take the road round and turn into a vacant ramp. I get out and walk down to the lake. It is still very hot. The water is sludge coloured. I note two wriggling "V"s making fast progress across the lake towards me. Large water snakes! Discretion, I decide! Carefully watching where I put my feet, I hastily climb back up to the car.

Darkness has now fallen. It's been another busy day. Time for sleep. And tonight, not much option. The Chevy's going to have to serve as motel—though once the engine's off, without air conditioning! With seat reclined, travel rug wrapped round my shoulders, and just dropping off, there's a sudden "rap, rap," on the window. I look up into a blinding light. It's the Park Ranger.

"I'm alright to park here for the night?" I ask. No problem, says he. But there's an $8 fee. I hand over the $8; he gives me a numbered identity card. We exchange farewells. I then resettle, and despite the humidity and closeness—windows are rolled up tight to keep the mosquitoes at bay—I soon drop off.

# 21

## *Chickasaw Homeland*

*Tishomingo, Miss.*—It's 5 am. There's grey light through the pines, and grey mist hovering over the lake. I release the seat from reclining position. Last night I noted a wash-house down the forest road. A short drive, and I pull up in front of the yellow-lit, screen-doored building. I get out of the car. A sudden excruciatingly sharp pain shoots through my hip joint. My right leg buckles. I grab the car door. Maybe it's just asleep?

Alarmed and puzzled I hobble up the path. I perform my ablutions. Rather than easing, the pain gets worse. I struggle to the toilet and collapse on the seat. I'm baffled. The cold sweat rolls. For 15 minutes I dare not move—and hope someone doesn't come in. I'm feeling very foolish.

Suddenly I have a thought. I check my right trouser pocket. I extract some change and a ball-point pen. I then lower my trousers and check my hip. There is a long purplish bruise just about the size of the ball-point coming up on my hip.

I am not pleased with myself. The moral? There's no such thing as an "$8 good night"—particularly if you're so stupid as not first to empty out your pockets! Gradually, the pain eases. I manage to get back into the car.

Back on the Trace Parkway I'm beginning to wonder whether I've caught a bug. My sinuses are throbbing; I've got a sore throat, a nasty hacking cough, my chest is tightening and I feel laryngitis settling in. Maybe it wasn't the ball-point? Maybe it's rheumatics in my hip? Maybe this is just the start?

There is a good deal of early morning non-human activity. All roads attract wildlife. This Parkway is no different. I pass two flocks of Wild Turkeys feeding on the verge. A little further, two deer, both nut-brown with big ears pricked, stand in the middle of the road. Only when I am close do they casually rock off, white tails flashing as they disappear into the bordering forest. Sadly, there are too a number of smaller animals which have not been so fortunate. Crows pick at mangled, scarlet road-side remains.

The grey does not lift. As I reach Tupelo Visitor Center, Headquarters of the Trace Parkway, rain starts to fall. By the time I've parked it's torrential. I make a limping dash for the door. Inside I discover yet another first-class bookshop. I wrestle with choices. Finally I settle on two books about Lewis and Clark, the celebrated American explorers. It was they who in 1804 brought back news of the Pacific Ocean and the cross-continental route by which it could be reached. Lewis is forever linked with the Trace. For it was on the Trace, not far from Nashville, that he met a mysterious and untimely end. He was 35 years of age. Perhaps sub-consciously influenced by my current maladies, I purchase also two small books on Indian Herbal Medicines.

Before departing I see the customary video. It provides a good idea of what's coming down the remaining 260 miles of corridor green I plan to travel today. Tacked in at the end are various "home truths." One in particular catches my attention. "Take your time on the Trace," it advises. "You just might surprise yourself; find a bit of yourself you never knew on those quiet trails."

Back on the Parkway, the rain continuing to thrash down, I turn off at Tupelo in search of a non-fast-food breakfast. I have just about given up, and am preparing to face up to a Burger King, when I encounter a Shoney's Restaurant—but by the look of the car-park, so have a hundred others! Inside it's busy, but there's room for me. I enjoy a slap-up Buffet Breakfast. Fresh fruit salad, blueberry muffin, cereal; then scrambled eggs, bacon, sausages, mushrooms, a bit of salad, tomatoes, pasta, home-fries and gravy; and finally fresh hot rolls, butter and raspberry jam, and as many cups of fresh hot coffee as I want. $5.99, all in. And if I want, the waitress tells me I can do it all over again. I decline and desist. I reckon I've consumed enough food for today—perhaps for several days! Others, I note, appear better to appreciate this opportunity for repeat bounty. And it shows.

Stomach well satisfied, I press on down the Parkway. The rain has stopped. I come to a site of historic (not pre-historic) Indian interest. It is a re-constructed Chickasaw Village. Here again a number of descriptive boards tell the story. After the break-up (1300-1500 AD) of the Mississippian system, it seems there were adjustments in resident south-east populations. New peoples moved in from west of the Mississippi, and perhaps also from the north. With the remaining local peoples they settled, shifted and re-settled into the basic tribal structures of what we know today as the Cherokee in the north-east of the region, Creek and Seminole in the south-east, Choctaw in the south-west, and here in the north-west, the Chickasaw.

All of these peoples, of course, were forced off their lands by advancing White settlement; this culminating in the notorious 1830s "removals" to "Indian Territory" (later, in 1907, to become the State of Oklahoma). It is interesting to note that the capital of the "removed" Chickasaw Nation in south-central Oklahoma is Tishomingo. It is worth noting also how descendants here of Chickasaw who evaded removal—like the residual Choctaw, Creek, Cherokee and Seminole in their respective pre-removal homelands—have re-grouped, re-strengthened and reinforced their positions. Each now has territorial holdings both west and east of the Mississippi, with more Oklahoma Chickasaw yearly returning to settle in their eastern homeland.

Making my way round the Village, what most catches my attention is the similarity to basic elements of Mississippian life. Pallisaded towns, circular and longhouse-style buildings, proximity to major waterways; similar games, agricultural practices, religious ceremonies and rituals; and a robust involvement in trade and warfare; all are shared characteristics. What seems to be missing is the structure, order, engineering achievements, the power and paramountcy of elite governance, the authority and reach of Imperial interest and design, and of course the magnificent items and icons of high art produced through the genius of Mississippian artists and craftsmen.

I ponder further. Is not what I am seeing here what I've seen and sensed elsewhere in Native American communities? A sort of Dark Ages of these Indian peoples? The Imperial Mississippian Center, like Rome and its Empire at the Fall, had collapsed. The Chickasaw and their fellow insurgent tribesmen were the fragmented take-over groups. It was each community for itself. Some would survive. Many wouldn't. It was out of this harsh crucible that the Chickasaw and the other principal tribes would emerge.

And who is to say that it was not this experience which prepared the Chickasaw for the ferocity of the White assault that was shortly to come? Spanish, French, English and finally Americans, all extended immense efforts to subordinate, then ultimately to destroy the Chickasaw Nation. That the Chickasaw maintained effective fighting resistance for as long as they did may perhaps be attributed to the fact that post-Mississippian life had turned their attentions to urgent practicalities, rather than aesthetic creations; to the requirements of leadership through skill, force of character and battle success, rather than heredity and rank

Having seen round the various exhibits, I am about to depart when I encounter another visitor. He is tall, broad, with glossy black hair, swarthy complexion and piercing black eyes. He has a small, dark, wide-eyed girl in tow. Somewhat hesitantly I greet him and ask if he knows whether there are other sites like this in the area. He pauses and solemnly observes me. "Many, many," he replies.

It turns out he is Chickasaw, and that he has returned from Oklahoma to this his homeland. He informs me that there are large numbers of villages, hunting camps as well as more settled locales throughout this region. I ask whether these are sites that were newly-created by the Chickasaw, or re-cycled from their Mississippian and earlier predecessors?

"Many of these sites," he states, "have been in continuous use, at least the principal ones, since the arrival of our ancestors some 10,000 to 15,000 years ago." He pauses. "This is the real American Heartland."

I mention Bear Creek, its ancient settlement and mound.

He measures me with a long hard look and asks me where I come from. I tell him England. He nods. "What you see here and throughout the south-east and south-west is little different from what's happened in your own country. London, York, Dorchester; people from earliest times; invaders from afar; all recognised the advantageous positions of these premier sites. On top of one layer was added another. Bear Creek is one instance." He then repeated to me what I already knew from the Bear Creek display boards; that people had lived there since earliest times; that more recently the Mississippians had extended it and built mounds. "Then it was the turn of our people. There were many sites like Bear Creek before you Whitemen came." He fixes me with those black eyes. "At least Bear Creek is one that remains!"

This is not quite the encounter I expected. This is a very well informed person. I ask if there is another site close by he can recommend. "Owl Creek is just down the road," he says. The child is now petulantly tugging on his arm. "But you'll not see it on your Parkway map. Divided jurisdiction. Owl Creek is maintained by the Mississippi State Government, not the Federal Government. The Trace Parkway and its sites operate under Federal jurisdiction." The little girl gives his arm another angry tug. "Of course, that's how you Whitemen and your governments work. Everything and everybody in his designated pigeon-hole! Practical common sense doesn't enter into it!"

Before the little girl finally has her way, he informs me that he is an archaeologist, and that he has worked on recent excavations at the Owl Creek site. "It's worth a visit," he says, as he now hurries off in pursuit of his small companion who has stomped off in a huff along the trail.

# 22

## *Owl Creek and Sites South*

*Davis Lake, Miss.*—Sure enough, there is no indication of Owl Creek on the Parkway map, or surprisingly, on my Mississippi State road map. Fortunately, about 20 miles on, a large sign indicates that Owl Creek is off to the right. A short distance, and there settled in a grove of pines and hardwoods, it is.

Once again, the display-boarding is excellent. This site, the five ceremonial platform mounds, plaza and outlying villages and camps appear to go back in time only as far as the Mississippians. Further, it seems that the mounded sites were occupied only for about 100 years—1100-1200 AD. Nevertheless, in its time it was a regional center of importance; another Moundville on a not-very-much-smaller scale. Intermittent digs—with FDR and the CCC once again playing a big part in the 1930s—have taken place. Student crews from the State University of Mississippi turned up many artifacts bearing stylised Mississippian motifs during excavation in the early 1990s. One prized find was a ceremonial axe, cut and shaped from the soft imported stone, limonite.

Seated on top of the principal mound, I settle down and tune in to the land. All is quiet. Only the gentle wind through the pines breaks the silence. Gradually, that familiar slow pulsing throb starts to come through. I sense the ancient presence. This is thought to be the largest Mississippian ceremonial center in several thousands of square miles. When the first Europeans took note of Owl Creek there were five principal mounds, all of platform style. By the 1960s only this Mound remained largely unaltered. The others were much reduced by repeated ploughing and crop production. And now a road divides the site; leaving two mounds on this side on public land, and three on the other on private land.

Back on the Parkway, I reflect on these and related matters. It is sad to see this important site broken up, the larger part of it left open to whatever further use or abuse to which the landowner may subject it. And yet, life does carry on. In Britain, ancient sites going back to Roman times and beyond have long provided useful stone "quarries" for building and rebuilding over the centuries. Much ancient material has been re-cycled many times. Is not the point, therefore, that what is important is to ensure preservation of "types"—as with Moundville, Etowah and here at Owl Creek? This can provide the opportunity for uncovering the full detail of the concerned specific culture. For the rest, one is able to observe location, often the size of similar or linked sites, this giving a good idea of the extent of a culture and its peoples.

But then I think again. I'm not so sure. What of sacred and ceremonial sites retained on private land? Surely further loss of sacred lands must be prevented? And can this be assured other than under public trust and ownership? But as *all* sites contain elements of the sacred does not this bring us back full circle to the "all site preservation" position? Clearly there are no easy answers.

The complexity of the situation was underlined early this morning when in the heart of "Mississippian Cultural territory" just south of Tishomingo State Park I encountered Pharr Mounds; mounds and a culture which date back 1000 years *before* those at Owl Creek. And now *a few miles south* of Owl Creek here are the Bynum Mounds of *similar antiquity* to those at Pharr. The implication is that each site is unique; that there is no such thing as a "period area."

It is a situation made all the more complex and problematic by the fact that, as mentioned earlier, one "period culture" is often built on top of another; and indeed that the *entire Mississippi Valley and its out-reach lands have been constantly, often quite densely inhabited over the span of many millennia.*

So what does all this indicate? Certainly it does *not* suggest that "period typing" can be applied *until* it is established that individual sites are *solely* of that period—which means that all individual sites must first be closely investigated. And as nearly all sites will be found to possess elements of the sacred, with many bearing the hallmarks of multiple-period occupation, the message would seem to be that *all* sites should be secured under public ownership *until* such time as close investigation and "period typing" may show that *some* may safely be released back into private ownership. Indeed this is a position put by many archaeologists. It is a position I think I now better understand.

Moving on down this corridor of green I am tempted by sites off the Parkway to left and right. I find it particularly difficult to resist the lure of the Winterville Mounds at Greenville on 'ole Miss, and of Spanish Fort near the Yazoo River. About both I have heard and read much. But I resist. By mid-afternoon I am at Kosciusko, about half-way to Natchez.

Suddenly the sky darkens and the rain descends in torrents. The lazy chocolaty streams and winding expanses of cypress swamp I pass seem little affected. The road is empty. I see several deer on the wide, green, immaculately mown verges. At one point I stop and remove three large painted turtles from the middle of the road. They appear not to resent the interference and make their deliberate ways to the verge-side ditch. I make steady progress.

By early evening I have passed the 10-mile-long Ross Barnett Reservoir near Jackson and pull into the Boyd Mounds site. Other than to indicate that structural and pottery remains suggest that the site was inhabited in the period around 500 AD, there is only the slight rise of the circular mounds to be seen. Nevertheless, a short walk round the site with my sensors activated, brings back that curious, warm feeling of power and presence that I am now finding common with all these places of ancient habitation.

By the time I have negotiated detours near Jackson and rejoined the Parkway, the evening is fast closing in. The map indicates another 80 miles to Natchez. I'd like to make it if I can. Only 25 miles on however I start suddenly to feel very sleepy. Time to stop. But where? A large sign looms. "Rocky Springs Site—Recreation Area and Campsite," it announces. I turn in. As at Tishomongo there are many camper-van ramps on the forest edge. Am I up to a second night in the car, I ask myself? At this point, a Ranger with headlights flashing cuts me off. I am driving the wrong way on a one-way system. I inquire about camping. "No problem," says he. And the fee? "No charge." I am about to settle in when I re-consider my previous night in the car and the result. I ask if there are any motels in the area, off-Parkway. The Ranger suggests Port Gibson another 15 miles down the road. I decide to have a look. I can always come back if necessary.

It is dark when I enter Port Gibson. A neon motel sign blinks. A quick run up and down the short town strip shows it is the only motel. I sign in. A young Black man named Mohammed is on the desk. He notes the English address. "First time in Port Gibson?" he asks. I reply I'm looking at Indian Mounds. He lifts an eyebrow. I then inquire if he has long been of the Muslim faith. "Ten years," he replies. And how do Muslims get on in Port Gibson? He taps his pencil and smiles wrily. "Bit of a minority. But we go our way." He pauses. "Not many Uncle Toms amongst our brothers." And is he a practitioner of polygamy, I ask? He laughs. "No! Not even *mon*-ogamy at the moment!" He is, he explains, in his final year of Business Studies at University of Mississippi.

My room is functional. There is a light, a wash basin, toilet and shower. And the air conditioner works. Before retiring I go next door to a Fish Bar. Three attentive young Black men—more students picking up a few evening dollars—quiz me on England and my travels.

Eventually they produce a large basketful of lightly-battered, medium-sized shrimps fried to hot, juicy perfection.

The flavour is delicate, the texture most toothsome. This, as it turns out, is to be my very best fish meal of the entire trip.

# 23

## *The Golden Spire*

*Port Gibson, Miss.*—Next morning my plan was to re-join the Parkway, and then to visit the renowned Emerald Mound along with one or two other ancient sites *en route* to the end of the Parkway at Natchez. But that was before I saw a distant golden spire rising above the mist and tree canopy. I decided a brief detour was merited. The road leading in the direction of the spire gradually broadened out.

*This*, it turned out, was Fort Gibson. In the dark of night I had mistaken the mini-fast-food strip for the town. It wasn't. Magnificent, corinthian-columned ante-bellum mansions, a wide green corridor, and about half-way down, the golden-spired church; this was another Selma, only more gracious, more regal, more awesomely magnificent. I drove a mile or so through the heart of the town, then back.

On the southern outskirts was posted a sign. It stated that Union General Ulysses S. Grant was so enchanted by the beauty of these splendid properties that he ordered they be "spared the torch." And so they were—though not before being thoroughly looted and pillaged by Union soldiers.

Back in town I stopped at one such mansion which displayed a B&B sign. Another night in this locality, I reasoned, would enable me to rest up and see a few additional sites.

I got more than I bargained for. This residence, Magnolia Hall, turned out to be an entire city block. In fact the property comprised a number of separate buildings linked to the principal residence. And this time I got not just a taste, but a full-flavoured mouthful of what the Old South was all about, without the tempering of a Beauregard Duke.

Mrs. Evelyn Lamar, my hostess, was a lady of late middle years, carefully and correctly spoken with all the grace and lyric expression of Southern speech. After preliminary pleasantries, and a number of courteously-phrased, but nevertheless probing queries, Mrs. Lamar turned discussion to the Civil War; to the causes of the War, "the Federal Tariff on Southern manufactured goods, *not* slavery;" to the extensive "mindless, malicious and vindictive" damage inflicted by Northern forces in their "rampage through the South;" to the post-War "Reconstruction" of the South which enabled "those Northern boys to stamp down their foot on our throat, a foot that has never really been removed."

Discussion continued. And as we talked, children, grandchildren, other family members, materialised from time to time, briefly hovered round the entrance to this big, high-ceilinged sitting room, were introduced, smiled, said "Hi," then floated off, phantom-like back into the dark silence whence they had come.

I felt much sympathy for Mrs. Lamar and her kind. Nor did this go un-noted. Finally, she nodded and smiled. "You know, Mr. Vickers, you're just like one of our boys." I paused. Yes, I could see myself, a spirited young cavalier in Confederate grey striding up those mansion steps, blood fiercely burning that any person should dare to challenge the continuity of this my heritage. And yes, no question. That young cavalier would fight to the death to protect and preserve it.

I pause and think again. I am drawn to Mrs. Lamar; she touches something deep, very close to my core. I would like to be one of her boys to please her. But I'm not. I feel the need to "come clean." I explain that I am a visitor; that I can listen; that I can feel; but that I'm just passing through; that I don't live here. "So many things divide folk. I've reached the age where I like to see us sharing, a family, together...."

"But Sir! That's just what we had in the old days!" And so Mrs. Lamar continues. I realise there is no easy way out.

Then, quite suddenly, the discussion veers sharply off to that other favoured and not-unrelated Southern subject—religion.

I learn that in recent years Mrs. Lamar has come to know Jesus. And she has come to love him greatly. I listen. It is a wonderful, a greatly uplifting account. There is enormous force, great spiritual yearning in the feelings and thoughts she conveys. And then it is my turn. In response to one or two queries by Mrs Lamar, I put my own position: the inescapability of guiding Christian ethics in a life lived in a Christian community; of my belief that the Lord God is all round and within us; that the natural world is the Lord God's Church; that I feel great wonder, great awe, great humility amongst these living presences, these unique creations of the Almighty.

For a few moments Mrs. Lamar contemplates me and my words. "Hmmm. Mr. Vickers, you are an intellectual. The toughest nuts to crack. Faith doesn't come easily to you." She sighs. "But if you will just relax, open your heart and your mind, Jesus will come to you...."

The Southerners, top to bottom, are a spiritually highly-sensitive people. And given what we have learned of the role of religion in Southern culture over the millennia, it seems clear they always have been. Added to the effects of geography and climate, this spirituality is no doubt enhanced by the deep persisting trauma of the Civil War—an open wound within all ranks of Southern society. Perhaps it is simply that great loss, great pain opens our beings to the consolation, the re-assurance and support that a passionate Christianity can provide. Simpler still, perhaps it is that Mrs. Lamar, like many of her Southern brethren, possesses a passion and a spirituality that are beyond my reach.

As it is Sunday, I decide to seek out a church service. Indeed after my discussion with Mrs. Lamar it seems timely. Once again there is no shortage of choice. I settle on the New Christian Reformed Pentecostal Church. Tucked away on a back street this is a much less grand place of worship than my last prayer stop in North Carolina. It is a large single-story building; there are no plush carpets. Also the clientele is mainly Black. People push over to make room for me on a back pew.

There are a number of lively hymns for a start. This is followed by an hour-long sermon by a stout, freely-perspiring Whiteman in shirt-sleeves and loosened tie. Like that Pastor in

North Carolina, he makes fulsome use of biblical quotations. It is about the only similarity. Here is Grand Opera compared to Gilbert and Sullivan. At several points he stops and mops his brow. The sermon is followed by powerful, reverberating gospel singing with an equally formidable Black woman providing the lead, the beat and the mesmeric refrains. For the finale, we are treated to a solo by this woman's daughter, a person of similar dimensions and an absolutely fantastic voice. What spirituality I possess is deeply stirred. There is no air conditioning in the church, and the heat and stifling humidity of the Mississippi Delta, as I am discovering, doesn't let up.

After recovering back at Magnolia Hall, I feel the need for an evening meal. I ask Mrs. Lamar if she can suggest a local restaurant. Things are a bit thin in town, she says, and it's getting late. But just south of Port Gibson there's The Old Country Store, a restaurant, she says, which should meet my needs.

It is dark when I get there. And the Old Country Store looks to be just that—no outward sign it's the eating establishment I am expecting. However, inside it's quite perfect. Lots of space, brightly lit, well-ventilated by lots of overhead "whip, whip" fans, many tables, not many people. In fact I am the sole customer. There is a well-stocked hot buffet. The principal offering is barbequed spare ribs in a medium-hot sauce—as many helpings as I want—along with hot vegs, grits, lots of green and fresh fruit salads. I consume two full rounds of ribs and salad. Well-filled and well-pleased, I chat briefly with the proprietors, an ebullient, fast-moving White woman and her Black partner; delightful, courteous and hospitable people. Finally I thank them for the meal and pay up—$4.50. They wish me well on my tour. This is the one and only time during my entire tour that I am to see a White woman and a Black man in "joint harness."

Back at Magnolia Hall, I settle down in my fringed four-poster, air conditioner on full. Sleep is not slow in arriving.

# 24

## *America's "Hot Corner"*

*Port Gibson, Mississippi*—By the time I appear, Mrs. Lamar is already finished her breakfast. Again I am the sole guest. A Black servant duly produces the cereal and toast I have requested. When I tell Mrs. Lamar I am today heading for Emerald Mound and Natchez, she searches out an area map. "You must see these!" She points out the "Plantation Trail" and one or two of the properties open to visitors. Then there's Jefferson College, a former academy, then military institute, "where our Jeff Davis (President of the Confederacy) went to school." And of course there's Emerald Mound; she points out the route to get there.

"And if you've got the time there are many beautiful antebellum houses in Natchez. You really should see them." She points to an item in a Natchez brochure. It states that "Prior to the Civil War, *over half the millionaires in the entire United States lived in Natchez.*" She laughs quietly. "An impressive record for just one small town in the Old South, I'm sure you'd agree!"

Car packed, farewells exchanged, and with Mrs. Lamar, a tiny figure waving a final goodbye from the stately, high-columned front entry to Magnolia Hall, it is back to the Parkway. I want first to visit a dual site I skipped on the way into Port Gibson. Grindstone Ford in the days of early travellers heading north on the Natchez Trace was regarded as the boundary between "civilisation" and the Choctaw "wilderness country". Mangum Mound, located a few hundred yards from the Ford on the opposite side of the Parkway, was a principal ceremonial centre linked to the Natchez state of the Mississippian period.

For the first time I am actually *walking* on the ancient Trace. A broad, leafy, tree-shaded path, it is probably little different now from the Trace 400 years ago when Europeans first used it—even perhaps 10,000 years ago when Indians from near and far regularly traversed these Mississippi lands. The Ford (named "Grindstone" because of a water mill once located on a nearby bayou) provides a shallow where the traveller, sometimes entire armies and war parties could cross in safety. And today it remains a ford; there is no bridge. Other than the silence of this steamy morning and the discovery of a few gravestones of settlers who had progressed no further, my visit is without event—with one exception.

I hear a rustling sound near some Trace-side trees. Constantly on the look-out for rattlers and other snakes about which I've been warned, I freeze and listen. There it is again! With cautious steps I move towards the sound. Another scuffling rustle. Then I see it. I breathe a sigh of relief. No rattler this, but rather, in full grey armour plate, an armadillo rooting round for grubs and insects.

Crossing the Parkway to Mangum Mound, the first thing that strikes me is its massive size. Atop the mound distant views are afforded in all directions. And settling down in the grass the feel of the place starts to flow up. I let my sensors extend. Like all prominent Mississippian ceremonial centres this is a place of peril, pain, terror and blood-letting. The signboarding tells the story. There was ritual killing, human sacrifice here; retainers, perhaps entire families dispatched to accompany a great leader to the next world. And amongst other remains are those which speak of personal tragedy; a young mother and her infant child likely lost at child-birth.

Yet these were just the hard days, the bad days; the days of howling grief, of bitter sadness. Life here in the Great Valley was generous, abundant. This too pulsed up from these lands. Mississippian farmers and their families in surrounding villages and plantation plots not only produced great bounty from these fertile, immensely productive lands, they enjoyed it. People lived well; they celebrated their fortune at a succession of seasonal and other ceremonies. While life had its discipline under the Priest-Suns, the generosity of these lands and waters, the living requirements they readily provided, left time for the artistry, the high crafts; for the creation of items of great beauty like the finely embossed copper ornament uncovered in this mound.

It is now mid-morning, very hot, very humid. Back in the car I am again very grateful for the air conditioner. Another ten miles down the Parkway, with little traffic, the wide verges mown to bowling-green perfection, and I take the turnoff onto the "Plantation Route," a 12-mile loop running close to the Mississippi (not visible), then back to the Parkway. Here, suddenly, one drops back into the Old South era of "King Cotton." My sensors quickly pick up the atmosphere, one of awe and apprehension little different from that engendered at Mangum Mound and every Mississippian site I have visited.

Here however at Springfield, at Oak Grove, along with another dozen or so plantations I have the chance to see and feel the power of a past culture with its physical remnants still fully in place. And such beautiful remnants. Here are statuesque, collonaded Plantation Houses in their original working environments. These are houses that survived not only the ravages of the Union armies, but also successive periods of turbulent rule under the French (from 1716), English (from 1763) and Spanish (from 1779), before the final American consolidation (from 1798).

These were indeed the "King Cotton" plantations, the packed heartland of the fabulous cotton economy—and of America's early millionaires—of which Beau had spoken. Each estate, its Great House, its intensively cultivated acres, its high-efficiency slave and share-cropper workforce, its enormous productivity of premium cotton at premium prices for a ravenous world market; it all happened right here. And here too, just as in Selma and throughout the South, wealth and greed and arrogance and pride had ensured that the decline and fall, when it came, was swift—a true Mississippian heritage?

Moving on now a short distance from this "loop," and with my senses still singing, I am confronted with an awesome sight, a mound of overwhelming size and presence. Not since

Monk's Mound at Cahokia have I set eyes on an earthen monument so vast in extent. This is Emerald Mound, one of the four great centres of Mississippian culture in pre-historic America, the largest in this Great Valley, and ceremonial home to the early Natchez peoples.

I stand in the shade of a broad-limbed hickory at the mound base and try to take it in. About the length and width of one-and-a-half football fields, the platform mound base, is about 35 feet high. Rising above it I can see two secondary mounds, one at either end. Now up on the first level platform in the full blast of Mississippi Delta liquid heat, I check a signboard. The mound site, I learn, covers over eight acres. And before erosion and plowing took their toll there were in addition, six secondary mounds set in pairs at evenly-spaced intervals along its length. No sign of 'em now.

For the rest, it would seem that what has been uncovered here at Emerald Mound reflects what has been learned from other principal Mississippian sites. And this is that here too a people lived and worked under the leadership of a powerful "Sun hierarchy;" a people who some 800-1000 years ago provided mass labour under the guidance of priest/leaders for the production of mounds—not cotton.

Certainly it is tempting to speculate. Both activities—mound-building and cotton production—needed elites with tightly-disciplined, highly-developed skills to design, to engineer, to organise and manage, often on a very grand scale and to a long-term plan. Both also required mass labour-intensive activity. We know about those who provided the labour in the days of King Cotton. But what of the Mississippian mound-worker? Was he a "volunteer," a person participating in a seasonal or annual "devotional" exercise, an exercise which would bring to him credit in the eyes of the Sun hierarchy and the ancestors? Or was he a conscript held permanently to back-breaking toil through physical fear of his masters, perhaps spiritual fear of his ancestors—perhaps both? In what ways was the position of the Mississippian labourer different from that of the King Cotton slave?

And what of the fate of these time-layered cultures? Is it possible that it was the arrogance and greed of those who dominated life here at Emerald Mound—just like those who ran things on those fine plantation properties on the "loop"—that were responsible for bringing the Mississippian civilisation to its sudden, sharp demise? Once again I am drawn to ask myself what was the darker, the contributory siren role of this richly productive land, this generous climate?

I ponder these matters as I now head for Jefferson College in the town of Washington, my last stop before Natchez. This turns out to be a site packed mainly with settler memorabilia and information. Not only did Confederacy President Jefferson Davis attend College here, but in earlier years the Mississippi Statehood Convention (1817) was held in its grounds. And earlier still, in February 1807, close to the "Burr Oaks" (still standing), a hastily-convened Grand Jury having considered the case of the "fugitive" Vice-President, Aaron Burr, decided to release him—much to the fury of President Thomas Jefferson.

As I look over the curricula display—Latin and Greek prominent—for what by then (1817) had become a full-blown College, I am reminded of the world to which these new European settlers were so steadfastly, even desperately clinging out here on the far South-western frontier. It was an alien world, with alien values being transplanted. It would help to ensure alien persons would remain committed to and shaped by alien ideas, aims and concepts in what they (the new settlers) themselves regarded as an alien and hostile land amongst inferior peoples. The irony was that the Natchez Indians held the European in a similar alien and inferior regard. As noted by historians of the Natchez, this mutual dismissive regard, no doubt strengthened by the language gap, ensured that "problems grew that might otherwise have been avoided." A masterpiece of under-statement!

# 25

## *Grand Village and Natchez*

*Washington, Mississippi*—Back in the car, the air conditioning on full, I re-hydrate with a luke-warm coke, and cast a final eye over these historic buildings and grounds. It is interesting to consider that this small corner of what is now Adams County, Mississippi, possesses perhaps the greatest, the richest density of culture, layer upon layer, ancient and modern—truly a "hot corner"—of any locale on this continent. But now? There is no surface hint of the alarums of earlier centuries, of past millennia; of so vigorous, brilliant and turbulent a past. The people are few, the streets quiet. Only the land speaks. And it speaks only to those who care to stop long enough to listen.

A short drive and I am in downtown Natchez. After a cooling Fresh Lemonade with plenty of ice-cubes in the Radisson Hotel bar, and then extracting some cash from a hole-in-the-wall machine that, thankfully, accepts my VISA Card, I attempt to follow brochure directions to the Grand Village of the Natchez. An hour later, after several false attempts, I finally locate it and pull into a shaded parking place. I note there are no other cars.

The Visitor Center is a rambling, modern, single-storey structure under a leafy canopy. I try the door at the entrance. It does not open. I check my watch. Damn! It's 5:02. A notice on the door states that the Center shuts at five. Blast! I've done it again. That hour of vain searching has cost me dear. Then a Security Officer appears. We chat. He commiserates. Finally he says he'll "see what he can do." He disappears into the Center via a side door. A few minutes later Site Historian Jean Simonton appears. I tell her my story. She sighs, smiles and leads me into the Center.

Once again, as at Florence, I have hit gold. Ms. Simonton is not only very knowledgeable, she has feeling and enthusiasm for all things pre-historic and historic. While most of the items in the many displays relate to Mississippian culture—with spear and arrow points of great variety, pottery shards, beads, clay and stone figurine pipes, along with copper and shell ornaments, plus much more—there are some artifacts reaching back to earlier ages.

I am a rapt student, she a compelling teacher. She also shows me the "work exhibits" they use with visiting school groups. Children can not only see and handle Natchez Indian-style items of clothing and ornamentation, along with utensils and tools, they can try their hands at fashioning their own "Natchez creations." Ms. Simonton lets me cast a quick eye over the Bookshop collection. It is a bit disappointing compared to the offerings at Moundville and Tupelo. Still I find one or two useful titles, and note down a few more for future reference.

What started as a "ten-minute peek," has become a full hour of quality time. I am both grateful and much-impressed. This Center, its displays, the events organised, the obvious efforts made to bring the story of this "hot corner" of the continent to life in new, challenging, different and constantly changing ways is a most reassuring delight. The State of Mississippi and its Department of Archives and History can take just pride.

It is 6:20 by the time Ms. Simonton and I part company. Parked by my car is the Security Officer. "Was the visit worth it?" he asks. I tell him it was well worth it, and thank him for making it possible. He purses his lips. "Well, you'd come a long way. And we're mighty proud of the Grand Village." He nods in the direction of some small mounds I can see in parkland beyond the trees. "Now if you've got the time, you might just have a wander round those mounds. Home of the Great Sun and his people, 'afore our folk came along and messed it all up!" I tell him I shall do just that. He departs on other business.

Even though the sun is well down, the shadows long across the green of this parkland, the heat is still sweltering. I look first round a re-constructed Natchez house and corn granary. It is what I now recognise as the customary Mississippian design—circular, mud and wattle walling, thatched roof and silled door. I cross the plaza, a modest space by Moundville standards, to the Great Sun's residential mound, then another 40 yards or so to the Temple Mound. Both are about eight feet high, and again modest in extent compared to Moundville or Emerald Mounds.

Still, the buzz, the tingle of power and presence rises as I settle down on top of the Temple Mound. With my sensors once again at full extension, I puzzle. Why did these Natchez peoples' ancestors vacate the grand and imposing Emerald Mound and shift to this location?—which is what the archaeological record appears to show. Why the sudden modesty? It is clear this Grand Village is but a small hamlet compared to the community that once existed at the Emerald Mound site.

Had the "Suns of Emerald" lost their Imperial hold? Had they pressed "royal absolutism" beyond the limits acceptable to their peoples? Had there been crop failure, pestilence, perhaps disease of plague proportions arising from lands too heavily lived upon by too many, for too long? Had they lost favour with *Coyocopchill*, (the Supreme Being), perhaps too with the *Coyocop-techou*, (the lesser spirits)? Why this apparent shift to this Grand Village site took place is but one of the intriguing mysteries we must wait for archaeologists of the future to reveal.

It is not so difficult to find my way back into Natchez. And in the evening light I view in passing the great houses of which Mrs. Lamar has spoken. Each is individual, each magnificent. Here not only are soaring, colonnaded elevations of high-Georgian style in the luxurious surround of extensive parkland properties, but also Plantation Town Houses of the Spanish (pre-1798) period; rambling, single-storied, white, frame-built structures with long, spacious verandas under lengthy roof overhangs. Amongst the many properties open to my appreciative gaze are Dunleith, Rosalie, Stanton Hall, Monmouth, and my particular favourite, Auburn (built 1812), a four-pillared, two-storey, Georgian neo-classical brick residence of simple symmetric design and graceful presence.

From high culture and the layered mysteries of a rich and powerful past, it is back to the realities of the present. In need of a bed, and finding none in town, I discover on the high bluffs on the outskirts, a motel. And a room is available. After checking in, and feeling the need of food, I set out in quest. On the fast-food strip not far from the motel I duly locate a Dairy Queen. I order up a Chocolate Thick Shake. It is cold, tasty and reviving. Pangs of hunger appeased, I return along the now busy strip to my lodging.

Not quite ready for bed, I decide to stretch my legs. Behind the motel is an elevated section of the high bluffs. Atop this promontory I first look to the west; the sun a distant fiery orb on a darkening lavender horizon. Then I look down.

And there at last it is.

A broad, shimmering ribbon extending to the north, and as I now turn to look, as far to the south. Here is America's steady, throbbing heart, pumping the continent's life blood through this mighty artery. Here is the great giver and sustainer of life, mid-wife to wondrous prodigies of art, of engineering, of human striving and achievement. And here too is the primary cause and vital force of all that has from earliest times brought terrible darkness as well as intermittent shafts of brilliant light to the lives of all who have resided here and for many thousands of miles distant. It is the Mississippi. I stand for a few moments and soak it in.

Across on the far side a huge, heavily laden barge labours up-stream. There is an acrid, foul smell of chemical pollutants in the evening air. My eyes and nose start to smart. Downstream, high industrial chimneys on the Louisiana side belch up great grey columns. A pulp mill, or some kind of chemical production plant, I reckon.

Upstream the air is clear and seemingly pollutant-free. A mile distant, the loops of metal lattice in the bridge across to Vidalia stand out sharply in the fading light.

Tomorrow, early, I shall be crossing that bridge.

Tonight is my last in these deep, brooding and powerful lands east of the Mississippi.

What, I wonder, awaits me in Louisiana and the West?

# 26

## *The Heart of Ancient America*

*Vidalia, Louisiana*—A heavy mist is starting to lift off the river as I cross the bridge to Vidalia. It has just turned seven. Past the customary fast-food strip I spot a non-glossy small diner. A sign announces, "Breakfast Special—$3.00." I pull in.

A full breakfast is quickly hustled up—fresh Florida orange juice, scrambled eggs, bacon, sausage, tomato, buttered toast, raspberry jam in little plastic packets, and fresh hot coffee—and as quickly consumed. It is my first serious food since The Country Store. And it is good. How, I wonder, do the glossy, plastic, fast-food emporia even briefly draw their breath against tasty, nourishing real food like this? The marvels of modern advertising and other forms of public mis-representation!

While sipping my coffee and gazing idly out the window, suddenly it hits me. I have arrived! Here at last I am in the very heartland of pre-American antiquity. I feel a rising buzz of excitement. I tidy up some escaped egg yolk with my toast and drain the last of my coffee. Did the fellow who was breakfasting here on these lands 6000 years ago enjoy as tasty a meal? Maybe more nutritious?

Already it is starting to heat up. Back in the car and further down the strip I see a "Louisiana Welcome Center." A car is parked in the lot beside the main building, an oasis of pristine white and green in this suburban belt of depressing light-industry drab. Must be open, I reckon. And it is.

Two neatly-dressed, middle-aged women are in attendance. I tell them my story: that I'm visiting sites of the Ancient Moundbuilders; that I've just crossed from Natchez; and are there any sites locally I should see?

They smile. One departs to attend to other business. "I guess you've come to the right place," declares the woman remaining. "And if I may ask, how local is local?" I explain that I am aware of Poverty Point and Marksville, and that I've heard of a few other sites. She laughs and reaches for a brochure. "Now this pamphlet says that Looseeanna has more than 700 sites with mounds." She flips through, then passes it across to me. "In fact, if anybody bothered to count 'em, we've probably got that many sites right here in Concordia Parish!" She laughs again and adjusts her glasses. "You're deep in the heart of ancient America. Folk have always just loved to live here. Good food, and lots of it. Things grow with very little persuasion. And as for the weather, well my, oh my. It's not very often a person is going to catch a chill down here! No sir!"

She then selects several more leaflets and hands them across. "These'll give you an idea of the sites to be seen." Here were particulars on Poverty Point, Marksville, the LSU (Louisiana State University, Baton Rouge) mounds. But not much more.

Helen—this I learn is her name—notes my dismay.

"I know," she sighs. "Not a whole lot after what I said about the hundreds hereabouts. The fact is that most are on private land. And owners are not that pleased to have the public tramping all round their property, and maybe doing a little speculative digging." She went on to repeat what I had heard from Ohio to the Deep South: the market in ancient artifacts; the vandalism, desecration and damage at accessible and unprotected sites; the determination of many landowners to ensure that any artifacts extracted went into their own "personal collections"—or the proceeds therefrom into their pockets. "So you see, the result is that unless you're well-connected in the archaeology world the actual number of sites you can visit is pretty limited."

Helen looks me up and down. She notes my disappointment. "Hmmm. You are *real* interested in these mounds aren't you?" She tears off a sheet of paper and jots down a name. "Now up in Catahoula Parish, just up the road from here, you might care to look up this man. Name's Davey Richards. He's an Attorney. Knows a bit about the mounds through here. You'll find his office near the Courthouse in Harrisonburg. Don't know exactly where. Never actually been up there myself." She sketches a map to show the route and location. "And another thing. There's a pre-history museum in the Harrisonburg Courthouse. You might find that worth a visit. They say it's very good."

Resuming travel, I am soon clear of this light-industry wasteland and heading west. In every direction the land lies flat, the shimmer of heat already rising from the black soil. I check one of the maps Helen has given me. Yes, I am well into the alluvial plain. Four hundred miles north-to-south, 50-100 miles east-to-west. No bluffs here to protect against the waters of ole Miss when she decides to ramble cross-country. The only escape is stilted houses. I see a few. But not many.

I make a brief stop at Frogmore, an ante-bellum cotton plantation restored to full operation and a local tourism feature. I note that the Plantation Mansion, a modest structure by Natchez standards, stands about eight feet clear of the ground. This, I later deduce, is the elevation considered adequate to keep residents dry when ole Miss is on serious rampage. Frogmore's slave cabins enjoy no such protection. They are planted solidly on the ground.

The young blonde in the Visitors Shop, trim in Frogmore T-shirt and short shorts, make-up carefully applied, informs me a tour of the plantation will shortly depart. I tell her I'm here to visit Indian mounds. She brightens and tells me about the Frogmore Mound. "It's not in any of the books. But there it is. Close to where you've parked." She notes the New York plates. "You come down here often, then?" I tell her my story. She regards me doubtfully.

I ask her about the Frogmore Mound's pedigree. She shrugs. "Just an ole Indian mound. Used to be lots through here. Guess those Indians didn't like getting their feet wet any more than we do. Most of 'em gone now. Plowed 'em up and levelled 'em." I pick up a couple of postcards and an ice-cold coke from the stand-up, glass-doored cooler. "Biggest mound round here used to be up the road at Jonesville. 'Bout 80 feet high, they say." She pops the cards in a bag. "Don't rightly know what happened to it. But ask anyone when you get up there. They'll tell you."

Outside I see the tree-covered mound. About 8 feet high, and 100 feet by 60 feet at the base, it is of platform style .I walk round the perimeter. The sun is now well up. I am sweating heavily with no exertion at all. Why, I wonder, was this mound spared? Application of a plow and a bit of slave labour would have levelled it in no time. Then I take another look. Eight feet in height. The same clearance as the Plantation Mansion. Maybe a place of refuge for chattels—cattle and slaves—during high water?

The land continues dead flat, with a few forested rises—more ancient mounds?—as I approach Jonesville. Into the town's outskirts, and over a bridge, the broad, light-chocolaty stream below in placid temper, I manage to dodge some sizeable potholes in the town's dusty mini-fast-food alley. Failing to find the turn-off to Harrisonburg, I double back. Beneath a strange enclosed tinted-plate-glass deck extending out towards the road, I see "Police Department" in modest white letters on the door below. Inside I ask directions to Harrisonburg. Directions received I inquire if they know of Attorney Davey Richards, and if so, where is his office? The officers are suddenly alert. "Across from the Courthouse," I am informed. "That's where you'll find him."

Before departing I ask about the tinted-glass room above. "What's that all about?"

One of the lawman grins and laughs. "We put the speed-gun on folk comin' through. It's got a camera connected. No need to chase violators. We get their licence numbers. Then send 'em a summons. Works real good." And what, I wonder, was my speed as I passed the gun? I have visions of speeding tickets popping through my letter-box at home!

# 27

## _Mounds, Snakes and Mystery Treasure_

*Harrisonburg, Louisiana*—Another ten miles or so on the instructed route up country and I am driving down the main street of Harrisonburg, "the second oldest town in Louisiana," the brochure tells me. I wonder what town is the oldest? It does not say.

It is nearly mid-day. I stop at a gas station to fill up. The heat is a blistering 97 degrees, the humidity stifling. I ask the whereabouts of the Courthouse. The perspiring attendant points to a large red brick building across the road. And Attorney Davey Richards, I inquire? "Mistah Davey?" He points to a brown timber bungalow next door with all its venetian blinds drawn. "If you're lookin' for Mistah Davey, that's where you'll find him."

I park the car in front of the office bungalow. No sign at all of life within. But his shingle's on the wall, so it must be the right place. Somewhat hesitantly I open the door and enter. It's a biggish waiting room. But nobody is waiting. It's deliciously cool. I cautiously poke my head through a doorway. A large young-ish woman is working on a word processor. I introduce myself, tell her my interest, and ask if I might have a brief word with Mr. Richards.

After ten minutes or so I am sitting down opposite a lean, greying, curly-haired man in white T-shirt and battle fatigues. This is Mr. Davey Richards. We exchange greetings. Rubbing a two-day growth he eyes me warily. The phone rings. He picks it up, raps out two or three truculent comments and bangs it down. "Never leave a man alone in this business!" he growls.

I fill him in about my interest in the mounds; what I've seen so far; and what I'm looking forward to seeing in Louisiana. He listens, fidgets with a pencil, then relaxes a bit and starts to tells me about "early residents" here in Catahoula Parish. As we talk another younger man comes in and pulls up a chair. This is Davey's colleague, Attorney Robert Jenkins. Robert, it turns out, is perhaps even keener than Davey on local and indeed Louisiana and Southeastern pre-history and archaeology. I smile to myself. The Vidalia Tourism ladies have done me a very large favour.

Within a short time I am made aware that in the immediate vicinity of Harrisonburg there are the signs, symbols and artifactual remains of man as he has lived here in Louisiana from earliest times more than 10,000 years ago, through every age and identified period, right up to the present. I am informed there are lots and lots of sites which are known to local people, but which do not show up on the maps. And some are very big. Davey and Robert volunteer to give me a quick whip-round of places of pre-historic interest in the locality.

After a light lunch—sandwich and chocolate milk-shake for me—at the local diner, we hit the back roads of Catahoula Parish in Davey's battered Four-Wheel-Drive (4WD) Ford Bronco. As with Mr. Beauregard Duke, air conditioning is provided by what comes in the windows. We keep 'em open wide. Finally, after yet another turn down yet another dirt road, then a bouncing dive down a forest tangle track, Davey hits the brakes." This is it!" he announces. "Mitchell Mounds."

All that I see is a jungle of green scrub, vines and trees on the banks and tops of a few sizeable knolls and hillocks. Davey leads, Robert follows, and I bring up the rear—keeping a sharp watch for snakes. It is not an easy climb. More like a scramble through the dense undergrowth.

On top now, Davey points. Through the dappled half-light and green tangle I can see to my left another mound about the same height as this one; then another large mound to my right. "And that down there," Davey points to an elevated path connecting this mound to the one on my right, "is something which has caused a bit of a fuss in the archaeological world. Some experts say it is a levee built by sensible Indians to keep out flood waters. Others maintain it's nothing of the sort, but merely a part of the ceremonial works constructed by our prehistoric Catahoula residents." He grins wryly and wags his head. "The latter view is currently in fashion."

Davey then points to other features well-disguised by the undergrowth. There is a smaller path connecting to the mound on our left. And with the guidance of Davey's experienced eye I am able to make out yet another path joining up to three or four heavily-overgrown smaller mounds in a dapple of sunlight opposite.

He explains that the site contains altogether seven mounds: the large platform mound on which we are standing, two large oval domed, and the four smaller mounds which may originally have been domed or platform, age and erosion making it difficult to tell. In the center, surrounded by these mounds, is what was once an open space or plaza.

I ask if the complex is Mississippian? Davey shrugs. "The experts maintain that our ancient Catahoula residents of the period were at best only *half* into Mississippian culture. The Great Suns of Cahokia, Natchez, Moundville, they say, did not extend their political influence this far. And while the general style and layout of this complex does suggest Mississippian cultural input, it's possible that what was constructed here was in fact built much earlier. Given this interpretation, it may be that these top layers visible to us merely represent the result of Aztec, perhaps late Mayan influence, as their 'imperial missionaries' probed up from the Gulf of Mexico."

As we now made our way back down through the undergrowth tangle, I noted two large, jagged depressions on the side of the mound; then a number of smaller deeper holes. I pointed them out.

"Pot hunters," said Davey. "Some serious and professional. But most just local hopefuls looking to add a few spear-points or pottery shards to their collections. The fate of most mounds not publicly owned and protected—like Marksville or Poverty Point. Folk just go in and dig to see what they can find. Even though there are now stiff legal penalties, it doesn't seem to slow 'em down."

Back in the Bronco, bumping and jolting back up the overhung track, Davey asked if I'd heard about the fabled "Natchez Treasure." I said no. "Well I don't know whether there is a Natchez Treasure, or there's not. But the fact is that just about everyone in these Northeast Parishes and many from far beyond—even foreign shores—" he eyed me evenly, "believes that ole treasure is hidden somewhere nearby, maybe in a mound, a cave, maybe stashed in a river bank. Solid gold, jewels, all kinds of precious objects just waiting for some lucky person to dig 'em up." He laughed. "Well this has stirred up a whole lot of trouble. A kind of 'treasure fever.' And it's been going on as long as I can remember. And a lot longer than that."

I asked how the story of the Natchez Treasure came to be. Davey explained it went back to a "little argument" the Great Sun of Natchez and his people had with the French colonisers. The French, he said, had pushed too hard. There was a dispute over a "land grab." The Natchez finally reacted and in 1729 killed many French colonists. The following year the French re-grouped and hit back. Some Natchez were killed. But most chose to abandon the Grand Village, cross ole Miss, and set up house in the remote back-country here in Northeast Louisiana. "And the popular belief is that they brought their treasury—known to contain fabulous wealth—with them." The Bronco bucked hard over another bump. "And where do you suppose they chose to set down roots?" Davey laughed. "Yes sir! Good ole Catahoula Parish! Near a place now called Sicily Island, not more than a few miles from here."

That then was the story.

"And that also is the reason why just about everybody gets jumpy and green-eyed when any of the archaeologists from LSU, the Smithsonian—or anyone else—starts to do a bit of diggin', or nosin' round any mounds, or suspected mounds hereabouts. Folk reckon that ole treasure just might turn up. And if it does, they're going to be right there. Kinda like their birth-right. Everyone's determined to have his share!"

Davey laughed again as the Bronco with a final violent buck and bucket regained the tarmaced road. "What's real sad about all this is that we've got us what are almost certainly the oldest settlements on the American continent—long before the Olmecs or the Mayans of Central America got into business—but it's just about impossible to do the serious archaeological investigations that are needed. The moment the archaeologist puts down his tools for the night, the local folk are in there. Anyone told you about the Great Mound at Jonesville?" I said no. "Well that's another story for another time. But same theme."

On the way back I noted a few big rambling bungalows close to the bayous, and all comfortably elevated to the customary eight feet or so above ground level. Then a little further on at a crossroads I was horrified by the sight of a withered head with big ears nailed to a telephone pole! I shouted at Davey to stop. Both Davey and Robert seemed amused, though they said nothing. Closer inspection revealed the head was that of an enormous catfish with big fins. What,

I asked, was this all about? Robert explained that it was a "local custom." When a fisherman caught one of these monsters, this was his way of advertising the fact. Interesting custom, interesting people, thought I, as we scrambled back into the battered Bronco.

Another mile or two and Davey pulled up by the side of a bridge. "Lots of big snakes round here. They love this kind of wetland and green cover," he observed as he edged his way down the bank towards a sluggish brown stream. Following closely I kept a sharp and apprehensive eye. Beneath the bridge, Davey used a rock to scratch away some rich, loamy soil. "Lookee here!" he called out and handed me two jagged stone chips. "One of our early residents has been at work here. He's just been sittin' here knappin' and knappin'. 'Damn!' he says—maybe somethin' worse—as he mis-hits or gets the line wrong." He picked up another chip, turned it over and examined it. "For every spear point successfully produced, I've often wondered how many were messed up?"

I asked how old these chips might be? Davey shrugged. "Maybe 11,000 years, maybe only 5000, but no less than 3000." He explained that the level—6 feet down from ground level—at which the chips were exposed suggested an earlier rather than a more recent date. "But it's never easy to be sure. You see Catahoula's pre-historic residents made use of a pretty standard lithic (stone) technology from very earliest days right up until maybe 700, even 500 years ago.

"These chips on their own tell us very little. But a bit of careful scientific work easing back into this stratum might produce some tools, utensils, pipes, ceremonial ornaments, maybe spear points which would enable us to know whether these folk were our recent or more distant cousins." He turned and chuckled. "That's what *real, proper* archaeology is about. They tell us something useful. Don't use it to inflame yet more theoretical argument in quest of fame, academic prestige, promotion and God only knows what else us human folk are prone to!"

Now carefully parting the profuse greenery with a stick as he headed back up the bank, he suddenly turned. "Seen any snakes yet?" I said no. "Funny," he growled. "Must be having a siesta. Usually one or two provide a nice welcome 'buzzzz'—just to let us know whose land this is!" I was very glad to reach the sanctuary of Davey's Bronco.

# 28

## *Safeguarding Catahoula Heritage*

*Harrisonburg, Louisiana*—It was late afternoon when we pulled into the office yard. With Davey and Robert getting back to office business, now was my chance to visit the "Catahoula Parish Museum of Natural History." Both had confirmed it was well worth a look.

Crossing the road I noted two Black men in orange coveralls doing a bit of scything in a ditch beside the Courthouse. We exchanged a few words. I told them I was a visitor from England and was much-impressed with what I'd so far seen of Catahoula Parish. They listened politely, then wished me well on my travels before returning to the slow rhythmic swing of their work. The heat was fierce and they were taking its full impact.

As I crossed the Courthouse lawn I noticed there were numbers on the backs of those orange coveralls; and under a tree was a man in uniform with a rifle in the cradle of his arm. He tipped his grey stetson as I passed. I later learned that this was a variant of "community service," whereby the inmates of Louisiana's penal institutions were kept busy, and the taxpayer got at least something in return for the enormous sums spent on the State's correctional facilities—the biggest employer, if not the biggest business in the State.

Once inside the Courthouse—beautifully cool—the Museum was not hard to find. On the ground floor close to the Police Department front office a set of display cases were ranged. Each provided artifact exhibits with accompanying era-by-era signboards. Thus there was coverage from palaeo times, through Marksville period, and into "modern" times—Troyville (400 AD), Coles Creek (900 AD), and Plaquemine (1300 AD). Much attention was given to these "modern" periods, as apparently they are well-represented in the archaeology of the area. I soaked it up.

There were also a few signboards devoted to the Jonesville Mound, about which Davey had spoken. I learned it was thought to be the regional center for the Troyville culture; that there had been a complex of sizeable platform mounds; indeed that the largest, at 80 feet high, was second only to Monk's Mound at Cahokia. The *denouement* was that in the summer of 1931, Governor Huey Long's Roads Department got busy. In three weeks or less, a few thousand years of Louisiana's history was obliterated when the Great Mound was levelled and used as dirt-fill in road construction.

One thing about the display cases puzzled me. Within most there were neat little marker cards naming and describing the relevant artifacts. The problem was that many of the artifacts described were absent. Well, I reckoned, maybe the artifacts were out on loan, or with a travelling exhibit? As there was no one else about, I inquired in the Police Department office.

No, I had not come to pay a fine or answer a summons. But please could someone tell me about the absent artifacts. The two women clerks stopped typing and regarded each other uncertainly. Then one spoke up.

"We had a burglary a while back. A lot of them things went missing." I expressed surprise that a burglary should have taken place in a Courthouse, and right next door to the Police office. The woman shrugged. "It happened." And were these valuable items, I asked? "No, not so valuable this time." *This* time? Had there been other burglaries? The woman nodded. "Been four burglaries to my certain knowledge." Her colleague nodded in agreement. "But we reckon there'll be no more problems. The security system's been up-graded."

I thanked the women for their help. Improved security system indeed! A bit late. Nothing left of sufficient value to secure! Still, the few lithic and pottery items were interesting. And the signboarding and descriptive markers were excellent.

On my way back across the Courthouse lawn I looked for my two acquaintances in orange and their minder. No sign. Home for a nap and a well-earned dinner I assumed.

Back in Davey's office things had picked up. A number of persons, informally attired, male and female, were silently studying newspapers and magazines in a well-filled waiting room. From the back office where the secretaries held court came the sound of raised voices, women's voices. There was a lot of hollering and shouting and stamping. Cautiously I poked my head round the corner. A very large White-woman was in full flow.

"He's not getting away with it this time! No way! It's now four months! Not a fucking dime! Says he can't pay me my alimony and look after his new family. *New fucking family*! Can you believe it!" The relevant secretary, of dimensions nearly as formidable, clucked sympathetically. "What about me? What about Josh and Bethany?" Bang! "I tell you he's not getting away with it this time! I'll sue! Put Davey onto the fucker! I want blood! He's gonna know what it feels like!" Sobs, tears, a chair gets bashed by a meaty fist. The secretary makes more soothing noises. The other pours a cup of coffee and hands it to the distraught women who now seems suddenly to have deflated. The second secretary guides the woman back into the waiting room and seats her.

Another client, a man in denim bib-and-braces and not much else, gets the nod. He follows the secretary into the back room. The others rustle their papers and magazines and continue their patient wait. I too take a seat.

By 7:30 the waiting room is clear. I venture into the back room. Davey and Robert appear from their respective offices. We talk for a bit. Then Davey casually reminds me of our "archaeological investigations" under the bridge in "snake country." He points to a picture pinned on the wall. It is of a rattlesnake (dead) of terrifying size. The caption below reads, "10 feet long, 96 lbs." Struggling to hold up the doubled snake is "Jake Wyatt's Daddy, Sam," a powerfully built Black man in fatigues and—appropriately—snake boots.

Davey notes that I am impressed. "Yep. They grow real big down here." He laughs. "Ole Sam got a bit of a surprise when he dug into that embankment with his 'dozer a few years back." He glances over at me. "Gives you an idea of the surprise a man may experience when he does a bit of diggin' round, like under that bridge we visited this afternoon." He laughs again.

Davey checks his watch. "Time's gettin' on. Any place you got lined up to stay tonight?" I say that I would be grateful for a good motel reference. "No problem," Davey declares. Jonesville, I am informed, is the place.

Leaving the secretaries to close up, Davey and Robert clamber into the Bronco and lead the way. With darkness nearly down, they pull in at Williams Motel. The very finest accommodation, I am assured.

I book in. It is indeed a fine room with all mod cons in the brand-new wing. I snap on the air conditioning. There is a reassuring purr. The cool air spreads. Lovely.

I have a final word with my Harrisonburg friends. They instruct me to come by the office about ten in the morning. I watch as the big Bronco swings back out onto the main road and growls off into the night.

# 29

## *The Ancients Are Present*

*Jonesville, Louisiana*—I am onto the road back to Harrisonburg by 9:30. Already the heat is into the 90s, the humidity about the same.

At Davey's office, things are off to a brisk start. A more or less continuous flow of customers is passing through, most, at a guess, at the lower end of the fee spectrum. I can practically see Davey's cordwood pile growing.

Then there's a break. I am summoned. Davey is not happy. He has a plea to enter across the road at the Courthouse. This means discarding his favoured T-shirt and fatigues for a shirt, tie and jacket. "Don't know why," he grumbles. "This fancy dress don't make no difference to a man's words!"

He then explains that he and Robert are going to be busier than they thought today; that he hopes they've given me something to think about; and "Why don't you drop by again after you've seen what you want to see round this part of the State?" With his secretary popping her head round the door, and papers flying back and forth, I realise I'm holding up the production line. It's time to go. "Now you will check up with us before you get back on the Trail?" Davey inquires. "We've still got a bit to discuss and see." I assure Davey I'll be back in his waiting room in a couple of days.

I decide to head south, visit the Marksville Mounds, and then the really ancient mounds, built about 3000 BC, at the LSU Baton Rouge Campus. This route should also allow me to have a look and a feel for ole Miss in her lower reaches, and perhaps catch a glimpse of a few of the many remaining old Plantation Mansions and ante-bellum houses in this pocket of fabulous pre-Civil War productivity and wealth.

The road west, then south to Marksville is relatively clear and straight. It's smooth driving. The main reason I had opted for this Monte Carlo with its big wheels was my concern about road conditions here in the back country of the Deep South. I needn't have worried. The roads are in fine condition. No pot-holes or washboard sections. Only in some municipalities for which the State Roads Authority is not responsible have things been a bit rough.

No grand residences through here. Rather a few large bungalows with wide, low tin roofs, many shacks and other domestic structures in a state of comfortable dereliction and dis-repair, and an equal number of large and small trailer homes, these often at a distance from the main road and without tree shade or any other cover for protection against the blistering heat. The bayous, streams and lakes I pass and cross make clear why this area has been largely by-passed by the big planters. Much more to the taste of hunters and fishers, and to those who prefer a more rugged and independent life.

Indeed with fish and game so readily to hand it is equally easy to understand why this had been a preferred area of settlement over the past many millennia, and perhaps why also those who lived here were very difficult to lure into the open, or force out. No problem at all to disappear. Locals knew the ground; newcomers and invaders didn't—as in modern times both Union and Confederate authorities were to discover. Catahoula Guerrillas, Alligator Rangers and Pinewood Sharpshooters were but three of the colorful Louisiana companies which fought hard for the Confederacy, but in their own way and often on their own terms. Other than resentment of Northern interference in Southern affairs many up-country Louisiana residents felt little but contempt for the influential "plantocracy" and indifference to their "Southern Cause."

I notice that here too all residential structures are elevated. The older, permanent dwellings are up the customary 6-8 feet; the others are 2-3 feet clear of the ground. I had heard about the last big flood. It was in 1973. Clearly, however, people today residing here on the floodplain can feel a little less fearful of *severe* flooding. For running parallel to the road is mile upon mile of earthen embankment providing what appears to be a perimeter of protection for isolated communities. I get out and inspect a section. Ten to twelve feet high, and about 50 feet wide at the base. This is an impressive structure. The Moundbuilders of antiquity would, I am sure, be impressed.

It was not easy to find the Marksville site. But at last, having located the turning and negotiated the quasi-shantytown avenue on the town outskirts, there, at the end, it was—or so the sign said. I could see no mounds, only the Spanish-style

Visitor Center. Out of the car, into the Center, then back out again into the wilting Delta heat, I started to make my way round the 42-acre site.

Though not of the scale, nor the dramatic presence of Moundville or Emerald Mound, here was a compact ancient ceremonial site. Facing onto Old River, and contained by a semi-circular earthwork rising to seven feet high, were five mounds. Nor as I made my way amongst them were these trifling. The largest, a platform mound rose to a height of 14 feet from a rectangular base nearly 300 feet by 250 feet. At the opposite end of the enclosed plaza-like area was another platform mound of similar immensity, this one 300 feet in diameter and 13 feet high. Close by were three smaller mounds, all conical, and none more than 100 feet in diameter.

I climbed up the first big platform mound and settled down in the grass. What was this place about? What did my sensors tell me? Gradually I started to feel the throb of the place. It was an even beat. And though the sun was screened by clouds, this did not ease the stifling heat. It was of at least equal intensity to that of the Niger Delta. That heavy wet heat. I remembered it well. The sweat was again streaming. Rich and productive though this region was, there was, and no doubt always had been, a human price to pay. And for the malaria mosquito, these steaming flatlands must have been heaven!

What I sensed here, rising up through the many-generationed layers of this mound, was simply a steady presence and power. No great feeling of fear, nor of overwhelming dominance. This was a sacred place. A place of ceremony, of magic, of sorrow and celebration. Here leaders and priests—perhaps one and the same—took counsel, and sought those divinations which would guide them and their peoples through the cycle of the seasons, through the natural and supernatural realities of their daily lives.

Back in the Visitor Center I made my solitary way round the display area. The exhibits were somewhat confusing, and perhaps a bit antiquated in their presentation format compared to others I had seen. Still, the information was there. And piecing it together a clear picture emerged. Though throughout this bayou country and alluvial floodplain—just as in Catahoula Parish—there were many ancient habitations, here at Marksville was a center of regional importance. With a life-span of about 400 years—0 AD-400 AD—the archaeologists (with once again the vital assistance of WPA workers in 1930s digs and restoration activity) had uncovered enough of this Marksville material culture to establish a framework of meaning, a framework with which I was now familiar.

From here, a wide trade network had extended; this indicated by the copper, imported stone, shell and other materials from which fine jewellry and ceremonial items had been created. Customary practices of elite burials in the mounds had been confirmed; primary and secondary interments, complete with grave goods had been found in one of the dome-shaped mounds. And in the finely-decorated pottery, platform pipes, copper ornaments, together with the low semi-encircling earthworks, a link with the distant peoples of ancient Ohio was suggested. The people of Ohio's Hopewell culture, at about the same time, were building earthworks and producing items very similar in form and function to these found here in the Mississippi Delta.

It was fascinating stuff.

# 30

# *Deep in the Delta*

*Marksville, Louisiana*—As I climbed back behind the wheel of the Chevy and headed on south towards Baton Rouge, I pondered. Clearly the archaeologists yet again had been hard at work. And from their findings, it seemed to me, three main questions had emerged.

First was this a purely Marksville period site, or did its origins stretch back 1500 years or so to the days of Poverty Point culture, perhaps earlier? Findings at the site suggested to some specialists that this was more than a possibility. Second, what of the Hopewell connection? Was it the Hopewells who were the "culture transmitters" to the Marksville and neighbouring Louisiana peoples, or was it perhaps the other way round? Third, was it possible that what had happened here had little to do with either Marksville or Hopewell peoples, but that in fact it was the Meso-Americans who were the principal engines of "culture transmission"?

The 3rd century Mayans, were bursting with energy, confidence and imperial zeal. It was but a short trip from Meso-America around or across the Gulf to the mouth of ole Miss. From this "port of entry" there would have been no problem in trade, perhaps "missionary" expeditions supported by the military moving up-stream and inland, spreading the Mayan "word" and customs as they went.

Though this view is not favoured by specialists who point out that no Mayan remains have been found in the Mississippi and Ohio catchments, I would be inclined to put the position the other way round. And that is, that *until* conclusive evidence is found which shows that Mayan influence was *not* present, then given the obvious similarities to be discerned—platform mounds, ceremonial objects, and ornamental items, etc.—it is reasonable to assume that Meso-American and Mayan influence in particular *was important* if not dominant in these regions at this time.

Suddenly on the road in front of me is an enormous brown bird picking at something. I swerve, it flaps off, and I get a quick glimpse of a snake of about five feet, its diamond pattern well flattened out on the tarmac. So much for my musings on Marksville.

What then, I ask myself, did this Marksville experience and these musings have to say to me? Well, it was not for me to say who had influenced who, and done what to whom, and when. That was for the specialists. But for me one thing at least had emerged. And this was that here as elsewhere in these Delta lands a great many people—perhaps more than reside here now in the 21st century—had been living well, involved in productive activity, and subject to group control and discipline. As for Mayan influence shaping the lives of these remarkable peoples, this seems to me an obvious certainty. Perhaps in time more will be revealed.

Across the mighty Red River, which was not red at all but chocolaty, and on along the highway which winds its way south through bayou, stream and mangrove, finally I caught sight of ole Miss. This was the old French District of Pointe Coupée. And there, conveniently, was a road-side snack bar. But sadly, no French cuisine. I acquired an egg sandwich and a chocolate shake and retired to the car. I had a good view of ole Miss. Broad and heavy chocolaty, she just rolled quietly along.

A bit further on this twisting and turning route, then a left turn into a heavy-trafficked dual-highway and I was into Baton Rouge. On the second try I picked up the turn-off to LSU; and a few miles down another busy road, and I was onto the Campus. It was then a matter of asking directions, and then suddenly there they were, rising to an impressive 20 feet, the LSU Mounds.

I spoke with a passing student. What did he think about living and working side-by-side with the ancients? He looked at me strangely. "Always been there. Always will be, I guess." He then hurried off. 5000 years, settled here beside ole Miss, and now a "living part" of one of the State's leading educational institutions. It seemed right. Each had something to give to the other. This, I felt, is how the ancients should live with us. A reminder, a presence always there. 250 generations at least had come and gone since those who had completed these mounds had passed on. In another 250 generations, who would be visiting?—that is, if by then we have not been reduced to atoms drifting through the infinity of the universe.

Perhaps a person seeking out the same roots of long past cultures as I am?

Somehow, in all the rush and hustle of our modern life these mounds as I reflect on them here in the steam-heat of an early summer afternoon, bring a sense of peace, a soothing stability. In their very presence they serve as a reminder that no matter the battles, bloodshed, horror and devastation they have seen—and they've seen plenty—life, just like ole Miss, is a continuity. It just flows on.

I climbed one of the mounds and settled down on the well-worn summit. I felt down for messages. I was fully expecting more than the customary buzz. But still after 15 minutes, nothing; just the intensity of this heavy wet heat. Perhaps it was simply that here the spirits of those who had lived before, whose remains and presence lived on in this soil; perhaps it was that they were content, their energies absorbed by the intensity of these life forces around them.

Back in the car and now heading north along the east bank of the Mississippi, passing through Port Hudson and St. Francisville, I reflected on the ancient presence in this tropic clime. Here were still-magnificent Plantation Mansions in abundance. And beneath many and surrounding all were the habitations, the ceremonial complexes, the monumental earthworks, and not in mere isolated scatterings, but in their 1000s. In New Orleans alone more than 600 sites of varying, often layered antiquity have been uncovered. It all attests to man's long-standing preference for residing in this region—even if, in my personal view, it must have required serious adjustment to accommodate this tropic heat prior to the days of "whip, whip" overhead fans and air conditioning. But obviously man did adapt, and continued to do so. Presumably I too would adapt, given time. In the meantime, I reached over, turned up the car air conditioner a notch, and said a prayer of thanks to modern technology and General Motors.

As for these ancient sites scattered in profusion throughout these Delta lands, available time and access opportunities meant I could not visit them all. I had to be satisfied with a chosen few. But in a way this was enough. I had seen and sensed and touched enough. Enough to satisfy my curiosity and my need to confirm the reality of the presence of these ancients; enough to allow me to confirm to myself that I had made direct contact with these real, living roots, the "first principle" of evolving civil culture and settled life of this continent. It was a good feeling. Despite growing time pressure—I was well behind on my tour schedule—I was starting to relax.

A road-side sign flashed out "Cajun-Style Shrimps—All You Can Eat—$5.99." I hit the brakes and pulled in. I was keen to try Cajun cooking. And the dish sounded good. Napkin round my neck, I tucked in. The shrimps themselves were good. But to get at them you had to peel off a thick coating of batter. I managed one plateful—the fatty batter piled on one side—before conceding defeat. I was informed this was the only way in which the shrimps for this "special" were served. "People like 'em this way." I didn't. Disappointed, but at least with a few shrimps aboard, I paid up and departed.

I tried for a bed at two of the fine ante-bellum houses in St. Francisville. But no luck. All were booked. And so I decided to push on up-river and across the State boundary into Mississippi. With a little luck I would be back in Natchez before dark. This would give me a good jump on my planned travels back into Louisiana, with my focus now on Poverty Point and the northeast of the State. I called the motel I had stayed at two nights before. Yes, they had a room for me.

Night was nearly down when I arrived at those now familiar bluffs rising high above ole Miss. The motel lights were on. I eased the Chevy into a space in front of the Reception Office. A refreshing shower, then a Dairy Queen down the road, and I was ready for an early night—the air conditioner on full. Though it rattled a bit, I slept well.

# 31

## *Poverty Point*

*Epps, North-East Louisiana*—By 7 am I was across ole Miss via the Vidalia bridge and heading north, the sky grey, the mist hanging low. Forty miles on I stopped for a good bacon and eggs breakfast. By 9 am I was, with difficulty, trying to follow the few and not-very-helpful signs to Poverty Point.

I had written before about Poverty Point. Books, brochures and a few research papers had been my guides. Seeing it now for the first time as I drove through the broad, open space towards the Visitors Center, it was as though I'd known it intimately for a long time, that we were old friends, that I was coming home. It was a marvellous feeling.

As I now duly made my "pilgrimage" round the site, the sun beating hard down, the sweat rolling, I again read through the principal Poverty Point brochure. Remarkable. What it said, measured against what I knew and now saw and sensed, was identical. As its words convey the essence of this great site—at least as well as any I can muster—they are worth quoting.

"The time was eight centuries after Egyptian slaves dragged huge stones across the desert to build the Great Pyramids, and before the great Mayan pyramids were constructed. The place was [right here] in what is now Northeastern Louisiana. The people were a highly civilised group who left behind one of the most important archaeological sites in North America.

"The Poverty Point inhabitants, like the ancient Mayans, set for themselves an enormous task as they built a complex array of earthen mounds and ridges overlooking the Mississippi River flood plain.... The central construction consists of six rows of concentric ridges, which at one time were five feet high. The five aisles and six sections of ridges form a partial octagon. The diameter of the outermost ridges measures three-quarters of a mile. It is thought that these ridges served as foundations for dwellings, although little evidence of structures has been found. However, features and midden deposits uncovered during excavations support this theory.

"Earthen mounds were also built on the site. Immediately to the west of the concentric ridges lies Poverty Point Mound, a spectacular [falcon] bird-shaped mound measuring 700 by 640 feet at its base and rising 70 feet into the sky. To the north is a 20-foot-high conical mound which was constructed over a bed of ash and burnt bone fragments.

"Poverty Point's inhabitants imported certain essential supplies from great distances. Spear points and other stone tools found [here] were made from raw materials which originated in the Ouachita and Ozark Mountains, and in the Ohio and Tennessee River valleys. Soapstone for vessels came from the Appalachian foothills of northern Alabama and Georgia. Other materials came from distant places in the United State. This extensive trade network attests to the complex and sophisticated society that built these earthworks.

"[Along with thousands of unique molded clay cooking balls] a large number of beads of various sizes and shapes, together with many small stone tools, called "microliths," have been found at the site.

"Poverty Point is indeed a rare remnant of an exceptional culture. It has been estimated that it took at least five million hours to build the massive earthworks. Considering that laborers carried this dirt to the site in baskets of about 50-pound capacity, it is obvious that this was a great communal engineering feat. The age, size and character of these Poverty Point earthworks place them amongst the most significant finds in America today. Dated between 1700 and 700 BC, this site of 400 acres is unique among archaeological sites on this continent.

"In 1962, Poverty Point was designated a National Historic Landmark by the US Department of the Interior, and is one of three World Heritage Archaeological Sites north of Mexico."

These words convey the essence of Poverty Point. What they do not convey is the awesome scale of the complex; the immense, pulsing power of the place. Only by walking round the mounds, standing on these ridges, climbing the lengthy tiers of steps to the summit of the falcon-effigy mound does the essence become reality. Standing and sensing, as I did, in the center of the extensive plaza ringed by these ridges, the images, the sounds, the busy vibrancy of life long past were conjured to the present. Secure on this bluff from the floodwaters of ole Miss, the residents and visitors—on trade, perhaps religious or ceremonial missions—were well-placed to order and conduct their lives here and in distant lands abroad.

And when I cast an eye round, I could but shake my head and marvel. What an incredible master plan the architects and designers had created. The ridges, the aisles, the falcon-mound; each bore a precise, symmetrical relation to the others. And then to get on with the awesome task of building these structures; clearly this entailed equal skill by superlative engineers and by those responsible for recruiting, organising, supervising and feeding the vast labour force required.

Nor, it would seem, was this a task quickly completed. From concept, to design, to construction and eventual completion might well have taken many generations. Hence the master plan, and its precise particulars would have been passed from one generation of specialists to the next. An incredible feat. And given that there was no apparent written language, is it really possible that in the absence of writing that this master plan, the details of design and all the precise engineering particulars were passed on simply by word of mouth?

Perhaps there's another explanation; one which could detour our thinking round these obstacles. For some modern-day specialists contend that, given the consistent applied labour of 800 persons, this formidable feat of design and engineering could have been achieved in *less than 10 years*. It is an interesting theory. If successfully validated, it could have important meaning for much orthodox thinking on Poverty Point.

The immediate, physical impact, the scale and precision of the works of this site, render it unique, compared with any other site, or residual structure of comparable antiquity I have visited. And yet the basic questions remain. Was this site a "one-off"; the creation of a remarkable people, under leadership of genius at this particular point in time? Was it a "spin-off" from perhaps the great Olmecs in Meso-America who by 1500 BC were building massive constructions and exercising their imperial muscle? Was it simply an evolution from earlier moundbuilder cultures and civilisations in the Great Valley of the Mississippi about which only recently, and gradually, we are starting to learn astonishing things?

As I now sat on the grass of the plaza, the heat fierce from the sun now directly overhead, these were the things on which I pondered. The questions they raise; the speculations about the larger and smaller issues they generate; all these and much, much more serve both to stimulate and encourage those like myself intrigued by the felt force, the slowly unfolding mysteries of America's "cultural first principles."

In this sense, Poverty Point is not merely remarkable in itself. More importantly, it is remarkable for the "windows of wonder" it opens; for the "intellectual fuel" it injects into the "systems" of all who are in quest of these first principles. Poverty Point has opened our minds to the reality of a past which until recently we dared not imagine. What has been done to reveal mysteries here can be done elsewhere. This is an important contribution.

Back in the Visitor Center—divinely cool!—displays of extensive ranges of artifacts were breathtaking; the marker signboards and other textual descriptions full and informative; altogether excellent. The Interpretative Historian on duty took me round the displays and explained. And when he was stumped on one or two points, he passed me onto Curator, Linda York. By mid-afternoon I was well topped-up with Poverty Point details. In addition, Ms. York provided copies of a number of relevant publications.

While the site lived up to everything I had hoped for, there was in fact more. Like the Grand Village of the Natchez, this Poverty Point site had that "something extra." And it was the Visitor Center Museum that provided it.

Briefly, no matter the quality, range and quantity of the artifacts, or the excellence of the the display and presentation; the key to the effectiveness of a Center Museum lies in the ability of those who deal with visitors to be able to bring the ancients of yesterday to full and vibrant life, "right here, right now, today!"

This is not easy. It requires imagination and ingenuity as well as skill and knowledge. It is this ability to create of the museum a "living place," a place that leaves a mark, a place to which one *wishes to return soon* for "the next chapter"; it is these attributes which set apart the extraordinary, from the merely good.

One might only suggest that the addition of a bookshop, of improved highway signboarding to the site, and of expanded advertising via the Internet and specialist international tourism media will serve further to ensure that this fabulous site gains the attention, attendance and recognition it greatly deserves.

# 32

# *The Golfing Ancients*

*nr. Monroe, North East Louisiana*—I checked my watch. It was already mid-afternoon. My next port of call was the site at Frenchman's Bend, 35 miles due west; and after that Watson's Brake about 30 miles south of the Frenchman's site. When I informed Linda of my intentions and asked for directions, her response was a long, low whistle.

"Oooo ee! You really *are* serious! You're talking about the grand-daddies of 'em all! This is heavy stuff. Mists of time and all that. They make our good ole Poverty Point here look like the new boy on the block!"

Frenchman's Bend, I was informed, had been a mounded communal site 2500 years *before* work on this site had started; indeed 1500 years before construction of the Great Pyramids of Egypt. Watson's Brake was said to have a pedigree of similar antiquity. These were the oldest known mound complexes in the Americas. "And you're going to visit them. Lucky man!" declared Linda.

Looking at the map, Frenchman's was a mere hop from Poverty Point, albeit with a few bends and jiggles. The reality was different. The route over this alluvial scrubland and bayou passed through a succession of shantytown hamlets, all with speed restrictions. There was road construction a-plenty; the labour here being provided by men *without* orange coveralls. And of course being hot and very humid the workers took their time. Long chains of vehicles, many of ancient manufacture, were in no hurry either.

Now within range of Frenchman's, according to my map, I stopped at one steamy crossroads to purchase a cooling chocolate shake. I noted an ambulance parked. The uniformed driver was relaxing with a can of Coke inside his air conditioned cab.

I knocked on his window. "Trade a bit quiet?"

"No, no, not really," the driver rolling down the window a few inches, informed me. "Busy time of day. This is a good spot. Pick up calls from Monroe, the Interstate and Ouachita Valley."

I mentioned I'd seen many sizeable, sleek, lawn-surrounded, seeming state-of-the-art Medical Centers as I'd made my way round the back roads of Louisiana and the Deep South. I had found some difficulty, I said, in reconciling these gleaming edifices with communities where signs of material wealth were not readily apparent.

He smiled and crunched his Coke tin. "Insurance jobs. Same for us. People come to these centers from all over." He lowered the window a little further. "Community health, largely, is for the community to worry about. Not the Medical Centers." There was a sudden sharp buzz on his intercom. Through the static crackle I could hear it. An emergency pick up in Monroe. He shifted the remnant of a sandwich to the passenger seat and straightened his tie. "Hope you enjoy that shake. Best by far round here." And he was off. The big machine rocking down onto the road, cut sharply into the rush-hour traffic and accelerated away, siren howling, lights flashing.

A short distance after passing through a particularly ramshackle shantytown corridor which followed the winding, heavily overgrown course of an extended bayou, I came to a large sign. "Frenchman's Bend Golf Club—200 Yards on Left," it announced. Linda York had told me, "Find the golf course and you'll find the mounds." Another 200 yards and I came to an elaborate open-gated and landscaped entry, complete with security inspection booth. I hesitated. It was the only entry I could see. There was no sign. Nothing about the golf course. The booth was unmanned. I eased the Chevy through the entry. No alarm went off. No security men materialised with drawn guns.

Suddenly I was in another world. The road broadened into a wide, winding avenue. Set well back along the heavy green forest perimeter were huge, brand-new, brick, neo-Colonial, neo-Georgian, neo-Classical style homes, complete with stately white portal columns. Each was placed within a vast expanse of carefully-mown lawn, and displayed on each black tarmac drive were at least three, shiny, late-model cars and/or SUVs (sports-utilities-vehicles). As I progressed, so did this surreal disney-esque tableau. I was in profound shock. It was as though that world out there beyond the gate did not exist. Was this, I wondered, the "New South?" Everything squeaky clean, neat, sanitary, not a person in sight?

At the end of the avenue a large, dark, timber-frame single storey building loomed. No sign, but a golf cart in the parking area provided a clue. I ventured inside. Plush beige carpets greeted me. No sign of humanity. I ventured further. There on the corridor wall was a large framed print featuring Jack Nicklaus in mid-swing, with Arnold Palmer, Tom Watson, and another no doubt golfing great looking on. And then I came upon a small dining room, then a bar. Both afforded wonderful panoramic views of the course through broad expanses of plate glass. An attendant in uniform appeared. I explained my mission: that I was interested in the Indian mounds; and was there anyone who could tell me about them? I was directed to the pro-shop. There a fit-looking attentive young man explained about the Ancient Mounds and the golf course.

In a lightly forested area between the 4th and 5th holes—he pointed to a detailed diagram of the course, and indeed of the entire Frenchman's Development, on the wall—and the 7th and 8th holes on the other side, the five mounds were clearly indicated.

"Now a local collector, when he heard about this development going forward, well he contacted the Louisiana State Archaeologist for this area, Joe Saunders. Dr. Saunders came out and had a look round. He confirmed the importance of the site. These people reckon these mounds we've got right here date back to around 4500 BC!" He turned to me, his bright blue eyes as big as pie plates, "*That's 6500 years ago! It makes 'em the oldest known Indian mounds on this entire North American continent!*—or so these experts say." He pointed to a rustic-looking crafted board etched with a series of date lines. "That puts 'em way, way back. Like back here," he pointed to one of the lines, "1500 years *before* the Egyptians got busy with their Great Pyramids!"

James—we were now acquainted, he was the Assistant Pro—now went on to show me the rest of this "Gallery of Antiquity." There were glass cases with stone artifacts recovered during excavation; photos of the archaeologists at work and their tools; there were large framed poster-sized illustrated guides detailing the development of the lives, manufactures and activities of Louisiana's pre-historic residents. I was impressed.

"So anyway," said James, "after Dr. Saunders had had a look round, he talked with the developers. The result was that the golf course was re-designed to ensure these mounds would be preserved." He ran his finger along the date-lined board. "And they've done a great job. Those mounds are all nice and snug and comfy." He laughed. "And let's hope they stay that way for another 6000 years! Golf's an important game, you see. Important conservation input!" I thought back to the Great Hopewell Mounds at Newark, Ohio, and their golf course protector. He was right.

Already it was past 5:30. There was nobody around, and I was very anxious to have a look at these "grand-daddies" of mounds. "What's the best way to get to them?" I asked.

James developed a sudden cautious reserve. He scratched his head and fidgeted with his pencil. "It's a private course, you know. And today's the Women's Competition. They're still on the course. Don't know it's possible."

I tried another tack. "Tell you what. Time I had a little fresh air. Is it alright if I just wander out by the first tee? Lovely evening. Cooling down a bit now. Take in the view?"

James eyed me, then nodded. "No reason you shouldn't do that. Fine course. We're very proud of it. Just take care to steer clear of the players." He reached out and shook my hand. "It's been real nice to meet you. I'll say goodbye now. I'm off home in a few minutes."

It was indeed a fine evening. The sun was well down and a light, cooling breeze was coming in from the west. There was no one on the first tee or fairway. An opportune moment to stretch my legs. It took only a few minutes to skirt the first fairway. Approaching the second tee and another lengthy strip of manicured fairway, I checked for player activity. All quiet. Another few minutes and I was circuiting the green and discreetly following the forest line, crossing towards the eighth fairway where I knew the mounds started. I had progressed only a few yards when I heard a sudden "whooosh!" and a "plop!" Less than ten feet from me rested a little white ball. I retreated quickly into the fairway edge thicket. Before long, two, tanned, fit-looking women, trim in blue shorts and sleeveless white blouses appeared. There was much chatter. Men problems. One stepped up and cracked the ball with a good-looking iron shot. And off they strode, golf trolleys in tow.

According to the course plan the first mound, I reckoned, should be about here. I thrashed about in the undergrowth, being careful where I put my feet, but found nothing—not even a snake! However, another 50 yards or so, and there tucked in behind the seventh green was what I was looking for. Oval and dome-shaped, perhaps 75 feet long and ten feet high, here was where people had congregated over 65 centuries ago. I drew closer. The wind had dropped. It was very still. I felt as I had one night at Chillicothe, an important center of the Ohio Hopewells. I did not need to ascend the mound. The power of the place was all round. The buzz of the ancients throbbed out.

I continued along the edge of the seventh fairway, and there was another, smaller mound; this one also oval and dome-shaped but rising to no more than four feet. Finally, round the bend and tucked just inside the forest perimeter, well-protected from assault by errant golf balls, was the principal earthwork. About 100 feet in diameter, conical, perhaps 15 feet in height, it was an impressive sight.

I stopped and pondered and sensed. The throb of this entire complex was immense. The ancients I knew were present. They had lived here when the waters of these bayous and the River Ouachita followed different courses in their lowland meanderings. As with all such habitations I had visited, from early pre-historic to late-Mississippian, this complex of mounds was on a terrace just high enough to keep residents dry during periods of high water. And of course these mounds had been occupied more or less constantly for several 1000s of years. Finds of clay cooking blocks, grinding stones, ordinary lithic and exotic chert points, bifacial and unifacial tools, jasper beads, these and over 4000 other finds turned up in early 1990s digs provided evidence that these mounds served as rather more than the customary seasonal camp. Indeed, discovery of postholes (indicating habitation structures) and firepits extending down several strata appeared to confirm this.

For a full 15 minutes I switched off my thought processes, forgot about the lady golfers, and opened wide my sensors. Gradually the message came through. And it was a simple one. The ancients were greeting me. They recognised in me a friendly spirit; a spirit into which they had now entered. There was nothing to fear. They would be my guardians. I thanked them.

Suddenly, round the bend I heard rapidly approaching chatter. Again I ducked back into the forest perimeter. Another pair of trim lady golfers—no sign of McDonald's excess on them!—strode swiftly past, trundling their trolleys behind.

I checked my watch. Nearly 7:30. I'd seen and sensed enough. I'd made contact with the ancients. I felt refreshed and lifted. It was time to go.

Having furtively returned along the route I had taken, I was back in the car and about to pull out of the parking area when I noted a slip of paper under the wind-screen wiper. I stopped and removed it. "Hope you enjoyed your breath of fresh air. Safe journey. James."

# 33

## *Secrets of Ouachita*

*Valley of the Ouachita, Louisiana*—A "Super 8" motel on the outskirts of Monroe provided me with a restful, air conditioned night. And after a complimentary coffee and sticky danish I stepped outside. The sun had not yet made its way through the watery industrial haze. But it wouldn't be long. The land was steaming. I mopped my brow and arms.

After several stops for directions, finally I found myself on Route 34 running south to Winnfield. My destination, Watson's Brake Mounds, was not on any of my maps. I had only the general location. This I'd determined from one of the technical articles on the "Mounds of North-East Louisiana". It appeared to be only 25 miles from Monroe, tucked away in the Ouachita back-country. The trick was to find it.

Eventually I found my way to Luna, a hamlet comprising three, white-frame bungalows in a clearing on a forested rise beside the road. I pulled in at the first. An elderly man, wearing only ragged shorts was busily hoeing his vegetable patch. The ordered green growth was lush, practically jumping out of the black soil. At a quick glance I could see beans, corn, beets, carrots and spinach, and all coming along very nicely. After due consultation I had new directions which were even more complicated. The man, hitching up his shorts returned to his hoeing; I returned to the road.

I found the first turn-off, as instructed. It was a dirt road which narrowed, dipped and twisted through scrubland, light forest and bayou. Then I came to the first fork; I kept to the left; then a triple fork; I took the center. There were more forks and junctions. I think I managed one or two more correctly. After that I hadn't a clue where I was, and as there was nobody about, I just followed my nose. About to turn back, and coming down off a slight rise, I caught sight of what appeared to be a river. Hedged between heavily overgrown banks, I could see movement of a sluggish, light-chocolaty stream. That should be the Ouachita. And if it was, then according to my directions, Watson's Brake must be close. But where?

Venturing further I spotted what I reckoned was a derelict shanty tucked away off the road in a jungle of green. However, the track leading in showed fresh tire tracks. Worth a try, I thought. I could find no front door. Round the back was a screen door. The inner door was open. I knocked. No answer. I knocked again. I could hear the "pad, pad," of bare feet. A man in well-worn bib-and-braces coverall and an engineer's cap appeared. He was large, fat, hairy and white. He did not open the door. "What you want, then?" he drawled.

I told him I was looking for the Watson's Brake Mounds, and could he please tell me how I could get to them? He didn't say anything for a bit. Then he pushed back his cap to reveal a near-bald scalp. "You lookin' for them old Indian mounds then?" I said I was. He eyed me warily. "And that's what you come all the way down from Yankee country to see?" Clearly he'd seen the Chevy out front. Once again I explained that I was English; that I was travelling round the South visiting many places with ancient mounds. "Mmmm," he said, and spat a large gob of tobacco juice into a pail by the door. There was a resounding "Dang!"

"Quite a few folk come this way. Them mounds seem mighty popular. 'Course," he regarded me furtively, "ain't nothin' to 'em. Just ole mounds, piles o' dirt." I said I wanted simply to see them, nothing more. There was another lengthy silence. He aimed another gob at the pail. Another "Dang!" He then informed me he'd never been out to the mounds. "The man you want to see," he gestured towards the road, "lives just down a ways. Biggish place. Doin' a bit of brushin' out front, bit of work on the house. Can't miss it. He knows lots about them mounds and Indians and the like. You'd best go talk to him." And with that, the man pulled his cap back into place, launched another brown gob at the bucket, turned on his unshod heel and disappeared into the interior darkness.

Sure enough, less than a half-mile down the road on a sloping rise of ground across from a bend in the river, there was a sizeable brown, timber house elevated the customary 6-8 feet above the surrounding land. A bulldozer parked at the far side of the property and several heaped brush piles confirmed there was serious clearance underway. An extension at the side of the house had reached joist-and-rafter stage. Again, there was no one about.

Round the back, up the steps, across a broad planked deck, and there again was a screen door. I knocked. A burly, grey-haired man in shorts and T-shirt appeared. I explained my mission. He swung open the door. "You'd better come in." He extended a powerful paw, "Jeremiah Jordan's the name."

Inside, the house was open, spacious and bright. Escorting me past a gallery of trophy heads, including a snarling bear, several antlered deer, an enormous catfish and a villainous looking wedge-headed diamond-back rattler that made me jump, we crossed to the far corner of the sitting room. I settled into the proffered armchair, Jeremiah into a rocker opposite. Two other men appeared. These were his "boys," Will and Jared. Both lived and worked in Monroe. Will was a doctor, Jared a land developer. A pot of fresh-brewed coffee was produced. I was introduced to Sarah, Jeremiah's wife. We helped ourselves.

I told them a bit of what I'd so far seen and experienced on my tour. The atmosphere eased. "Well," said Will, pointing to his father, "you've surely come to the right place. My daddy may have worked in the pulp mills all his life, but this place, this land round here's where his heart's always been." He stroked his coffee mug. "For him, the ancients have always been family. In fact, they've been family to all of us." He looked across at Jared. "Anyway, we'll leave the explanations to him. Afraid we've got to go." He and his brother got up and shook my hand. "Due back in Monroe."

The boys having departed, I asked Jeremiah when he first learned about Watson's Brake and its mounds. He took a sip from his coffee mug, then turned round and extracted a long roll of paper from a pigeon hole in a wooden frame mounted on the wall behind. He rolled it out on the coffee table, anchored it with books at either end, and gestured for me to come over and have a look. It was a map of the Ouachita Valley.

Jeremiah's finger traced traced round an extensive area. These, he said, were the four parishes through which the River Ouachita in this locality flowed. "And there's not many creeks or bayous I've not fished, land over which I've not hunted, in fact any bit of this area I've not tramped over and explored. Done it all, time and again, since I was a boy." He lit up a cigarette, took a deep pull and grinned. "Despair of my Momma! Why she reckoned for sure I was going to sink without trace in one of them swamps; that is, if I didn't first get et by an alligator, or ambushed by some riled up rattler—we've got lots and lots of 'em round here!" Casting an eye at his trophy, I said I had noted. "But as you see, I have survived!"

He grew suddenly serious. "In fact, I've never had no problem at all with this land and water. We've always got along just fine. Always felt safe and secure." He slowly shook his head. "But of course not all have been so lucky. This land, these waters of Lady Ouachita," he paused, his eyes black and gleaming, "they make their demands, take their toll. Always have. It's wise to be respectful."

He then ran over the map in closer detail, pointing to about 30 different locations. "All of these places, they've all got old mounds or earthworks, often both. And there's lots more down on the submerged shelves and terraces in many of these lakes and bayous. Where the water's clear enough you can see 'em. Every fisherman knows. The water level's lifted maybe four feet over the past 6000 years, maybe more. So, you may ask, how many old sites, mounds, habitations, ceremonial works, camps have been submerged in this Ouachita Valley alone? Maybe 100s? In the whole of the Mississippi Valley, maybe tens of 1000s? That's my guess. But, of course, nobody knows." He took another long sip from his mug. "Our ancient forbears are specialists in mystery!"

Having digested Jeremiah's observations, I asked whether it was then fair to say that that the Watson's Brake mound complex represented only one of such settlements known to local people; that there was perhaps nothing so very special about the site; that perhaps its importance was being greatly overplayed?

Jeremiah contemplated me for a moment, then hunching forward, he waved his hand over the map. "You can see this area." He again traced out the line of the Ouachita and its extensive adjacent lands. "Now these are mainly back-country terraced lands. They rise just clear of the Mississippi flood plain. At least mostly they do. Now a day like today, hot, humid; this more or less is how it's been the past 6000 years or so." He looked at my beaded brow and grinned. "And folk do adjust to the heat and wet very quick!" He turned again to the map. "Now where you clear a bit of ground in this valley, there's not many places where things don't grow. All kinds of roots, grassy plants, leafy vegetables, and maize loves it. Add plentiful fish and game and you've got as good a diet as you can get; a diet which fed probably more people then, than live here today.

"You see it was a very good life for these early residents. And the fact of the matter is, it still is. Folk today can get along quite nicely. Bit of fishin', bit of huntin', grow a few crops, build yourself some kind of house and you can get along just fine." He laughed. "And that dole cheque, well that can keep just a few coins a-jinglin' in your pocket!"

"Course," he confided, "none of this makes us back-country folk very popular with the taxman, nor local officialdom. *They* feel we should play by *their* rules. And every now and then they get a little heavy. But in the end everyone seems to simmer down, and we all manage to get along alright. A nice chunk of fresh catfish, or shank of venison in certain freezers can remedy a lot of problems. Life here has a way of just carrying on."

All this was very interesting. And it confirmed yet again what I'd been repeatedly told and indeed deduced for myself. But what about the Watson's Brake Mounds? For whatever reason, Jeremiah seemed most reluctant to talk about them.

I tried another tack. I referred to Poverty Point, to Marksville, to the fact that since becoming public sites both had drawn a lot of tourists; that this had brought in money and boosted employment. If the State decided to open up Watson's Brake, the same thing, I suggested, would happen here. And would not the people of the Ouachita Valley welcome such a development?

Jeremiah let out a long sigh. There was a hint of exasperation. "Let me ask you this. If you lived out in this fine backcountry, if you valued the independence, the solitude and freedom that have been the stand-bys of folk who have lived hereabouts since the beginning of time, how would *you* feel about a whole lot of strangers invading *your* quiet space, bringin' all that noise and nonsense from the outside world to *your* doorstep?"

"But surely," I replied, "the numbers would not be that big, and the State purchase of land would amount to only a few hundred acres, if that?"

Jeremiah eyed me for a long moment. "The point is that there's plenty of sites for folk to see if they want to. Round here there's not just Watson's Brake, there's lots and lots of them. Common knowledge to us locals. Part of the scenery. No need to shout and make a fuss about 'em. All these sites are old, who knows how old. We've found things….And of course all these specialists, these professors and pot-hunters, they make all kinds of noise about the antiquity of this place, of others. Right now they're gettin' themselves all lathered up over a new 'find', the Conly site—again well known to locals—in Bienville Parish up towards Shreveport. Say it pushes the date of 'known habitation' in the Americas back another 1000 years to 5500 BC. This, at any rate, is what their carbon-dating procedures tell 'em!"

Again I stuck my oar in. I made the point that these sites provided a vital link to the roots of this continent's culture; that as such they provided a window into America's ancient past which until recently no one knew or believed even existed. And given that in so many places important sites had been destroyed by farmers, developers and the like, it was surely important that those few that had been positively identified should be preserved and protected?

Jeremiah scowled, fidgeted, then broke into laughter. He turned and fetched out another much longer roll of furled paper from another pigeonhole. He rolled it out on top of the other map and anchored it. I saw the heading at the top: "Watson's Brake Mounds—A Survey." He smoothed the wrinkles. "Maybe this will help to fill you in."

The Survey showed an 11-mound complex, seemingly connected by earthwork ridges. Immediately bells rang. This could be a large-scale replica of what I'd seen at Florence in northern Alabama, or those back-country Mitchell Mounds near Harrisonburg, only a few 1000 years older!

Jeremiah took me round the map. The complex was roughly 280 yards in diameter, the largest mound 25 feet tall, the ten others ranging in height from three to 15 feet. He indicated the circular line of the connecting three-foot earthen ridge. "So that," said he, "is the layout. And for the rest, the experts have come up with the obvious: that our early residents ate not only lots of fish, shellfish and various species of game, but also a pre-historic equivalent of Quaker Oats; that this mound complex was likely inhabited seasonally when folk came through to fish and hunt; that they had plenty of tools and gear, including lots of spear points; that the mounds may have had some kind of ceremonial purpose; but that they seem not to have been used for burials.

"In other words, while having to adapt and adjust to changing drainage patterns and a rise of some 3-5 feet in the water level, the folk here got on with their lives much as we do today. The only difference is that maybe they moved around a bit more. All these river valleys of the lower Mississippi catchment were well—in some instances, heavily—populated from a very early date. But there's no sign that people started getting territorial and nasty till well up towards historic times and the appearance of our European predecessors."

He lifted the weights from the maps. First one, then the other snapped back. He popped each back into its pigeonhole. "So that's the story of Watson's Brake mounds. Up to date!…Now I'm afraid I've got to get moving. Business up in Monroe."

I checked my watch. It was already 1:30. I too had a date. A colleague of one of the Poverty Point Guides who lived down Route 34 at Winnfield had some papers for me to collect. I was due at 3:30. The drive I reckoned would take me about an hour. That left me with an hour to have a look over the Watson's Brake site. So where exactly were these mounds, I asked Jeremiah; and how could I best reach them?

He explained I need only return to the last fork on the road, then take the left branch, and then about 300 yards along on the left, look for a trail cut through the forestry pines. It was then just a matter of following that trail for a quarter of a mile and I'd come to the site. It all sounded simple enough, so having said my farewells to the Jordans I made haste to follow the directions given.

I found the specified fork, followed the left branch, then looked for the trail. I could find no trail. Finally after nearly a mile I did find a trail; but this one passed through hardwood and scrubland, not pine. Nevertheless, I locked up the car and headed off. The trail was very rough. It twisted, it dipped into marshy wetland. A little further and I heard a sudden angry

"Buzzzz!" I froze. Then "Buzzz!" I heard it again. About five feet to my left I saw him. A big, diamond-back all nicely coiled and warning me not to get any closer. I took the message. After a few moments of pure terror, I very slowly skirted the snake and continued up the trail. Another 100 yards and it came to a dead end. No sign of anything but stumps, scrubland and a few hardwoods. Keeping a very sharp eye on where I was putting my feet, I finally made my way back to the car.

So near, but apparently still so far! I wanted so much to see and sense these mounds, these "grand-daddies." I might still have time. Back at Jeremiah's house for re-direction I had no luck. He had already departed for Monroe, and his wife could only look apologetic. "Jeremiah's department, I'm afraid."

Dame Fortune, the ancients and their local representative, Jeremiah Jordan had, it seemed, decreed that I was not to visit this ancient sanctum. I was disappointed, but still I had ventured into the immediate territory, I had got a feel for it, and Jeremiah had provided much detail and an equal amount on which to ponder. So my attempt was not without benefit. That at least was my consolation.

The route back out to Luna was not easy. There were forks and junctions to be re-negotiated. It took time. Finally I reached what I recognised to be the last fork. What I did not recognise was whether it was the half-right, or the straight-on road I should follow.

There was a weather-beaten shack set back in the trees close to the junction. I pulled in and got out. On the front porch was a big wooden rocker. And in it, gently rocking back and forth, was an elderly woman in a faded cotton print dress. I told her I'd been up the road, that I'd got in alright, but that I couldn't now remember how to get out. She laughed. "So what's a feller like you, all the way from New York," she nodded at the Chevy, "doing out here on the back roads of Looseeanna? Don't see too many Northerners down this way."

I went through my customary patter of who I was and where I came from. "An Englishman!" she exclaimed. "Never met one before. Only knowed 'em by reputation." She coughed and laughed. "My grand-daddy was Irish. He had some pretty strong views. No doubt he's still got 'em, wherever he may be!"

When I told her about my visit with the Jordan family and my subsequent failure to find the track to the mounds, the old woman started to laugh and cough and shake so much, I thought she was going to fall out of the chair. "My, oh my! You surely did knock on the *wrong* door! Why Jeremiah, he don't want *nobody* round them mounds, if he can help it. Government people managed to get a bit of the land, but Jeremiah's got his eye on the rest. You see, his son Jared's a big developer. Wants to build some fancy big houses down here." She cocked an eye at me. "Probably suspects you're after the same property. Where he sent you wasn't even close!"

I told the old woman that at least I'd not come away empty-handed; that Jeremiah had given me lots of very helpful information, even if his directions were not entirely accurate; and that I'd had a bit of a taste of these Ouachita terraced lands, including my encounter with one its reptilian residents.

"There's plenty of them critters round here," she said. "But what you really want to watch out for are them pretty little copperheads. Like to get nice and snug in your boot during the night. When you put your foot in in the morning, why many's the person who's got a nasty surprise!" She noted my shudder with apparent satisfaction. "By the way, the road you was askin' about?" She pointed. "It's that one; the half-right."

Another two miles down the half-right fork, and I was back to the main road. Winnfield was further than I thought. And there were the usual construction hold-ups. By 5 pm I had located the pick-up address, collected the papers, and had had a quick look round the locality. It was a most uninspiring experience, though a recently built Supermarket did add a little commercial flash.

One writer has described Winn Parish as "poor from birth." Another added, "It hasn't gotten any better!" And this was the hometown of the legendary and colourful Huey "The Kingfish" Long, Governor of Louisiana in the 1920s and 30s, and his brother Earl K. Long, a somewhat more surreal figure, who also served as State Governor in the 1940s and 50s. One could only surmise that this drab, depressing surround was an active provocation to the high and vigorous spirits of the Longs. Was their extraordinary, larger-than-life behaviour simply a statement of rebellious defiance? As I now got on the road heading back to Catahoula Parish and Jonesville, I wondered.

It was dark when I pulled into Williams' Motel. I was greeted by Mayor Williams' wife, Carol. She was tending to the laundry, gradually reducing a mountain of sheets. We chatted as she ironed. Then I got a nice, cooling chocolate shake from the stand down the road. I didn't realise how tired I was till I stretched out on the bed. Sleep came quickly.

# 34

## *That Ole Alligator!*

*Jonesville, Louisiana*—Attached to Williams' Motel was Williams' Restaurant. I was ready for a good breakfast, and I got one, though still I evaded the favoured customary dish o' grits and the nearly as favoured Hotcakes. Good old-fashioned bacon, eggs, sausage, tomato, toast and several cups of fresh hot coffee was good enough for me.

There was only one other customer in the restaurant. And this person, I was informed was Mr. Williams himself, proprietor of the establishment and Mayor of the City of Jonesville. I introduced myself. The Mayor was busy counting up yesterday's cash take. He preferred informality; "Just call me Bobby." Count completed and cash safely bagged, Bobby and I exchanged a few words.

"Lots of mounds through here," he said. He made special mention of the Jonesville Mound, as was. I said I'd heard about it. "Supposed to be the second biggest mound in America," he added. He watched as I drained the last of my coffee. "Like to have a look at the site?" I said I would, very much. "Well, it'll only take a few minutes. Just down by the Black River bridge."

We parked near the bridge and got out. To the ignorant eye there wasn't much to see. A road, a bridge over a sluggish river, plenty of traffic. To the awakened sensors however there was an immediate and powerful buzz rising from the land like an electrical charge. It was extraordinary.

The sun was already creating cruel heat, the humidity a dead weight. "All round here, 1000, maybe 1500 years ago, this was part of the place they called Troyville; that is before it became Jonesville," said Bobby. "Don't know exactly how far it extended. But some experts reckon it may have covered a square mile. It was some kind of regional center. There were up to 15 small mounds, most like upside-down bread loaves; some with earthen cones on top."

Bobby mopped his brow. "And the Great Mound, all 80 feet high, was bang in the middle. In fact we're probably just about standing on top of the base site now. Strange construction. Bit like a smaller version of one of them Aztec pyramids in Mexico. Two separate, terraced platforms, one on top of the other, then a 35-foot cone mound on top. At about 200 feet square it must've been quite a sight." He laughed and mopped again. "Jonesville in *those* days was maybe the Baton Rouge or New Orleans of its time. He pointed towards the Four Rivers' confluence of the Tensas, Ouachita, Little and Black rivers. "And all these rivers must have made it a kind of a hub. Busy place." He chuckled. "And no Williams' Motel in those days!…Often wish we could 'open the book' on the past here. The experts can tell us a bit, give us an outline. But all round and beneath us here, all sealed up, there've got to be some amazing stories."

Bobby then spoke briefly about the levelling of the Great Mound in 1931. "It was sad to lose it. But then Huey's boys (Huey Long, then Governor of Louisiana) needed dirt fill for road construction, and that mound had some of the finest fill you could get—all 600,000 cubic feet of it!" As for the antics of the locals when Smithsonian Archaeologist Winslow Walker had attempted a few digs on the now-levelled site, Bobby shook his head. He repeated the story about the fabled Natchez Treasure, and the belief of local people and landowners that it just might be here. "Poor old Walker. Why he thought this was just a straight-forward dig job. Well, it wasn't. Finally, things got so bad, Walker had to pack up and go home. Of course, don't know there was all that much more he could have found out. But the point was, he didn't get a chance to try!".

It was now past nine. Bobby had business to attend to and so did I. Back at the Motel, I thanked him for the guided tour, then collected my bags, packed the car, paid up and by 9:30 was past the "Leaning Tower of Jonesville", and on the road to Harrisonburg.

By ten I was in Davey's office. A quiet day, said he. A chance to tidy up a few things; one of these concerning a "bit of a boundary problem" with his family property outside town. We would have a look at this later. "So how'd you get on?" he inquired, leaning back and arranging his feet on the corner of the desk. "Make lots of contacts with our early residents?"

"Lots and lots," I replied. "Even had a word with the ancients of Troyville this morning, thanks to Mayor Williams." I then provided a recount of my travels. Davey found particular amusement in my distaste for prawns in batter—"Only way to eat 'em!" he declared; the 'breath of fresh air' I had taken with the Golfing Ancients at Frenchman's Bend; the Secrets of Ouachita and Watson's Brake that had so artfully *not* been revealed by Jeremiah Jordan; and my encounter with the big rattler—" 'Bout time! They've just been a'waitin' to shake hands!" he pronounced with satisfaction.

"And do you *now* understand why this part of the country has been the livin', thumpin' heart of America for the past 6000 years?"

I said I thought I did. But I said also that in this modern day I found something important missing.

"And what is that?"

"Where are the mound-building designers? The engineers? Where are those highly-skilled, foresightful people who managed those building works, who recruited and organised the labour to construct Poverty Point, Watson's Brake, Frenchman's, Troyville, your own Mitchell Mounds here and the thousands and thousands of other mounds and earthworks, great and small, throughout these Louisiana lands? I see people like Jeremiah, eminent, resourceful individuals who clearly draw on the power-reservoir of ancient life, who provide this unbroken line, this connection between ancient and modern man. But where are those people who once drew all these back-country people together, who gave shape, identity and force to their respective collective presences? Where are they?"

Once again Davey was much-amused. He rocked back on his chair. The phone suddenly buzzed. He shut it off. "That is an interesting question. Maybe some are working as NASA astro-physicists in Houston, plotting our next leap into the heavens; some in the big financial houses of New York and San Francisco; some in the legal stew-pots, the courts of this State and further afield; some in our leading universities and research institutions messin' about with just such questions as you seem drawn to grapple with." He laughed. "And some may be at home, just gettin' quietly on with their business."

He now dropped his feet off the desk, leaned forward and doodled with a pencil on a pad of paper. "You may have heard the saying; 'comes the time, comes the man.' Now at present we're just coastin' along, nice and easy. Everybody's got their troubles; life's not good for us all; but then it's not that bad. And it has, as you have noted, its consolations up here in the back-country."

He paused and elaborated one of his doodles. "Going on present and past form, it may be we'll just tick on like this for another 500, maybe 1000 years. And then it will only be at that time, a time of crisis, some imminent cataclysm, that the residual DNA, or whatever you want to call it, will out; that the successors of those gifted persons who first emerged from the ancient forest perimeter, from the midst of those mists-of-time groupings, will come forth in whatever form this future call may require; and they will perform with equal breathtaking brilliance."

Davey looked up and grinned. "Course, that's just one man's opinion!" He got up and stretched. "In the meantime, it's just a matter of keepin' a man's rasslin' and wranglin' skills in shape! And folk round here have no trouble with that a'tall!…Speakin' of which, it's time you and me paid a visit!"

After just a few minutes driving, Davey had turned down a dirt road; then after a lot of banging and bumping down another track and over a field, he wheeled the Bronco to a halt close by a forest-ringed bayou. A team of surveyors was at work. Davey got out and shouted and fussed with them a bit. They returned to their task. I asked him what it was all about. He explained.

Over the years, the bayou had crept further and further into Davey's property. And the encroaching margin of the bayou had become the effective boundary between his property and that of his neighbour. In Davey's view, the bayou had already extended too far, and he wasn't about to concede more property should it extend further. Hence the surveyors. He had called them in to establish and mark what was the old property dividing line according to the Deeds.

I asked him whether in Louisiana the law took the position that such a dividing line, if maintained over 12 years, did not then become the legal boundary? He cocked a belligerent eye at me. "That's what my neighbour's sayin'; even my own lawyers. But I'm sayin' the *legal* boundary is what's *set down here in these deeds*!" He folded up the bundled papers and banged them down on the seat beside him. "They've pushed me too far. That's my family land. And if they don't back off, I'll fight!"

We took a careful scramble through the undergrowth round part of the bayou. Davey's young son, Luke, who'd been with the surveyors, joined us. Once again I was informed, "This is snake country. They just love it through here!" With Davey and one of the surveyors in deep converse in the lead, young Luke and I followed up.

"There's a big ole alligator in that Bayou!" Luke announced. And he shouted and pointed at least ten times in the next half-hour. "There it is!"

And we did look. But clearly those wide, ice-blue eyes of Luke's were better than ours.

A little further on and we were into nettles and brambles. I looked behind. There was Luke in his short pants trying to pick his way through.

"They hurt!"

He reached out his hand. "Carry?"

I lifted him. He settled on my hip, arm round my shoulder.

From up here he could keep a better eye on that ole alligator, he said.

It was up to me to keep a wary eye for snakes.

# 35

## *No Fishin'!*

*Harrisonburg, Louisiana*—Back in the Bronco, and bumping and bucketing down the track, Davey made a sudden detour. "Someone I want you to meet," he declared. After a mile or so of slow progress along this dipping, winding and ever more jungly track, we pulled up at a modest, timber-boarded cabin tucked well back in the trees. "Jacob lives here," said Davey. "He's a man I'd like you to meet....And you!" he pointed a finger at Luke, "You can stay right here and take care of the car! You hear?" Luke was not happy with this instruction. He pouted and whacked the seat. But he stayed put.

Two cement breeze blocks provided the front step. Davey knocked at the door. Eventually a tall man, gray-haired, trim build, two-day growth of whiskers, appeared. He broke into a big grin, seized Davey's hand and literally pulled him in. I followed. This, in patched grey trousers and torn white singlet, was Jacob.

As the two small curtained windows didn't let in much light, Jacob lit a kerosene lamp. I looked round. This was no timber cabin, but rather a converted trailer. Clever job. Jacob caught my examining eye. "Yep. It's all here. Sink, bathroom, couple of bedrooms. Looks after us just fine." At which a short, blonde, well-built woman appeared from one of the bedrooms down the corridor. This was Jacob's partner, Lois.

Tins of cold beer were produced. We all cracked 'em open. They tasted good. Davey explained I was a visitor from England, just passing through.

"And what's brought you up here into Catahoula Parish?" inquired Jacob. I explained. "Well," said Jacob, "as you will know from Davey, there are lots of them mounds round here. This was a busy place in the old days; alot of activity up and down all these rivers." He grinned. "No shortage of folk. And no shortage of fish either!"

"Speaking of fish," said Davey, "any more problems with the Fish and Game people?"

Jacob laughed. "Hell no! But then I ain't been doin' no fishin'!" Jacob went on to explain how he'd got into a "bit of a wrangle," with the State Fishery officials. All his life, he and his people before him had netted fish from the river and one or two nearby lakes and sold the catch locally. It was a steady trade. Then one day a few years ago one of the Fishery officers appeared, examined his catch, then charged and arrested him for catching fish from "protected species."

"I told 'em I'd caught these fish all my life, and that there was certainly no shortage of 'em in these waters up here. As for any law about 'protected species,' this was news to me!" Jacob went on to say that had it not been for Davey, "Why they'd have banged me up and thrown away the key!" He gave Davey's knee a friendly slap. "Yep, Davey here made 'em sit up and take notice. And he got me off with just a warning."

He laughed. "It was a great performance. This man's a wizard with words! But that new law they made is still there. And while it don't make no damned sense at all—least so far as these waters and my kind of fishin's concerned—the State says I can't fish no more. Course I can do a little sport-fishin' like any other man; put a few fish on the table. But that's it. Only job I ever knew; and my daddy and grand-daddy. Gone. By some law made by some man in an air-conditioned back office in Baton Rouge."

"So what do you do now?" I asked.

"Well, a bit of this, bit of that," he said obliquely. "Sometimes people need things. And sometimes I can help. And, of course, we've got us this fine, rich earth down here. It grows up all the beans and peas and corn and squash we need. And lots of berries too. And there's no shortage of nuts, hickory, walnuts, pecans later on. And every now and then we get the odd bit of venison, and I can assure you roast possum ain't bad a'tall. In fact, The Lord, he looks after us pretty good. And every month now I get the dole cheque. So we get along. But it still don't make no sense to me. No sense a'tall. And I miss the fishin'!"

I asked Jacob whether he'd ever thought of moving out; maybe into Harrisonburg, or one of the towns close by. He laughed quietly. "But what about my garden here? What about the river? And these are the hills and this is the valley that I know." He looked over at Davey. "Now I don't mean no disrespect to the fine people of Harrisonburg, and I've got some very good friends there, but the things that I've got, that I know, that know me, well they're all here, not anywhere else.

I like it here. Lois likes it here. There are other folk round here. We all know each other, and we get on, most of the time. In fact we both learned just recently that there's a good shot of Indian blood—Natchez and Tunica—in our veins. So maybe we belong here even more than we think!"

He reached over and gently took Lois' hand. "No, this is home to us. We're happy here. We'll stay. O' course," he grinned, "I'd like to get back to my fishin', and so do the folk we've always supplied. Town and Supermarket quality and prices ain't quite the same!"

Before we left, Jacob took us over to his vegetable patch. Luke, who'd been playing with Dinah, Jacob's brindle pit-bull bitch, and her new pups, fat and round as four-legged butterballs, joined us. It covered a small area on a low rise of ground no more than 20 feet from the tangle of undergrowth bordering the river. And there it all was. Burgeoning leafy green plants in neat rows in the black moist soil. He picked us six ears of corn and a plastic bagful of long, succulent-looking beans. He gave Luke the bag to carry. "Should be enough for your dinner there."

Davey knew that these vegetables were valuable to Jacob, either for his own table or for barter elsewhere. He also knew that Jacob would never take cash from him. Back now at the cabin and getting into the Bronco, Davey rummaged in the back. Two six-packs of beer were produced. "Maybe you can get a chill on these. Next time I'm down we can have a frosty one or two on me."

Jacob laughed and passed the packs to Lois. "I expect we can manage that."

Davey reversed the Bronco, we all gave Jacob and Lois a wave, and after another lurching drive down the track, which didn't seem nearly so long, we emerged from the undergrowth and forest canopy into the bright glow of late afternoon and onto the road back to Harrisonburg.

It was a great relief to step into the air conditioned cool of Davey's office. It was nearly 5:30. No one in the waiting room. One of the secretaries handed Davey a list of calls. "They need attendin' in the morning," she said.

Two mugs of coffee were shortly produced. Davey stirred in a spoonful of sugar and took a sip. "Well I reckon you've had a pretty good look and feel round this land, round us Southern folk the past week or two," he observed. "So is the picture coming into focus?"

I replied that a lot had gone into "the computer," but that it would be a while until I discovered what would come out. I added that his and Robert's efforts had helped greatly.

"I was glad you met Jacob. Bit like that Jeremiah fella you encountered, and one or two others. People round here, in fact throughout much of the South back-country, well they're well settled in. And like all folk the world over, there's more crossed-blood than many may admit to, or even know. The roots do go deep down here, for all of us.

"You talked about modern America, about the thin surface 'cultural coverings' on the ancient mounds. Now we down here are partly of that surface covering, but we go deeper. And some of us go right down to the base. You talked about New Echota, the Cherokees in Georgia, about their 'removal,' about the 'Roman occupiers having come but not yet left.'

Well you could say that the Romans came here too. But the difference is that the Ancients have risen up, ever so gently, and drawn 'em down. Ancient and Roman are effectively one."

He paused, checked one or two of the names on the message list and quietly cursed. "Maybe that's what makes us a bit different from our Stars and Stripes brethren elsewhere in this huge country. Your ordinary Catahoula man may not always be able to put it into words. But he *knows* his roots, he's *aware* of his instincts. He knows he *belongs*, he knows he's *kin* to those ancients of the mounds. And knowing's enough.

"And maybe that's why he doesn't take all these shouts and claims and 'discoveries' of these professors and antiquity adventurers all that seriously; in fact why he sometimes gets a little bit riled. You see, to Jacob and many folk like him, these experts aren't saying anythin' new. Just statin' the obvious and causin' a lot of strangers to come buzzin' round who they could get along very well without."

Davey cast an eye in my direction. He could see a furrow of doubt. "Now I'm *not* sayin' these experts don't mean well—most of them—and that it's not good that people beyond this State, indeed beyond this country should know there's more to America than John Wayne, McDonald's and Disneyland. It's just that your ordinary back-country Louisiana man doesn't like being interfered with, stirred up. He doesn't like some of his cherished bits of property being put on public display. He just wants to get on with his own life in his own way."

I considered raising the issue of Huey Long, of his 1920s and 1930s programmes of "social democracy," of the building of roads, and bridges, and schools, and hospitals, all principally designed to meet the needs of people like Jacob. All these programmes meant intrusions, interference in the lives of back-country people. But they all, virtually to a man, had voted for him. Huey was a hero in back-country Louisiana. But I decided to leave well enough alone. Basically I accepted Davey's argument. And indeed, given what I'd observed in my Louisiana travels it wasn't too clear that Huey's programmes *had* resulted in any great intrusions. Was Huey, like most politicians, more talk than action? And if what I had recently viewed was the product of the *actions* of Huey and his successors, one could only surmise what things must have been like *before*!

"Which reminds me," said Davey. "Some years ago a friend of mine who lives up in the Ozarks foothills a few miles from here found a long-abandoned well on his property. He tested it. It went down 120 feet. Now he was afraid that one of his kids might fall down it. So he got a man to come with a big ready-mix truck filled with cement, and he just poured it in and filled it up.

"Now I've often thought to myself; my, oh my, what is some antiquity hunter or archaeologist maybe 2000 years hence going to make of this 'buried column?' To what people, to what great feats of engineering, for what ceremonial purpose may he surmise this impressive column was constructed?" He chuckled and took a long sip from his coffee mug. "I have put this point to one or two of our local antiquities experts.

They have not been appreciative. And when I have gone on to suggest there may be parallels with current archaeological work they've got downright frosty." He laughed and stretched. "But then I guess we've all got our professional pride. And it's only natural to protect your patch."

At last the time had come. I needed to get back on the road. I was heading for Shreveport and the Texas border and wanted at least to get onto the Inter-State and run up a few miles before dark. It was difficult leaving Davey and Robert and little Luke. In the short time I had been with them I had come to realise we shared much. And these were basic things; things which had as much to do with a respect, a feel for these lands and bayous as for the ancient and indeed more recent residents who inhabited them. There was life and freedom and vigour and great energy here. And it all came up from these lands and these waters. It felt good to Davey and Robert and indeed to Luke. And it felt good to me.

I asked Davey whether he'd ever thought of moving on to a "bigger stage;" maybe in Baton Rouge, Shreveport, New Orleans. Did not things sometimes get a little confining up here in Catahoula Parish?

His answer came as no surprise. "Michael, this is my home. And I love it here. This is where I was born. This is where I want to be. And this is where I'll stay, and one day—not too soon I hope—be buried." He pushed off a flashing button on his phone. "Besides there are many of the important things in life here that no self-respectin' man would willingly give up; like fishin' and huntin', even the occasional bit of diggin', just to shake hands, you might say, to see that everythin's alright with our early residents. And of course if me and Robert lived in one of those big cities, just think what you'd have missed here in Catahoula Parish!" Davey laughed and slapped his palms down on the desk.

"Michael, I wish you luck in your remaining travels. And you can relax a little bit, 'cause our Catahoula Ancients have taken to you." He seized my hand and gave it a firm shake. "And there's no better protection than that!" After a few farewell words with Robert I was back in the car. It was now past six. I realised it would be dark by the time I reached the Inter-State.

# 36

## *On to "Indian Territory"—Oklahoma*

*Calhoun, Louisiana*—By the time I reached the Inter-State, night had settled in. I tried pushing on, but my eyes were drooping. Having checked and rejected two very bleak and costly motel opportunities, I spotted a huge Walmart's Super Store close to an exit. It was already past eleven. I pulled in to the vast flood-lit parking lot. I had a snack in mind.

Inside, which seemed the size of an aircraft hangar, I found the bakery section. I was interested in buying two, perhaps four doughnuts. But they were available only in bags of ten. Then, I thought, perhaps a few soft rolls. Same problem. Everything was available, but only in huge quantities. And then I discovered just what I was looking for; a great mound of big, beautiful, tasty-looking Blueberry Muffins.

"Special Offer!" said the display sign. "Box of 2!! $2.50!!"; and in small print below, "$1.25 each." I puzzled over this offer. Was I missing something? Perhaps a sales language I didn't understand? Eventually I found a Sales Assistant. Could she please explain the "Special Offer?" She looked at the sign, then at the Blueberry Muffins, then at me. She straightened the boxes. "Looks alright to me." But as there was no saving, what was the special offer, I asked? She regarded me in that long-suffering way of Sales Assistants world-wide. "Not everyone likes their muffins *single*, in a *bag*. The *box* is special!"

So there I had it. I purchased a box of two muffins and a half-gallon of "Fresh Florida Orange Juice"—the smallest size—and retired to the Chevy. Having consumed the muffins, washed down by two plastic cupsful of Orange Juice, I was again feeling very sleepy. It was now nearly midnight. I had a look round. Not many cars about. And with these overhead floods it was as bright as mid-day. Why not have a few hours of sleep right here, right now? So for the first time since Tishomingo State Park, way back on the Alabama/Mississippi border, I eased the seat back, this time *removed* the loose change and other articles from my pants pockets, and dropped off.

It was already light when I awoke. The lot was virtually empty. After a clean and wash-up in the Walmart Restroom, then a reviving cupful of orange juice, I was onto the Inter-State by 5:30 and heading west. After all the intricate ins and outs, and ups and downs of back-country driving, this steady running was both a relief and relaxing. And I was making good time. By mid-morning I was circuiting north of Shreveport and making for Texarkana, just over the Arkansas border, and again on a good, straight dual-highway.

Pulling in to fill up at a gas station, I checked my maps and notes. There were two well-known sites of the Mississippian period, Toltec and Parkin, I was keen to visit. Unfortunately, in my planning I had misjudged distances. Toltec, near Little Rock, was about 150 miles east; and Parkin, up towards the Mississippi flood plain, was getting on to 300 miles distant. I poured myself an orange juice and pondered the situation. I was sorely tempted. I flipped through my notes and Internet printouts. They showed what I would be missing. That wonderful head-effigy vessel at Parkin, the product of great artist/craftsmen impelled over 1000 years ago by who knows what driving fervour; and at Toltec, those surviving mounds—at one time 18 of them!—and remnant protective earthwork ring, close to that pulsing artery of the American heartland, the Arkansas River; I wanted so much to see them all. But the distances were simply too great in the time available.I had to keep moving. Perhaps, I sighed, another time.

Back on the road, the driving was more difficult. Travelling over broken-up roads, on narrow lanes weaving through numerous shantytowns and more prosperous urban districts, the heat shimmering, intense, I now cut across the top northeast corner of Texas. Finally. after negotiating more narrow roads and heavy traffic through scattered suburban settlements, I reached the very un-Parisian town of Paris. Turning north onto Route 271, in another 20 minutes I was over the broad, labouring Red River, Texas' northern boundary, and into the old "Indian Territory", now (since 1907) known as the State of Oklahoma.

In my initial tour plan I had intended progressing no further than the Mississippi Delta and Louisiana. That, after all, was where my "Phantoms of the Ancients" were mainly to be found. But then I noted the proximity of Oklahoma. And as I was very curious about this 19th century dumping ground of over 50 different Indian Nations removed from their homelands mostly east of ole Miss., I decided to extend my visit.

There were, of course, "phantoms" here too. But in my mind, these were of a very different nature. They were phantoms of tragedy, of despair and desperation, of bitterness, devastation and defeat. They were not phantoms I greatly wanted to meet. Still, I told myself, if I didn't look, didn't feel for myself, I wouldn't know.

These were my thoughts as I drove with ease and at speed up the Indian Nations Turnpike, over surprisingly green and rolling lands. In fact these were the "removed lands" of the Choctaw. And while there's no place like home, it did seem to me that these lands—albeit a fraction of the territory they once controlled in southern Alabama and Mississippi—of forest, hill, low-rippling mountain and broad meadow did at least bring to the removed Choctaw the compensations of refreshing variety and a less oppressive climate. Oklahoma heat, as I was to learn, can be very hot indeed, but seldom does that heat carry the weighty burden of humidity its does in the Deep South.

As I continued north on the Turnpike, passing now through McAlester, I was aware there was another important habitation of the ancients 70 miles to the east. This was the Spiro site and its Mounds on a bend of the Arkansas River close to what now is the State line with Arkansas.

This, the furthest reach of the old Mississippian culture, stood at the lowlands gateway, where the Great Valley met the Great Plains of the West. The Spiro people, like their Mississippian counterparts at Cahokia, Etowah, Moundsville, Jonesville and elsewhere, had evolved a high and dominant culture. Spiroans reigned supreme between 900 AD and 1450. This site, Oklahoma's sole National Historic Landmark and Archaeological Park includes the remains of a village and 11 earthen mounds. Spectacular artifacts, so my books and articles told me, have been uncovered. Some of the most breathtaking are fine, highly stylised designs worked with great artistic skill onto shell, beaten copper and stone. And while much of this heritage has been lost through customary looting, treasure hunting and private "appropriation," a good deal also has been safeguarded and preserved.

How much I wanted to *feel* this ancient ground—which in fact had served as an encampment for perhaps many 1000s of years before the powerful Spiroans took a sedentary hold—and *see* the celebrated collection in the Spiro Interpretive Center. But again, sadly, with time not in my favour, it was not to be. I would have to "feel" from a distance.

# 37

## *Cherokee "Green Country"*

*Tahlequah, Oklahoma*—My planned destination was the Capital of the removed Cherokee Nation, Tahlequah, in the north-east of the State. I still had a long drive ahead of me. My bones were aching; my head groggy. Tonight I did need a bed. But as this was the Memorial Day Weekend, I was aware that accommodation might not be easy to find.

Having first passed through Muscogee and surrounding Creek territory, I reached Tahlequah in the easing heat of late afternoon. A heavy rainfall had just cleared. I was astonished. Contrary to my expectations this was no arid, brown desolate place. Here were rich green flatlands and rolling forested hills cut through by bright, clear streams. And here too were houses and stores and a sizeable fast-food alley just like any small middle-American town. Indeed, without too great a stretch of the imagination this could be the town of Cherokee in the heart of the ancient North Carolina Cherokee homeland. There was, however, one thing missing. I saw no Indians—or so I thought.

Sure enough, all the local motels were fully booked. I thus decided to deploy my standard fall-back tactic. Having found the local Police Station, I explained my plight. To my great relief, the Desk Sergeant took a compassionate interest, and within a half-hour I was sitting in the shaded front room of his "close friends," Elizabeth and George Downing.

I had landed on my feet. Elizabeth took it upon herself to be both hostess and guide. In the course of the next two days I met many of her friends and family. They were a lively, bright, mainly professional—doctors, lawyers, accountants—assortment of people. Grand-children seemed always to be popping in for one thing or another. All were part of a busy local community. It was refreshing. Gradually that oppressive psychic weight of Southern culture started to lift.

Elizabeth showed me the high ground looking out over the Valley of the Illinois River; then south of Tahlequah, we toured a magnificent new development of luxury homes with stunning views over the broad, blue, forest-fringed expanse of Tenkiller Lake.

Nor was the Cherokee presence overlooked. We visited the Murrell-Ross House, a memorial and museum dedicated to the works and memory of the great Cherokee Chief John Ross. In the 1830s, Ross had fought long and hard—using the Courts, Congress and the Georgia legislature—to prevent displacement of his people, the "Civilised Tribe of the Cherokee," from their North Carolina and Georgia homelands. In the end, however—and as I had earlier learned during my visit to the New Echota site in Georgia—Ross was forced to concede removal.

Surviving the fateful "Trail of Tears", and arriving here in these Indian Territory lands, he then rallied the remnant of his people and led in re-creating a progressive and purposeful community; a community which flourished and burgeoned until the next calamity, the Civil War. Though the Cherokees were divided in loyalty—a substantial element under Stand Watie supporting the Southern Confederacy, while Ross and his supporters favoured the Union—all were to pay a heavy price under post-war Union Administration. Ross survived the War, but only by one year. He died in 1866, aged 76.

As I looked through the huge collection of photos, sepia prints, other artifacts and Civil War memorabilia I began to feel that heavy, depressing presence starting to re-gather. The South; the vivid memories of that Confederate Veterans Home in Alabama, were stirring. And yet, and yet; I could only shake my head in wonder. What an extraordinary people were these Cherokee. Once again they had rallied. Would that the White Southerners could have learned from these Indian people the lessons here writ large! Repeatedly they, indeed all members of the "Five Civilised Tribes", had suffered tragic betrayal and savage treatment by the Whiteman. But time and again they had bounced back, refused to be defeated, determined to make successful lives for themselves. Here was real courage, true heroism. It was a powerful and humbling statement. And it all was contained here in this simple display in these dark, musty-smelling rooms of this old, tree-shaded house.

Chastened, yet spiritually refreshed, we moved on to the Cherokee Nation Museum. A spacious, modern, single-storey building, it contained yet another treasure-house of artifacts, memorabilia—and shelves upon shelves of tantalising, puchaseable books! After extensive perusal, and agonising over choice, I finally selected two volumes not likely available in Britain.

Back at the Downings', I took an after dinner walk round the neighbourhood. Most of the houses were similar to the Downings'; comfortable, middling-sized, non-pretentious, practical, with small front lawns and larger back-gardens packed with flower-beds or neat rows of vegetables with beans, peas, carrots, corn and melons much in evidence.

As I extended my walk, I entered other areas. The houses themselves, mostly clap-board, timber-frame, were little different, but up-keep was more casual. Discarded bicycles, a rusty old refrigerator, a derelict car minus wheels, doors and headlamps on one front lawn space; these triggered memories of those Southern shantytowns in Selma, Greensboro, Cartersville. And yet, they also triggered memories of those sobering, *corrective* reminders—'what you see is *not* always what you get!'—of the Rev. Jesse Greer.

I stopped at a Convenience Store. A cold Coke from the stand-up cooler went down well. I asked the man at the counter whether he'd been here long. A few years, I was told. Business was good, I inquired? "Steady trade," he declared. It turned out he had three stores in Tahlequah, of which this was one. As we talked, a tall, rangy man came in, purchased a six-pack of beer and departed. "Steady customer," said the shopkeeper. "Lots of them live round here," he observed.

"Them?" I inquired.

"You know, Indians. Mostly Cherokee here in Tahlequah. A kind of capital city for them."

His comment came as a surprise. The man who had purchased the beer, was fair-complexioned, with sharp, almost Nordic features and didn't look anything like Indian people I knew. I said as much to the shopkeeper. He adjusted some gum packets on the counter. "I guess there's not much Cherokee left in most of these people. Cherokee women are very attractive to the Whiteman's eye. Have been since our people first encountered 'em. Not really surprising they look more like Whites than Indians." He delicately scratched his pink, balding scalp. "Funny thing is, though, they're still Indian at heart. Just like these folk who live round here—and round my other stores—they don't take easily to the Whiteman's ways.

"Now don't get me wrong." He raised a cautious eye at me. "They've got some very clever people. And they do well. Get on. But for most, it's a bit like these people round here. They just seem to be satisfied to get by on their Indian perks and state benefits. All of which we pay for!" He sighed. "Can't go on forever; at least not in my view. But that's how things are at the moment."

My return route took me through the centre of Tahlequah. There were plenty of people about. The men were mainly tall, tanned, fair-skinned, with lean, strong-looking bodies; the women of similar features, with large dark eyes, smiling and animated. Having merely looked before, I now saw. This indeed was Cherokee country.

Back at the Downings' I raised the subject of Indian numbers in Tahlequah. I was told, "This is an Indian town, with a fair sprinkling of Hispanics and Blacks to put added strain on the welfare system!" I was further informed that the Whites had their own communities and networks; that the two communities lived largely separate lives.

When I asked what was the role of the Cherokee Tribal Government in reducing the distance between the communities, and in moving the Cherokee people forward, George Downings' reply was abrupt. "Nothing!" He then corrected himself, saying that "for some people there was some movement." But most time and attention, he said, had been taken up with "financial complications." It was alleged that large sums from Federal and other official bodies had entered the Tribal Government Treasury, "never to be seen again." Things had happened; functions and projects seemed perennially to fall short of budgeted and allocated monies. And for whatever reasons, he added, Government Audit officials seemed not to be unduly concerned. "And of course, as members of the White community here, we know, and are told nothing."

This then was my introduction to the old "Indian Territory", Oklahoma, and the "removed" Indian Nations. As I lay in bed beneath the "whip, whip" of the overhead fan, I reflected. I had expected to find here a brown, arid, dust-hole; a scorched, desolate prairie with Indians living in a state of impoverished wretchedness. This was the picture that my readings, and experience from a distance had painted. Instead, I had found Choctaw, Creek and Cherokee territories which were green, well-watered, forested, productive. Indeed it seemed to me these lands were in many respects an improvement on their native territories east of the Mississippi. As for the Indian inhabitants themselves, none showed signs of physical or material impoverishment. And the Murrell-Ross House visit had provided a sanguine reminder of the phenomenal power and buoyancy of spirit these remarkable people had repeatedly shown. Finally, in relation to adjustment and adaptation to the conflicting demands of residual heritage and the modern American work ethic, clearly what applied elsewhere, applied here. Cherokees were working to find their place, their accommodation with the modern world. They had made progress. There was a distance yet to go.

# 38

## *Wyandotte Encounter*

*Wyandotte, Oklahoma*—I had hoped before leaving Tahlequah to have a word with former Cherokee Principal Chief Wilma Mankiller. I had acquired her phone number. But several calls produced only a busy signal. So having said farewell to the Downings I headed off north into more Green Country; my destination Miami in the North-east top corner, close to the Kansas and Missouri borders.

The Miami Agency of the BIA (Bureau of Indian Affairs) was firmly implanted in my mind as a place of legendary notoriety; the font and symbol of all that was evil and corrupt in the Whiteman's "guardian" relationship with the Reservation Indian. Here banished peoples from myriad removed tribes—including Ottawa, Wyandotte/Huron, Seneca/Iroquois, Quapaw, Shawnee, Peoria, Modoc—struggled to survive on often starvation rations, in wretched conditions, on lands not only alien to them but already occupied by existing native inhabitants. It was a nightmare period in the history of a defeated and demoralised race. Once again, therefore, I was not looking forward to facing up to this reality. Yet once again I was curious. Though I was aware that the seriously bad old days were long past, with so many of the "ward" nations now operating their own Tribal governments and with the BIA in a much-diminished role, still I feared the presence of evil phantoms.

The route through the Green Country was again a revelation. The road wound steadily northward, at one moment hugging the banks of a broad, brown-flowing river, then into and through lightly-forested hill country, and finally down and past the multiple bays and inlets of the 30-mile Grand Lake o' the Cherokees. Docks, cottages, boat-ramps and large numbers of outboard motor-boats, along with huge raft-like catamarans containing entire families on boating and fishing expeditions confirmed that this was indeed, as advertised, Oklahoma's playground.

I pulled in at one of the recreation areas advertising "trout fishing," and parked under the trees. Many other cars and pick-ups were scattered about, their occupants relaxing in camp-chairs with several "frosties" (cans of cold beer) in large, portable cooler-boxes close to hand. I inquired about the trout fishing. "Help yourself!" declared a rotund camp-chair occupant. He pointed to the small, dammed-up pond where children and adults were happily swimming, shrieking and splashing. I put my hand in the water. It was luke warm. So much for trouting!

In the Park Convenience Store were two women who doubled as Park Attendants. I purchased a cold Sprite and we got to chatting. I duly told them what I was about; that this was my first visit to the old Indian Territory; and that I was keen to visit the old Miami Agency. It turned out that one of the women was a Wyandotte mixed-blood; and that she was a teacher working for the Wyandotte Tribal Administration. "The man you want to see," said she, "is Chief Leaford Bearskin. He's been around for a bit." As for the Miami Agency, "When you get to Miami, you'll find it, right enough!"

Another hour and I had reached the town of Wyandotte; and shortly thereafter I had located the rambling, brick-built, strikingly modern Tribal Administration Building. However, neither Chief Bearskin nor anyone else was about. I checked my watch. It was already 5:30! Too late again! But could I track down the Chief? A man mowing his lawn next door paused to give me directions. A few minutes later, after negotiating a long, winding, leafy lane, I turned into a drive. This was the Chief's residence. It was a sizeable, single-story, timber-frame house, set on a high bluff at the back of a large property lightly-wooded with maples and other hardwoods.

Chief Bearskin was at home. Dinner was just about on the table. I was not popular with his wife. She did not appreciate the interruption. Besides, the Chief had to have his insulin shot. Finally, after a good deal of clattering and banging and shouting, she settled down. The Chief and I had a useful talk. A former USAF (US Air Force) pilot and retired Civil Servant, he had been Chief of the Wyandotte Nation since 1983. The Wyandottes, though small in numbers—only 400 locally, 600 in the State, and 2000 nationally—were, he pointed out, nevertheless fortunate to have very effective teams working in all areas—education, health, housing, employment and business support.

"We get the best," said he. I cavilled at the word "best." What did he mean? "Best," he said, "is defined by the Wyandotte definition of its foremost principle, which is a four-letter word, and is spelled, CARE!" The Chief explained in detail and at some length the efforts made and consistently needed to "restore and retain traditional values" at the root of modern Wyandotte and Indian life. "Not easy," said he. "Television, the media, McDonald's and the American Dream project powerful images and messages." I said that it might interest him to know that such images and messages created an equally powerful impact on the youth, and not-so-youthful in the small English town where I lived!

Conversation then turned to values and lifeways, and the persisting conflicts these generated between White and Indian communities. We spoke of the natural link of Indian man to the spirits and rhythms of the land; and of the Whiteman's inability to sense this fundamental link and its importance not just to Indian man, but to the White American himself. I spoke of an experience in *Phantom Ship* where Renée, a Seneca woman, sensed the presence of deer, when the Whiteman sensed nothing at all. Chief Bearskin related an identical experience when he was deer-hunting with White friends. "Not only did I sense it before I saw it; I knew instinctively *where* to look when it appeared. My White friends neither sensed, nor indeed were they able even to see it!"

Before I left, the Chief took me out onto the timbered deck at the rear of the house. It provided fantastic rippling views over distant forests and meadows, as well as a breath-taking sweep up and down the deep wooded river valley far below. I noted a long section of PVC down-pipe projecting from the railing at one end of the deck. It dropped 60 feet or so to a small wooden platform at the edge of the forest canopy. The Chief noted my puzzled gaze. "Feeding chute for the raccoons. They come every night. I like to watch 'em. I release the content of a tin of dog food down the chute; then turn on the floods and watch 'em snack it on that platform where it pops out from the down-pipe."

It was now a short run through still-green, rolling, well-watered country to Miami. Chief Bearskin was much in my thoughts. Strange, yet perhaps not so strange. We had made almost immediate spiritual contact. The inner language was identical. I felt at one, at ease with this Indian man; both refreshed, yet disturbed.

I had phoned ahead and booked in at the local Great Western motel. The room turned out to be air-conditioned and comfortable. I did not, however, sleep well. Chief Bearskin remained close in my thoughts. His role had been central to Wyandotte achievements over the past 20 years. Programme attainments had not been easily won. But now he was a man old in years. How, I wondered, would the Nation fare when he had gone? When I had asked him what provision there was for a successor equally capable of dealing with the modern world, he did not reply.

# 39

## *The Miami Agency—At Last!*

*Miami, Oklahoma*—The Miami Agency of the BIA turned out to be *not* so easy to find. I made inquiries. I checked the phone book. No sign. Then someone said I might try the Federal Building. I duly found the Federal Building in the downtown business area. It was a sizeable brick edifice. On the ground floor was the Post Office. Above it, I noted, were another two floors; and I could see office strip-lighting. Bit big for just a Post Office, I thought. Inside I checked for an Office Directory. There was none. And then I had a thought. I had stamps to purchase. I went to the counter. Having acquired the stamps, I put a question to the counter clerk. "The BIA is on the *second*, or *third* Floor?"

"Second," said the clerk.

There was an elevator in the near-end lobby. I stepped in and pushed "2". At "2" the doors opened and I stepped out into a totally different world. A strip of highly-polished brown lino led down a long corridor. On each side, at regular intervals, were gleaming mahogany-brown doors with brass numbers on them. There was no sight or sound of life. I smiled.

This was just like any government office, be it in Washington, Whitehall, or the smallest Local Government Authority. That strange sense of detached busyness; the sense that *something, somewhere* is going on; but that there's no actual physical indication that it's *happening*.

An arrowed sign on the wall directed me to "BIA Inquiries." At the end of the corridor I found the Inquiries Office. The door was half-shut. There was subdued chatter and laughter from within. I knocked and entered. The chatter stopped. Two women and a man regarded me uncertainly. I explained who I was, and what I was doing. I said I had long heard of the "Miami Agency," and being in the area did not wish to miss the chance of visiting it. I stated that I had not found it easy to locate the Agency; that it certainly did not advertise its presence. I felt myself bristling. I couldn't help it. These people were the bureaucratic descendants of those who by their cruelty and greed, by their criminal fraud and dishonesty had destroyed the lives of 1000s and 1000s of Indian people; lives they were obligated to aid, nourish and protect! These were my feelings. And they were noted.

"So what is it you want?" one of the women asked.

I replied that it would be helpful if I could talk with someone who had some knowledge both of the history of the Agency, and of what it was doing now. They consulted. A phone call was made. Shortly after, a tall, dark-skinned man appeared. His name was Alberto. He asked me to follow him. Well down the silent corridor he opened one of the numbered brown doors. Inside was a large-ish office. Two big windows let in much light. There were many maps and papers scattered on side tables. He gestured me to a chair, then drew up another and sat down.

Alberto, it turned out, was Italian-Cherokee/Shawnee, third generation. He was well-versed on the activities, fair and foul, of the Miami Agency of old, and indeed expressed some very heated un-BIA views. His Shawnee kin had been amongst those who had suffered. I spoke of the Quapaw, Peoria, Ottawa, Wyandotte, Shawnee, Miami, Seneca and Cayuga peoples, amongst others, for whom the Miami Agent, at one time served as Guardian and Trustee. What was the BIA relation to these nations now?

Briefly, Alberto explained that the extent of Agency concern here was no longer great. Leasing, development, funding and so forth, had largely been taken over by Federally-recognised Tribal Governments. Still, he explained, the Agency was active on matters of health, welfare and education. Alberto's speciality was "Environmental Health Protection," with particular attention to "Hazardous Waste Materials." This North-east corner of the State had once been a big producer of zinc and lead for US industry and armaments. Remnants were still about—surface and sub-surface, old sites—and still toxic.

I asked Alberto whether he had always been an "Environmental Protection Specialist?" He glanced across at me. "Depends on your definition of 'Environment' and 'Protection.' My first job was at the Fort Sill (Oklahoma) Indian Boarding School."

He saw the look on my face at the mention of "Indian Boarding School."

Things, he hastened to add, had changed. The "reform school mode" had long passed. That was the late 1970s. Most children, he explained, came from family backgrounds of abuse and violence; from situations where there were often contributory problems of alcohol and drugs. Single-parenting (mother only, no father) from pretty depressing Reservation situations was the norm.

When I asked whether things were really that bad, he sighed and examined his fingers; the moons on his nails were very white against the darkness of his skin. "Schools are not home," he said. "But what the Fort Sill School did was at least to provide some stability and security for these children; to offer them the chance to learn basic living skills; to give them the opportunity to equip themselves for the fight that we all of us have to face out there." I then asked how graduates from the school fared in later life; where did they go? He had no information.

Alberto asked where I was off to next? I said I was heading West, but was open to suggestions. "Well, you've seen a good bit of the Green Country. Time for you to see a bit of the Brown Country." He indicated a route on my map that went South-west via Tulsa, then on past Oklahoma City to Chickasha (pronounced "Chick-a-shay" by Oklahomans), across to Anadarko and finally down to Fort Sill at Lawton. "You're well into Brown Country through there." The Fort Sill Museum, he said, was a "must." And from Lawton west to the Texas border was "a straight run through some of the most beautiful Brown Country you'll ever see. You don't want to miss it!"

# 40

## *Route to "Brown Country"*

*Miami, Oklahoma*—Departing the Agency and the Federal Building, I found a Milk Bar and Burger Grill. Ordering up a double-chocolate shake, I checked my route. It looked like easy driving. The Will Rogers Turnpike to Tulsa; then the Turner Turnpike to Oklahoma City; just a matter of pointing the car in the right direction, putting it into cruise control, and letting 'er roll. I finished up the last of my shake and was on my way.

Approaching Tulsa, I saw a sign for the town of Claremore. "Visit the Will Rogers Museum," it said. I knew of Will Rogers as the celebrated American humourist and home-spun philosopher of the 1920s and 30s. What I didn't know was that Rogers was a Cherokee, and that he got his opportunity for show-business fame from the humble beginnings of a cowboy trick-roper.

This and much more I learned at the Will Rogers Home at Claremore. The Museum was packed with Rogers memorabilia. Rogers, it seems, did not make a big show of his Cherokee credentials, but he was not averse to making appropriate comment when occasion arose. Once, asked about his family pedigree, Will pondered for a moment, then made the following reply. Referring to the Mayflower (Puritan) immigrants, Will observed that "while my people weren't *on* the boat, nevertheless, they were there to *meet* it!"

Back on the Turnpike, and past Tulsa, the miles clicking past at a steady rate, I approached the Stroud exit. It was about half-way to Oklahoma City. Prague (pronounced locally, "Pray-gg"), birthplace of Jim Thorpe, America's Greatest Athlete of the 20th Century, was 20 miles due south. Thorpe, of mixed Indian, Irish and French blood, was brought up on the nearby Sac and Fox Reservation. I had seen the awesome bronze sculpture of Thorpe at the NFL (National Football League) Hall of Fame at Canton, Ohio, a few years before. It would be good to visit the land where he was born.

The road ran flat and straight. This was farming country. There were occasional barns and houses. Then on my right I passed a complex of new single-storey buildings. I hesitated. The rambling style was familiar. Not unlike the Wyandotte complex. I doubled back and turned in to the spacious parking area in front of the main building. This, it turned out, was the Sac and Fox Tribal Administration Center.

I stepped out into the late afternoon heat. There was no one about. Then a Tribal Police vehicle pulled up. I explained to the uniformed officer that I was passing through, but that I would appreciate a few words with anyone who might be able to inform me about present-day activities of the tribe. He eyed me, then got on his mobile. After a brief chat with an unseen party, he shut off his mobile, climbed out of his Patrol Car, instructed me to follow, unlocked the Administration Office front door, and led me down a hall to an open door. A large, greying man looked up from his desk. I was introduced to Merle Boyd, Second Chief of the Sac and Fox Nation.

There followed a long and enlightening chat. And it provided encouragement. The Sac and Fox were, like the Wyandotte, a relatively small tribe. And they were a far cry from that great trading and warring tribe that had held sway over vast lands in Illinois and along Lake Michigan; a tribe that had achieved stunning feats of arms against the encroaching Whites under their renowned leader, Chief Black Hawk. The Sac and Fox now numbered only 400 on the nearby small Reservation, and 600 off-Reservation in the local area. Another 2000 were scattered round the rest of the United States.

Determined, and it seemed, passably successful efforts were being made to work to the requirements of both the modern and traditional worlds. Clans were operative under un-paid Clan Heads. Duties were heavy. Many ceremonies, including Naming, and various Seasonal Festivals were held. Over the past 5-10 years, observed Chief Boyd, as "Indian" had become a "fashionable designation," there had been greatly increased interest and participation.

"And what of the educational front?" I asked. "Are things moving ahead?"

The Chief smiled wryly. "Most of our young people leave formal education after high school. They reckon that's enough."

"And do you?"

He wagged his head. "Well, there's a lot of book-learning in our colleges and universities these days that seems to me just common sense. But there's also a lot of specialised training, advanced skills, that a person can really only get through pushing on into higher education." The Chief tapped his pencil on the desk. "Our young people need to recognise this; that you've got to equip yourself with modern tools to compete successfully in the modern world. We do what we can to push 'em. Not easy."

I asked the Chief how he himself had managed with education and the modern world. "High School and a bit of book-keeping training." He told me he had worked many years as Warehouse Manager for a big publishing company in Oklahoma City. "But today nobody'd get in the door with my qualifications. A BA's the very basic requirement." And were there other Indian people who worked for his company, I inquired? "One or two. But they're Osage; and they work in another part of the company. I never see them."

The Chief then talked about his work with the tribe. Clearly this took much time and was very demanding. "But a man knows where his heart is, if he will stop and take the time to listen. I hear the words, the wishes of my people. Their spirit is my spirit. We go forward together. We share each other's burdens. It is not easy. It takes time."

And did this complicate things with his "day-time work," I asked?

He laughed. "A man has to be a bit of a head-case! Two separate persons occupying the same body; a sort of split personality, or whatever the head doctors call it." He paused. "I am a Whiteman during the week, and an Indian at the weekend—and during the evenings, like now. And there's nothing special about me. All American Indians live in two worlds. There's a lot of conflict and confusion inside," he tapped his chest. "Some manage this, and some don't. Guess I'm one of the lucky ones."

And would he prefer to live in the Indian world full-time, if he could?

The Chief took his time replying. "The fact is that the Indian has to learn to function in the Whiteman's world so he can eat. There's no point in trying to deny this. Even businesses run by Indians; these have to compete with businesses run by Whitemen. So there's no escape. Many Indian people are re-discovering their roots, the ways of their families, their people. They use their non-work time to learn. Today the numbers keep increasing." He laughed again. "It is fashionable to be an Indian."

And what, I asked, was his biggest challenge in dealing with tribal business?

"Don't know I'd call it a challenge. More like a headache! It's about Royalty payments on tribal lands. As you may know, under the old Dawes Act (1887), land was divided. Today many families still retain at least a part of their original 160 acre allotment. There are cases where 250 relatives now share ownership! It's our job to see that each one of these relatives gets his share of the Royalty received. It can amount to only a few dollars. It costs more to process and send, than the amount of the cheque!"

And did he see any solution?

"Try to reduce multiple ownership by naming the senior son, or a family member as inheritor; then let the inheritor make arrangements with family claimants." He hitched his considerable bulk up in his chair and gave out a great sigh. "But there's no easy way. For so long as the relatives believe there may be 'Black Gold' (Oil), or development potential—which has happened with many lands—they're inclined to hold on tight to the old arrangements."

I noted the Chief was suddenly getting very tired. His eyelids were drooping, and his skin had taken on a nasty pallour. It was time to go. I thanked him, got up and headed for the door.

"Sorry about this," he said, patting his chest. "Diabetic. Like many of our people. Still can't handle the Whiteman's diet. The Indian is not designed for high sugar, fat and carbohydrate content. Time for my insulin jab."

I told him that my object in taking this particular back-country route was to visit Prague, home town of Jim Thorpe. Was it far? Another few miles down the road, said the Chief; though the Jim Thorpe Memorial, he pointed out, was about 50 miles in the opposite direction, near the banks of the Cimarron River. I said it was the land of his early years I wanted to sense, to sound and to feel. He smiled and nodded. We bade our farewells.

What Chief Boyd didn't tell me was that there was nothing to mark the past presence of the great Thorpe in Prague. It was dark when I got there. I tried the main drag and a few side streets. But nothing. Just a small scattering of weather-beaten bungalows under the eery orange glow of a few street lights.

There was not a soul to be seen. Finally, I encountered a Prague Police Patrol car. I asked the officer the whereabouts of Thorpe's home.

"Nothing here," he shrugged

"Nothing at all?"

He shook his head. "Not a thing."

I knew Thorpe's family had first—perhaps throughout his early years—been based on the nearby Reservation and not in the town. But surely there must be some sign, some direction, something to indicate that this was his birthplace? But no; nothing. So far as these people in this strangely unsettling night-time ghost town were concerned, Thorpe apparently did not, nor had he ever, existed!

As it was getting late and I needed a bed, I asked the Police officer if he could direct me to a motel. No motel, said he. Then what about a Guest House? No Guest House. It was a very hot night. The officer removed his hat and mopped his brow. "There's a good motel at Shawnee. It's about another 20 miles down the road." A call came through on his radio. He put his car into gear and started to move off. "Best you'll do round here."

Before I departed I got out of the Chevy to stretch my legs. I walked up the main street, then took a turning up one of the residential roads. The footing was tricky in the orange half-light. I didn't see the potholes until I was up to, and several times with a jolt, into them.

Finally I stopped, stilled my mind, let my sensors extend round and down into this strangely vacuous land. I waited for some response; some small tingle. But nothing. The spirits of

Thorpe, of his people, did not make themselves known to me. Beetles of prodigious size and moths whirled round the few street lamps. There was the occasional "Smack!" as yet another beetle performed its kamikaze act against the light housing.

All the roads here are straight, the country very flat; the monotonous regularity of the American grid system—everything straight lines, or running off at precise right angles—depriving it of what little individual character it possesses. Another half-hour and I had found a "Motel 6" on the outskirts of Shawnee. There was, however, no nearby Dairy Queen or Milk Bar. Food would have to wait till morning.

Still, I was assured by the stout young woman in T-shirt and baggy shorts at the motel desk—whose ear appeared to be physically attached to her mobile—there was a "great diner" just south of the town on the route I intended to follow. "They put up a very good Breakfast Special." With visions of scrambled eggs, crisp bacon and tasty, grilled sausages dancing in my head, air conditioning on full, I settled down. I slept well

# 41

# *Indians and the "High Rollers"*

*Shawnee, Oklahoma*—It is another hot day; already over 95 degrees. And it's dry, very dry. There is much traffic here on the outskirts. Huge trucks are rumbling through *en route* to somewhere. There is much dust swirling. And I did find the diner. It was tucked away, as usual, behind its more glamorous relations on the fast-food strip. The "Breakfast Special" measured up to expectation. The fresh hot coffee was particularly welcome, as was the air conditioning.

I had an address for the local BIA Office. But again, finding it was another matter. Finally, after three dead-end leads, there it was, no bigger than a motel room, tucked away towards the end of a parade of offices in an off-street mini-mall. Hardly an imposing presence. A small BIA emblem on the door provided sole identification.

Inside the cramped, but bright, modern office, a tall, blond, somewhat hesitant young man spoke with me. His name was Brian. He dealt with Environmental Protection and Agricultural matters. He also informed me he was one-eighth blood Cherokee.

So what was the job of the Shawnee BIA, I inquired? Brian explained. This took some time. Its actual Trust duties in this 60 by 40 mile tract for which it was responsible were, it duly became apparent, virtually nil. Tribal Governments—Sac and Fox, Potawotami, Iowa and Absentee Shawnee—now saw to all their own business. Only with the Kickapoo did the Agency retain some direct administrative involvement. For the rest the BIA here worked in an advisory context. Brian pointed all this out on a section-grid map.

My, oh my. There it all was. The Great Plains and Grasslands of Central Oklahoma chopped up into symmetrical chunks. Each identical square-mile chunk belonged to somebody. And of the 2400 or so chunks, very few appeared to remain in Indian hands.

This map said more than any number of books about the fate of the Indian Territory. The Whiteman wanted all the land. And here, as elsewhere, he got all but a tiny remnant fraction of it.

Brian suggested I visit the Office of the Special Trustee for American Indians. The local office was close by. "It might be interesting." The main job of the Special Trustee, a Federal Office, is to check that funds from Government allocations are going where they should.

I was already aware that audits of Tribal Governments throughout the US had shown that several billions of dollars had "disappeared;" and indeed that the Indians of Oklahoma had made their due contribution. I found it difficult, however, to work up any moral indignation. After all, when one considered the awesome extent, the millions of square miles of

Indian lands stolen, expropriated, seized, or otherwise removed from their original occupants/owners, "several billions" was a very small price. The fact that there had surfaced relatively little shouting about this suggested to me that America's White Governments and politicians thought so too.

As for the Special Trustee's Office, once again I hunted. But this time in vain. After a half-hour and another four dead-end leads, I gave up. It was time to move on. Time to meet, or attempt to meet, representatives of one of the resident local tribes who had moved in where the BIA had moved out; the Absentee Shawnee.

As difficult as it had been to find the BIA offices, it was impossible to miss the Indian Tribal complexes. First there was the Citizen Potawotami Nation main building, a vast, sprawling, modern, single-storey structure, set in a beautiful *green* parkland—something of an achievement in this otherwise cinder-dry Brown Country. It had all the appearances of an exclusive golf club, but without fairways or flags. Yet that said, flags were not entirely absent. On a pole in front of the building, Old Glory was fluttering above a more modest Potawotami Nation flag on its royal blue background. It was an interesting statement.

Next door was the Absentee Shawnee complex. It too possessed extensive, beautifully maintained, green, rolling acres of which many a golf club would be envious. Amongst the various buildings I found the Administration Office. And there, after a bit of negotiation with an imposing and very striking Shawnee woman Secretary, guardian of the inner *sancta*, I was duly directed to Jonathan, one of the tribal officials.

After a cool start, he started to warm up. There was a glint in his eye. Here was a not-so-young Indian on the warpath. Only now the weapons were words and deployment of the Whiteman's games, not tomahawks. Jonathan had an appetite for battle. And clearly he was greatly enjoying getting his own back on the BIA and the Whiteman. He spoke with amused contempt of the greedy squabbling engendered amongst White businessmen competing for a casino tender. "Those Whitemen would kill each other for a single dollar! You can see the greed in their eyes!"

He then repeated to me what I had heard elsewhere: the growing fear that the Federal tax concession on proceeds from the highly lucrative Indian casino and gaming operations would be repealed. "Same old story," said Jonathan. "The Whiteman makes a small concession to the Indian. The Indian does well. So the Whiteman wants to cancel the allowance and take over the business himself."

These fears, I knew, had led to mini-wars in upper New York State and amongst Indian and State/Federal authorities on the Eastern Seaboard. I only had to observe the fire in Jonathan's eyes when discussing this subject, to recognise that here in Oklahoma any serious move towards repeal would be regarded as a declaration of *full-scale* war. "We've been through it all before. We know the script. It's our history. The Whiteman and his never-ending greed!" He banged his fist down on the table. "But this time it'll be different!. I only hope the Whiteman doesn't try! We pay up our local and State obligations. But that Federal tax component is ours! And it's going to stay ours!"

I was impressed with Jonathan's fire and his hunger for money—albeit on behalf of the tribe. No Whiteman could have done better. So what was this Gaming Casino money spent on? He pulled out a number of brochures. Health, education, social welfare, housing, occupational training. There were detailed programmes for each. Indians, he told me, filled out most of the staffing, and now many of the professional posts. Clearly, these programmes were providing a tremendous lift to the community. "The thing is," said Jonathan, "our people had been knocked so far down, it's a long way to come up. The first level is restored self-respect and confidence. For a good number of our people this alone is a big struggle."

He took me on a brief tour. First, there was the major generator of tribal wealth, the *Thunderbird Casino*, an enormous cement structure with an equally vast car park. Already, in mid-afternoon, it was half full. A large sign at the site entry reminded patrons that "No Fire Arms, Weapons…Concealed Or Carried, Allowed on Tribal Land." Clearly the Absentee Shawnee were keen there should be no return to Wild West behaviour!

"And over there is just one of the benefits which Thunderbird—supplemented, of course, by tobacco and gas—profits, has spawned." He pointed to a huge and magnificent brick and glass single-storey building across the car park from the casino. "That's our Clinic and Multi-Purpose Building, the home-base for many of our programmes." As he spoke, a group of five persons emerged from the building. In the lead was a short, stout, dark-skinned woman. Obviously agitated about something she was waving her arms and shouting. The man beside her walked hunch-shouldered. Three small children followed behind, one with a long, glistening, black pigtail; they all kept their heads down. Jonathan grinned and shook his head. "Just in for a bit of Family Counselling, by the look of it. Early days!"

Back at the Tribal Office, I asked Jonathan if he was happy with the progress of the various support programmes. He shrugged. "Some could do better. But all are doing quite well. We're consistently improving." And then the funding. Was he happy that this should come mainly from the proceeds of gambling? Was there not a risk that this "infection" of the Whiteman could pass to the Indian? Jonathan laughed. "The Shawnee, like all Indians, is no Puritan! Nothing he likes better than a bit of dicin', bit of gamblin'. He was 'infected' long before the Whiteman made his appearance. The point is that the Indian is no more a gambler now than he was then. The only difference is that now he's got a bit of money to gamble with!"

Before leaving I asked Jonathan whether he had any dealings with the Eastern Shawnee and other Shawnee bands I knew of in Oklahoma, Kansas and Ohio. He shrugged. "We all go our own way. Some have chosen the traditional way. Some have chosen the Whiteman's way. That is for them." He waved his hand in an emphatic gesture. "We Absentee Shawnee have found the best way, the right way. We know our traditions and are restoring them. But we also know the Whiteman's ways. We have constructed a path to the future for our people. Others would do well to follow!"

I had one final question. It had been niggling at me since first I heard the name "Absentee Shawnee." What did it mean? Were not all Shawnees "absent" from their "Old Northwest" homelands up and down the Ohio Valley? Jonathan explained. "When our people were rounded up and removed by the American Whitemen from our homelands, most Shawnee ended up in what is now the State of Kansas. Then, still in the early 1800s, when the Whitemen decided to round up those Shawnee again to shift 'em into the old Indian Territory—that is to a place here in Oklahoma that didn't sound too appetising—a third of the Shawnee broke off and 'absented' themselves from the Reservation. Hence the name 'Absentee Shawnee.' After first settling in the Deep Fork Valley north of here, the Whiteman's Army came along and drove my people down here into what is known as the Little River area." He grinned and nodded, "And here we remain. The Absentee Shawnee."

# 42

## *Raptors of the Plains*

*Shawnee, Oklahoma*—The temperature had settled into the low 100s by the time I got back on the road. Even with the air conditioning on full, the heat beat through the roof of the Chevy. My shirt was soaked, my head banging. Heading south to Tecumseh, then west towards Norman on the southern outskirts of Oklahoma City, I was surprised to find there was still a good deal of Green Country. Here were broad stretches of lightly-forested grasslands, without too many wire fences to break up the gently rolling rhythms of these magnificent, horizon-reaching expanses.

Once round Oklahoma City and heading south-west towards Chickasha, the country started seriously to "brown up." And when I stopped at Chickasha there was another change I noted. The non-fast-food restaurant I eventually located served mostly Mexican dishes. I tried a *Tortilla con Carne*, with some trepidation. I was pleasantly surprised. It was tasty, light, superb; and it ignited me only slightly. Having then tried for local accommodation and failed, I pushed on.

About 20 miles due west, just before reaching Anadarko, the rangeland changed from "brown" to "red," and most of the forest cover gave way to sagebrush, a variety of spiky plants, and bright patches of desert flowers. Occasional buttes now rose sharp up, pulsing blood-red in the rays of the setting sun.

In Anadarko I quickly found good air conditioned motel accommodation. I also discovered I had landed in the "Indian Capital of America." Seven Indian Nations had resident bands in the area; six of which—Apache, Caddo, Kiowa, Wichita, Fort Sill Apache and Comanche—were of South-west origin; the remaining Delaware from much further afield.

It was an interesting mix. In earlier days it would have guaranteed inter-tribal violence and bloodshed. But not now. Each tends to its own business through its own Tribal Government Administration. And at "Indian City," a permanent exhibition on the outskirts of Anadarko, tribal representatives concentrate their competitive efforts on creating separate dazzling displays of their individual tribal cultures. Each tribe has its separate village. Everything, from dwellings lived in (tipi, to longhouse, to hogan), to varied clothing, to food, crops, weapons, fine artwork—sacred, ceremonial and decorative—; it's all there. This, at least, was what the brochures informed me.

The girl on the motel desk also told me about the nearby "Southern Plains Indian Museum and Hall of Fame." The Hall of Fame was outdoors. I went to have a look. Here were marvellous bronze sculptures not just of great warrior chiefs, including the Comanche Quanah Parker, the Apaches Geronimo and Cochise, Osceola of the Seminoles, but also of such modern greats as Will Rogers and Jim Thorpe. Sequoya, the brilliant Cherokee linguist and originator of the Cherokee alphabet was also present. I went back and took a second long look at the busts of Geronimo and Quanah Parker. Tomorrow I would be visiting their final "home" and resting place, Fort Sill.

As I looked out over this rough, rolling Brown Country, nearly all now cloaked in the deep shadow of nightfall, I stilled my thoughts and let my sensors probe. It was very quiet, and also still very hot. I waited and listened. The land did not "speak." Here, as elsewhere in Oklahoma, my sensors picked up little. There was a slight tingle in my arms. But no strong or clear messages.

In a sense it was a relief. My mind and spirit were freed of their earlier weighty burdens; burdens emanating from powerful spirits which had come up so strongly from those Southern soils. But perhaps this was only to be expected. For this, after all, was Plains Country. Earlier peoples had moved seasonally, following the food animals; the buffalo, the deer, the antelope; and before that the Woolly Mammoth, the bear and other animals of an earlier age. There were no great ancient cities of empire here, no great mounds or earthworks leaving the impress of their presence, their dominance. No. People lived *lightly* on the ground here, on these Great Plains; their presence and their passing all a part of the rhythms of this wonderful, wide-reaching land.

Next morning I made an early start. Sadly, it was too early for Indian City. As I passed the site, all was quiet. Not even a wisp of smoke rose from the many tipis.

The land started now seriously to open up. More jagged buttes, more torn wounds in the red earth, more open range, sagebrush and spiky shrubs with intermittent bright pink and yellow floral effusions. Other than the occasional truck or pick-up, the road through this rugged rangeland was empty.

Passing through the town of Apache, the last small habitation before Lawton and Fort Sill and its Military Reservation, I caught sight of a building of now-familiar design. Modern, brick-built, single-storey, it was settled into a small rise of land not far from the road. I turned in. This was the Tribal Administrative Centre for the Fort Sill Apache Nation.

I was again lucky. One of the tribe officials was present. In fact this Tribal Government dealt only with the affairs of its own branch of the Apache tribe, the Chiricahua; one of the seven Apache Nations. We had a lengthy chat. It was the same old, bitterly depressing story. When finally the Whiteman, after stiff Indian resistance, gained control of the territory in 1886, the Chiricahua resistors—all 400 of them—along with their Chief Geronimo, were removed and sent by railway cattle cars over 1000 miles to Florida as prisoners of war. Their homeland, the Chiricahua territory, *all 15,000,000 acres of it* on the Arizona/New Mexico border, was taken over by the Whiteman.

After 27 years of sweltering captivity in Florida, then at Mt. Vernon, Alabama, and with nearly half their members dead, the Chiricahua, together with Geronimo, were sent to Fort Sill to start a "free" life on the Military Reservation. There they remained. In 1988 four acres of sacred land were returned to the Chiricahua people through "a generous gift from a concerned private citizen." By 1998 the Fort Sill

Apaches had restored their numbers to 425, all descendants of prisoners of war.

Though it was very dry, still the sheer force of the heat now rising again to over 100 degrees, was punishing. As I drove on to Lawton and Fort Sill I spared a thought for those American soldiers, many of them Easterners of recent immigrant origin who were sent to this territory in the mid-to-late 1800s. Not a pleasant fate. Yet if it was an ordeal for them, what of their Spanish predecessors? *Conquistadores*, soldiers in full body armour and visored helmets vainly traversed this land 300 years earlier in search of their *el dorados*. If I in my air conditioned Chevy was freely perspiring, how must they have felt?

Stepping out of the car on arrival at the Fort Sill former Trading Post, now museum/gift shop, I got a pretty good idea. The heat from the mid-morning sun was not merely very hot, it was blistering. And yet, whether on military sorties, or Fort duties, those soldiers in the days of the Indian Wars and Frontier Expansion put in long days of hard work. While disease and illness took a heavy toll—a far larger number than those killed in the Frontier Wars—the Fort continued in operation. It remains in operation today. Very simply, soldiers had to adjust, adapt, hang on, and hope—often with little prospect—for early transfer to a more temperate region.

The Fort Museum provided graphic, gruelling evidence of how those soldiers managed their lives. Blacksmiths, harness and saddlemakers/restorers, cobblers, carriagemakers, gunsmiths and many other skilled persons; all had steady, demanding work. Then there was the Trading Post. A permanent display showed the range of goods available for sale, barter or exchange to soldiers, and to Reservation Indians.

What, I wondered, must a soldier have thought when he saw a new Remington, with several boxes of shells, being sold to an Indian—perhaps to a Comanche with whom he had only recently been in mortal combat on the Open Plains? What too must the Indian have thought?

Perhaps it was the heat, perhaps the fact that sweaty and sweated labour no longer was conducted in these dark, cramped premises; perhaps it was simply that like so many of the Whiteman's constructions on these lands, these buildings had but a temporary relevance that had now long passed; perhaps it was the sense of loss, of Indian despair, of desolation that permeated these stone walls, these timbers, this atmosphere; for whatever reason(s), Fort Sill was an oppressive and depressing place. I was relieved to depart.

And as I left, I noted a few modern military exhibits near the main entrance. Several huge artillery pieces were on display along with other items of high-tech lethal hardware used by the Americans during the 1990s "Desert Storm" campaign against the Iraqis and Saddam Hussein. I looked, but didn't stop.

Certainly it all conveyed a powerful message. And this was that there was *no way* that that Indian in the Museum with his bow, lance and small arms could have held out with any even slight hope of success in the face of such fast-accelerating military might. In less than 100 years, this was the awesome warfare capacity the Whiteman had developed. These fearsome weapons said it all. The Whiteman was simply too inventive, too determined, quite apart from being too numerous.

I had asked the lady attendant about Chiefs Geronimo and Quanah Parker before I left the Museum. Where had they lived? Where were they buried? Both, I was told, were buried in Fort Sill's "Indian Arlington," so named because of the large number of famous warrior chiefs buried there. As for their places of residence: about Geronimo, she merely shrugged; but about Quanah, she volunteered that his substantial home, "Star House," had in the 1950s been moved off one of the hills on the Military Reservation to make way for an artillery range. It had been re-sited near the town of Cache, just down the road.

Time was short. It was a choice. Would I visit the "Indian Arlington," or try to find Quanah's re-located Star House? I decided on Quanah's house. Besides, it would be a convenient stop-off on my way west towards the Texas border.

The directions I had been given were not precise. I got to Cache. But there was no sight or sign of Star House—so called because of its red roof emblazoned with large white stars. I stopped at a gas station, filled the car's tank, and inquired of Quanah's house. The woman who took my money at the till asked me to "wait right here!" and disappeared through a curtain into the back of the building. She duly re-appeared with an elderly Whiteman wearing a battered panama hat. I was introduced. This was Herbert. We shook hands. He would show me Star House. That said, he climbed into an equally elderly, seriously battered blue Cadillac, and with great solemnity told me to follow him.

After a number of turnings up one dusty back street after another, then entering a gated compound, there in front of me it was. It was indeed a "Star House." Not quite the size of the original I had seen in photos; nevertheless the roof was very red, the four stars on it large and very white. And the fresh white of the timbered exterior of this two-storey residence in its substantial grounds clearly indicated it remained the subject of close human attention.

Herbert now took me inside and showed me round. Even in the bright of day the rooms were dark. The kitchen was large and long. And there was a long kitchen/dining table where guests joined Quanah and family for meals—there they all were in a sepia photo on the wall. And then we looked round the other rooms. There were various oddments of furnishing: a bed, a wooden chair, a dresser, various framed photos and calendar pictures. It was in fact very much like any big rancher's house of the period. But there was one major difference. Most of the rooms in Quanah's house provided accommodation for his many wives, which, to the consternation of the resident missionaries of the various Christian Faiths, were said to have reached a total of seven at one time.

Star House was a strange and uncomfortable place. A curious attempt at blending the life and customs of Plains Indian with domiciled Whiteman. One could feel the crash and jangle of these conflicting cultures. No harmony, no balance here. Only dissonance. The two didn't mix; just like Quanah, "the great assimilator," but at the end neither Indian nor Whiteman.

And yet, I checked myself, surely accommodation, regardless of severely limited options, had to start somewhere? And had not Quanah, like many other leading Indians, made that start? But yet again, where had it led? What was the evidence that accommodation on these lines had worked, and was working?

Having bade farewell to Herbert—and deposited a $5 bill in a small sweet-grass basket near the door marked "Donations Welcome" to which he had drawn my attention—I was soon back on Route 62 West. It was now a straight run through this rolling High Plains country to the Texas border.

The panoramic sweep of this rangeland, the Wichita mountains rippling up in the distance to the north, was breathtaking. Occasionally there were red dirt roads running off at right angles, arrow-straight, mile after mile, gradually narrowing to the eye till they melted in the horizon heat-shimmer. These were awesomely vast lands. And yes, they were hard and cruel lands to the unwitting and unwary. But Alberto, back at the Miami Agency, had been quite right. These border lands were indeed stunningly beautiful.

And there was something else.

It was *here* that the spirit of Quanah belonged; to which it surely had returned.

Here, like the sudden wind, the spiked cactus, the cruel, searing heat from an unforgiving sky; here was the home spirit of Quanah and the Comanche.

A large house, four-square, with red roof and big white stars was but an alien intrusion; partly an irrelevance, partly an insult to a raptor spirit it could never grasp, let alone hold.

This was the message conveyed strongly and directly by these lands.

# 43

## *High Plains Treasure*

*Amarillo, Texas*—Shortly after crossing the border into Texas, the sky darkened. A big storm was sweeping in over the High Plains. And it was coming my way. I had just turned onto Route 287, the main road to Amarillo, when it let fly. Not satisfied with one downpour, it loosed three torrential bursts driven by fierce westerlies which rocked the car, then moved on. The external temperature gauge showed a drop of 35 degrees—95-60—in just a few minutes. Very dramatic. I laughed—respectfully. The spirit of Quanah, no doubt, was reminding me, and in no uncertain terms, that I was passing through his Comanche domain. "You are warned! Take care!"

Arriving in Amarillo in the late afternoon, another storm suddenly descended. It loosed not only violent driving rain, but also hail and sleet. The roads flooded. Traffic ground to a stand-still. I pulled off at a Burger Bar for food-refuelling, and to wait out the storm—memories of my first hour at Charlotte! Topped up with burger and chocolate shake, and the sky easing, I got back in the car and headed up-country.

Forty miles distant was the town of Fritch, home of the celebrated (in archaeological circles) ancient Alibates Quarries.

This was the (Newark, Ohio) "Flint Ridge" of the South-west. It was from this High Plains outcrop that man for the past 12,000 years and more had been quarrying beautiful, highly-prized, pink-marbled flint. Alibates points have been found as far afield as the Great Lakes to the North, the Columbia River Basin in the Northwest, the Carolinas in the East and Mexico to the South.

Regardless of the weather, which remained overcast and uncertain, I was keyed up. What would these quarries look like? Perhaps a series of large bowl-like depressions—up to 50 feet in diameter—as at Flint Ridge, where ancient man had laboriously chipped out the chunks he required? Maybe a vertical rock face? Perhaps the flint stone was hacked from above-ground or under-ground caves?

It was a long drive in from the main road to the quarries—officially titled the "Alibates Flint Quarries National Monument." And once again the clouds had started to gather. By the time I reached the quarries and was climbing one of the strange, peaked, rocky hill-outcrops, the rain came again in sudden bursts; this time accompanied by heavy rolls of thunder and shafts of lightning released from what seemed to be a few hundred feet directly overhead. Someone, it seemed, did not appreciate my after-hours presence! I retreated down the hill.

With the storm moving on, I resumed my solitary explorations. Investigating a number of hill peaks I found the "chipping workshops" where some 12,000 years ago visiting miners/craftsmen had applied painstaking, highly skilled efforts to produce "weapon tips and tools which often achieved an aesthetic standard far in excess of functional need." I checked my Alibates literature. Yes, many exquisite points, long of blade, bi-facial, beautifully fluted had been produced right here.

Then along the bluffs above what was once the Canadian River and is now Lake Meredith Reservoir; there were the quarrying sites. And just like at Flint Ridge, they were shallow bowls, some small, about 5 feet in diameter; some larger, up to 25 feet across. Before departing, I examined one or two chunks of the hard pink-marbled stone. The warm rainbow hue, the weight and density of these rocks were impressive.

Back on the main road I drove on the few remaining miles to Fritch. My object: food and a bed. Getting food—good, non-fast-food—was no problem. Not so a bed. There was no local accommodation; or so I was told by the lady proprietor of the diner where I ate. But the attendant at the gas station next door suggested the motel outside town, though it was officially closed, might be worth a try. I did try. The owner, a young-ish man, was initially reluctant. But then we got onto pre-history and the Alibates Quarries. Suddenly a bed was available.

Jonathan, geologist by training and oil-man by occupation—currently shouldering the added burden of overseeing the sale of this motel owned by his family—was a keen archaeo-hunter with a particular passion for local flint points. Since childhood he had hunted palaeo items on the High Plains flats, and up and down all the flash-flood drains and cuttings running out of the surrounding hills. We discussed collections. I told him about the exquisite Florence "ceremonial points;" the collections—some of palaeo, some of more recent pedigree—built up by keen archaeo-hunters I had met in Selma, Moundville, the Mississippi out-reach. He was fascinated.

And then came the shift—the shift for me. To this point, archaeo-hunters I had met sought their treasure largely below ground. Here on the High Plains and throughout the Southwest, however, much of the treasure remains on the surface. Clearly, to Jonathan's mind, these High Plains items said more, were far more appealing to the aesthetic taste than the items to be found down in the alluvium, the swamps and bayous of the Mississippi out-reach. Besides, while the Deep South mounds might tell you lots about the development of communal life in pre-America, it was, he stressed, here on the High Plains that man left clear markers of his *earliest* presence. "You *must* see our South-west/High Plains archaeology. *Wonderful* experience! *Exquisitely beautiful* points and pieces." He was serious. Jonathan loved his archaeo treasures with a passion.

When I told him time would not permit, he insisted I at least visit the Museum at Canyon, just south of Amarillo. "*Fantastic* displays! You'll not regret it!" Somewhat reluctantly, I agreed. And next morning having followed the recommended route through hanging mist and intermittent heavy rain, I arrived at Canyon and found its Museum.

The Museum—its full title, the "Panhandle-Plains Historical Museum"—is a large brick edifice located on the campus of the West Texas A&M (Agricultural & Mechanical) University. The entrance is a bit of an eye-stopper. But what at first glance appeared to be stone-engraved Egyptian hieroglyphics, turned out to be "Famous West Texas cattle brands." I had reckoned the Museum would not be a big deal. And this very naff entrance seemed to confirm it.

I was wrong—again! The Museum was a very big deal. I duly discovered splendid exhibits from early-palaeo, right through to modern times. Amongst the modern exhibits was a breathtaking display of paintings centered on Taos, a vernal paradise in the mountains near Santa Fe. The artists who first visited—perhaps the best-known being Georgia O'Keefe—were so stunned by its clear, bright, air, its forested beauty at all seasons, that they stayed. And they loved it till their dying breath. Also there were some interesting historic Indian bits and pieces. And there was more immortality here for Quanah Parker. His War-Bonnet and lance were on display.

I then met Janice, one of the Museum's Assistant Curators. She was working on a section of the Palaeontology display. Here in their constructed environments were the alarmingly realistic creatures that roamed these lands some 150-400 million years ago, including the dinosaur, ground sloth, sabre-toothed tiger and shovel-toothed Mastodon, amongst others. There were also models of the nearby Palo Duro Canyon and the long-buried Amarillo Mountains which brilliantly took one's eye and mind back to these earlier ages of a vigorous antiquity. It was altogether a mightily impressive display.

I noted, however, that one thing, one creature was missing—*man*!

Would it not be nice, I asked Janice, to bring man into this palaeo section? She agreed, strongly. But the Museum Board took a different view. *Wild animals*, they were prepared to allow, *may* have been around for hundreds of thousands of years. But some were not quite ready to accept that *man* has been round that long. The concept of *Palaeo-lithic* man (10,000-30,000 years ago), let alone the existence of *Neanderthal* man (100, 000 years ago), *Homo Erectus* (500,000 years), *Homo Habilis* (2 million years), or *Proconsul* (26 million years); all are regarded with great reserve in this western extension of the Bible Belt.

I suggested it would greatly help ordinary people, visitors, if they could *see* themselves in *some* relation to the palaeo exhibits. And it would be equally helpful to see modern man in some kind of time relation to ancient man—who is really *not* so ancient.

Janice handed me a brochure. "You'll see we're shortly opening a new exhibit. *'People of the Plains: Experiments in Living'* will approach the contention of 12,000 years of human occupation of these lands from an interesting angle." She pointed to the relevant brochure section. "Artifacts and information will be arranged *not* chronologically, but *topically*. Major sections will be devoted to water, food, clothing, shelter; some of these items taking us well back into the palaeo period. The exhibit also will explore 'relationships and developments arising from trade, creativity and cultural transmission.'"

She folded up the brochure and gave it back to me. There was a twinkle in her eye. "It should be remembered that we are basically scientists—well, human scientists—here. One must present one's proof. This is what we're doing with this exhibit. It's up to the viewer or visitor to make up his or her own mind."

Janice went on to vent her feelings on another basic issue. It affronted and greatly irritated her that this museum—not unlike many others—is set up to provide about 90 per cent of its space and attention to what's happened in the past 125-150 years. "It's as though everything of significance on this continent happened solely during this period." She laughed. "Nearly all that you see here—settler lore, cattle ranching, oil discovery and exploitation, and so forth—set up and displayed with great ingenuity and equally great expense, reinforces this view on the visitor, old and particularly young."

She rapped a brochure on her palm. "I guess it's our hope, in a small way, that the 'Experiment in Living' exhibit will cause 'em to think, to open some doors.

"But then again," she rolled an eye up at me, "maybe those Southern Baptist and Bible Belt people are *right*. Maybe the Earth and all things on it *were* created during those biblical seven days and seven nights—with one day and night off for rest. And maybe all this *did* take place just 6500 years ago—I believe that's the customary figure calculated from Genesis in the Bible. *But* if that *is* the case, then such persons are going to have to come up with some pretty imaginative reasoning to explain away what our exhibits will suggest about man's palaeo presence hereabouts! They'll face a bit of a challenge!"

# 44

# *Clovis Encounter*

*Clovis, New Mexico*—After lunch with Janice and two of her colleagues, I was back on the road and heading west. Destination: Clovis; site of arguably America's most extensive range of palaeo remains, just over the New Mexico border.

The road was busy and the rain continued. I kept an eye on the land. It was now flattening out. Even through the sheets of rain I could see some big sky-scapes and landscapes opening up. I passed several huge cultivated fields soaking up this precious rain. But a far greater expanse was open, lightly-brushed range. Approaching the New Mexico border the rain eased, then stopped. The clouds cleared. And as I pulled into the Welcome Centre at Clovis, the sun re-appeared. Quickly the temperature jumped up. It was now back in the high 90s.

There were two places I wanted to visit. Both were close by. One was the *Blackwater Draw Museum*; the other the *Blackwater Draw Site*—from which the museum drew most of its artifacts—where the celebrated Clovis palaeo remains were located. Once again, however, time was shutting down on me. And it was not easy to find my first stop, the museum.

I arrived at 4:45; closing was at 5 pm. Here again were superb, well-mounted displays covering a range of mainly ancient and very ancient remains and artifacts. Bones, stone, even remarkably preserved wooden items, a startlingly life-like Mammoth; it was all here; fascinating stuff. I needed at least two days to soak it all up; but 15 minutes would have to do. Amongst the exhibits were some of the finest palaeo points—bi-facial, elongated, exquisitely fluted—I'd seen since Florence in Alabama. I noted the pinky hue of one or two. Alibates flint, no doubt. The very helpful attendant gave me a few extra minutes, but stressed that I'd have to move quickly if I was to tour the Blackwater palaeo site which was several miles distant. He made a phone call. The Site Curator, Joanne Dickenson would be present if I got up there now. At least the rules here could be bent a little to accommodate a distant visitor!

Briefly, what I saw at this fabulous site was enough to convert even the most fervent Bible Belt believer. The evidence? The remains of a Woolly Mammoth, a Clovis spear point well-embedded in its rib-cage. And this did *not* happen some time during the past 6000-8000 years. Stratigraphy and other dating techniques placed the demise of the unfortunate Mammoth at about 12,000 years BP (Before Present). In addition the remains of several other Mammoths, and Bison too, have been uncovered. In each case, Clovis points apparently did the job.

Joanne explained to me how since 1932 when excavations began in this gravel pit—a former ancient watering hole that dried up about 7000 years ago—palaeo artifacts and remains had been regularly uncovered. The unique value of this particular site was that it not only provided clear stratigraphy, a kind of "rain gauge" of cultural sequence for the past 12,000 years; but also that it held substantial numbers of artifacts, both stone and bone, in most of these strata. For the archaeological researcher concerned with the full span of American pre-history—a span which provides the added bonus of "strata deposition" going back 2 million years—the Blackwater Draw site was, is, and no doubt will continue to be a gold-mine of information and hard evidence.

I could happily have spent the rest of my life here. And I might just get closer to the "first principles" of Ancient America that intrigue me. Indeed, at least I now better understood the "High Plains palaeo passions" of the Fritch geologist/motel salesman, Jonathan. For while those sites I visited in the Mississippi Valley may provide the best and most promising evidence of man's *communal* growth; clearly it is these Great Plains sites, like this one, with their drier, hence non-biodegradable climatic conditions, which may eventually tell us much more about *when* man arrived here—a date perhaps much earlier than 12,000, even 30,000 years ago—or perhaps even provide confirmation that pre-American man had his origins *right here*, as many Indian Nations have confidently believed all along.

Before departing I walked the site trail down in the draw—once again keeping a wary eye for snakes about which I'd been warned. And though it was still bright day-light, there was what I can only describe as an unsettling "occupied silence." I could sense something. My sensors were gently throbbing. I felt neither apprehensive nor elated. It was a neutral feeling. But it was distinct and it was there in the lands of this draw.

I had a brief look inside the Interpretive Area Building. Again fascinating. Here was the famous stratigraphy; sharply delineated, very clear. Excavation was ongoing. And here too were exposed bones of the ancient Bison. Intriguing hands-on stuff. To me, this made the impact all the greater. This was a "living museum"; the best possible kind of museum. And the display boards were excellent. I could interpret for myself. I checked my watch. It was time to depart this remarkable site; to bid farewell to these fromidable ancient Clovis people who have left us such intriguing memorials, such powerful markers of their presence.

Joanne gave me directions to Route 60 West for Vaughn and Albuquerque. This involved an initial short-cut via an unmarked road round nearby Cannon Military Air Force Base (AFB). Her directions were easy to follow. I passed an unmanned Sentry Box and was making good time round the perimeter of the field, admiring some of the strange, predatory-looking aircraft, when I saw two Police cars, lights flashing, coming directly at me. One pulled in front; the other went past and pulled in behind. Two MPs with sub-machine guns stepped out and signalled me to get out of my car. I was directed to turn round, put my hands on the roof of the car, and "Don't move!"

Having been duly frisked I was asked for papers and identification. The MPs looked doubtful and puzzled. I explained. It turned out that there was a road bearing to the *left* at the

Sentry Box. *That* was the road I *should* have taken. Keeping a watchful eye on the sub-machine guns, I apologised. I then asked how best to get to Route 60 from here? The two front MPs said, "Follow us!" jumped into their car; and with the second car following close behind, I was escorted through the base—it looked like a good-sized middle-American town from a 1950s film set, *without* Doris Day!—then out to a roundabout and onto the ramped entry for Route 60. In the rear-view mirror I could see the two MP cars pulled into a siding, clearly watching to ensure I was departing. I looked again and the cars were turning and heading back in the direction of the Base.

It was well past 6 pm. I knew there was now no hope of reaching Albuquerque, some 225 miles distant. Besides I was tired. It had been a busy day and I had taken a lot on board. Still, as there remained many sites and "foreign phantoms" with which I wanted to make at least passing contact before departing Phoenix for my return flight to England in three days' time, I was anxious to clock up as many miles as possible. Perhaps there would be a bed at Vaughn, another 120 miles or so due west.

Once out of Clovis, the highway took me suddenly into another world. It was a stunningly beautiful world. And for the next two hours, except for this narrow highway and the occasional pick-up coming the other way, there was neither sign, nor sight of modern man, indeed of any man, or woman. It was just this land, this car and me.

This was the *real* High Plains, the High Plains I'd heard so much about. The air was very clear. To the south, the land ran out, and slightly down to the horizon some 50 miles distant. Great vibrant patches of lemon yellow from some hardy flowering plant, and the grey-ish green of sagebrush, huge expanses of it, provided the principal cover. And then as I travelled at speed across these open spaces, rocketing through one, then two long-abandoned ghost towns, then past the burial site of Billy the Kid, intermittently I caught glimpses of distant craggy buttes, of luminous, half-lit panoramas of the lower plains. How many Clovis', I wondered, lay settled below the arid surfaces of these lands; sites safe from the prying eyes of modern man, of people like me; safe—so far—from the excavating tools of archaeologists, of treasure-hunting opportunists?

At Vaughn there was a diner, but no accommodation. Having consumed a hot-beef sandwich while perusing an innocent-looking "news" handout that positively breathed right-wing fire at President Clinton, I consulted my Super 8 Motels Directory. The closest facility was at Moriarity, another 70 miles to the north-west and only 40 miles short of Albuquerque. Though it was now past 9, I phoned. To my relief, a room was available. I booked it.

Turning out of the car park, I noted several huge Road-Train trucks parked in a lot across from the diner. Curtains were discreetly drawn round the cab windows. No accommodation problem for them, thought I, as I headed back up onto the high rangeland, just a rim of pink light, now fading to purple on the far western horizon. It had come as a shock when checking my maps at Vaughn to find that these High Plains were very high indeed—7000-8000 feet above sea level!

About 10 miles out of Vaughn, darkness dropped. The road became twisty, with many sharp ups and downs. And then from the west, the wind started to blow. It grew stronger. Large bundles of tumbleweed rolled and bounced across the road. Then not far to the west the darkness was lit with spears of lightning. It came quickly closer. Then came the rain. Torrential, mixed with sand, it was driving horizontally in the car's lights, and as it intensified, rocked and buffeted the body. I slowed to 25 mph so I could see. And still this fierce prairie storm raged and roared. At times I felt the lightning was following me 200 feet overhead.

Emerging from this back-road onto IS 40 for Moriarity, the wind was still howling, the rain thrashing down. There was flooding on the road. The traffic slowed. At last I saw the turn-off and made my exit. Not far was the bright neon of "Super 8." It was still thrashing down as I shifted my bags to my room. I was grateful for the bed. I slept well.

# 45

## *Heart of the Sierras*

*Albuquerque, New Mexico*—Next morning I was up early. When I stepped outside I noted the road was dry. Only a few puddles remained. And the wind had dropped. Overhead a few high-billowing white clouds were making stately progress to the east. For the rest, the sky was bright and already very blue.

And there was something else. I took a deep breath. There was a light and pleasing fragrance in the cool morning air. I was puzzled. A costly perfume perhaps? Stretching my legs in the field next to the motel, I took another deep breath. Again that fresh, sweet yet tart scent; clean, refreshing and exhilarating. And then a light gust of wind rolled over the field from the nearby range-land. That delicious scent again. And then I realised. This scent was not man-made. It was Nature-made. Pine, juniper, cedar, the high, dry lands of these Sierras, these tablelands, the rarefied air at these high altitudes, the heat; it all combined to produce this unique, this wonderful scent. Indeed it was to accompany me for the rest of my tour.

Packed up and paid up, I was back on the Inter-State by 7:30. Hardly was I underway than to the north, in the distance, I caught sight of an extended line of jagged black "hills." I checked my maps. No hills these! I was getting my first sight of *The Rocky Mountains*! It was an exciting moment. These, the "lower lumbar" sections of the chain seem to rise out of a dead-flat plain; then to grow in height and presence. The early light from the east lent added power and drama.

The road to Albuquerque and beyond passed through green pine forest; it dropped down into deep winding gorges, into sudden yawning canyons, wild, primeval; but mostly it rolled over high plateau rangeland. These vast, bright, clear expanses beneath an intense royal blue sky; it is magical, refreshing, enlivening land. A very far cry from the enervating weight of heat and humidity of those lands of the Mississippi out-reach and the Deep South.

There were so many sites I wanted to see. And these Southwest people were quite insistent I "must" see them. But the sad reality was that I was hard up against the clock. I simply didn't have time. Signs to the celebrated Indian Petroglyph National Monument, to Laguna Pueblo flashed by. The fabled Acoma Pueblo (Sky City) came briefly into view. Far off to my left, atop a vaulting, near-400-foot high-rise of stone, there it was; the radiant white of its buildings, solitary and distant in a vast expanse of arid scrubland.

It was over these hard lands that Coronado and his *Conquistadores* not so long ago had marched and sweated, ever hopeful that the fabled gold treasure *must* be close. The glint from afar of their shining armour, their steel weapons stirred both fear and fascination amongst Acoma residents—and many another native people who encountered these Spaniards in the course of their bold explorations north from Mexico. They had yet to learn the cruel lessons in blood and carnage that these brutal White strangers, in the name of Christ and the Spanish King, would shortly bring to their homes, to their communities.

I drove on. All round was land vibrant with the spirits of people who had gone before; who had lived here since man's earliest habitation on this continent. There, the sign said, was the road leading north to the lands of the "Four Corners" (ancient sites and urban/pueblo remains on the "junction lands" where the States of New Mexico, Colorado, Utah and Arizona meet). I flicked through the pages of memory. Ancient man, some 30,000, perhaps 50,000 years ago had found here green lush meadows and valleys. Mammoth, long-horned Bison, the Giant Sloth were big game challenges. He learned to move with the rhythms, the cycles of the seasons. And then as the millennia passed, the glacial frontier edging relentlessly northwards, the big game disappeared, the lands dried out, and the people here had to adapt, to work at ways to survive and grow under their new living conditions.

And now coming up to the Continental Divide (at some 8000 feet), another sign flashed by: Chaco Canyon. Many millennia had followed before the people of this dynamic and creative culture arrived. Sandia, Clovis, Folsom man, still migratory, still following the seasonal movements of the food animals; each with his unique adaptations; each with his increasingly efficient and effective "tool kit"—whose beautiful and deadly fluted spear points I'd seen at the Clovis site—; each had long come and gone. What then had caused their successors, these 12th century Anasazi people to create these large, lavish, magnificently designed and brilliantly constructed cities out here on the arid heights of these plateau lands?

Here art, engineering, ceremony, organised urban living were brought to impressive new levels. Then suddenly it had all vanished—or at least the Anasazi people had. Why? What had happened? Where did they go?

I laughed. It was no different here than at Moundville, at Poverty Point, at Etowah, Spiro, Cahokia, Newark, Chillicothe and many another ancient site I had visited. The Ancients knew. But they weren't telling! At least not just yet!

Just over the Continental Divide and past more cruel temptations—signs to El Morro, the massive sandstone up-thrust formation, to Zuni Pueblo and Black Rock just beyond the Cibola Forest and mountain range to my left (the south)—I passed through Gallup, and in another 20 miles was over the border and into Arizona.

The light here was even brighter, the air clearer and drier, the sun very hot, the land back to the dip and ripple of "brown country" open range. Despite the frustration that time imposed, I was in high spirits. It was difficult in this climate, this atmosphere to be otherwise. I stepped on the accelerator.

I had progressed only a few miles when coming over a rise, there down in the dip between the two carriageways was a Smoky! At first I thought I was alright. There was a lot of fast traffic. However, another look in my rear-vision mirror and there he was. He flashed his lights, signalled me to pull over. My first encounter since coming over the border from North

Carolina into Georgia. Border crossings, I reckoned ruefully, must be productive Smoky hunting grounds! Fortunately, after a thorough interrogation, I again escaped with a warning.

All my life I had heard of the Grand Canyon, one of the Great Wonders of the World. As it was on my route towards Flagstaff, more or less, it would be criminal not to visit it, at least a part of it, however briefly. I stopped at a road-side Tourism Centre, checked the listings, and inquired about accommodation at one or two Grand Canyon sites. Nothing doing, said the uniformed girl at the desk. What then might be a good route for a drive along the South Rim of the Canyon? I could see from my maps that this might not be too arduous. The girl cast a thoughtful eye at the map, then at me. "Can I make a suggestion?"

"Please do," said I.

"Well, the Grand Canyon is a BIGGG place! You need time. And also at the moment there are big forest fires burning. Smoke has reduced visibility."

"Not a good place to go right now?"

She shrugged. "You can always give it a try. But there is another very interesting site. It's on your way towards Flagstaff, close to the Inter-State, and no forest fires or smoke visibility problems."

"And where is this?"

"You've heard of the Petrified Forest?" I said I had. It was the name of a well-known Humphrey Bogart film. "Well, actually, it's been around a bit longer than Bogie. About 250 million years, give or take 10 million years! There is a park. Petrified Forest and Painted Desert. Well worth a visit." She opened up some brochures and a booklet. The photos of this surreal, stratified moon-scape were spectacular. It might not be the Grand Canyon, but it seemed a very good second best. I asked directions. "Keep going on the Inter-State. Another 30 miles. You'll see the signs."

# 46

## *Trees of Real Antiquity*

*nr. Holbrook, Arizona*—It was mid-day when I reached the turn-off to the Petrified Forest National Park. And after paying the attendant at the entry booth—$5, as I recall—it was a short drive to the Painted Desert Inn. I stepped out. Here one was afforded awesomely magnificent views up and down the Canyon valley. The sky was cloud-less and again very blue, the heat intense, nearly 110 degrees. And how stunningly beautiful was this lean and demanding land. Nor was it shy about its history. There in rich terra-cotta of varying hues, in ripples of grey and slate-green, in folds of velvety brown and deep purple, in parched sandy hill-crests rolling away into the shimmering distance; there it all was.

Some 200 million years ago all this area had been part of an extended inland fresh-water lake. Layer upon layer of sediment had settled. And then as the lake had gradually receded, the land dried out, and indeed with volcano and wind making their due contributions, there across from me was the evidence of Nature's artistry. Run-off floods from then up to the present day cut and filled, and cut again, and filled again, deep courses through the sediment strata. The entire area is a fossil and rock-hunter's paradise. Though only a few small selected areas have been systematically investigated, the petrified fauna and flora returns have been rich.

Back on the Park road, and with the air conditioning on full, I had a chance to relax, to cool off, to take in the strange, compelling beauty of this High Plains moon-scape which rolled down and out in every direction as far as the eye could see. A few miles further along, there on a little rise of land was the ancient village ruin of Puerco Pueblo. Throughout the Park I was to read that indications of the presence of man—mainly projectile points of various kinds—back to 10,000 BP, perhaps much earlier, had been uncovered. But these earliest traces had been of man the perennial migrant-hunter on the move. Here, however, was evidence of *settled* habitation. The signboards and my brochures told the story.

This was a village first occupied about 1100 AD by 60-70 people. The plaza layout on a rise of ground with surrounding rooms and several kivas (underground ceremonial chambers) seems to follow the tradition of the Anasazi, a people dominant in this area of the Four Corners at that time. The form of construction, placement by the River Puerco—something of a misnomer for the trickle today!—and apparent utilisation of the floodplain for cultivation, perhaps ready irrigation of crops; all suggest Anasazi influence if not direct presence.

As for the sudden demise of Puerco Pueblo in the early 1400s? The specialists suggest it was most likely climatic change that forced them out. In fact they declare the village was twice hit by severe droughts; the second forcing the residents finally to move northwards. It is believed these Puerco villagers eventually settled in Hopi pueblos, towns that exist to the present day.

Standing on the rim of the ruin, the sweat streaming, I looked out over the small dip of the Puerco Valley. The plain extended to the west, sandy brown and shimmering, a good deal of green and grey-ish scrub dotting the range. On the horizon was the brooding, jagged thrust of the San Francisco Mountains.

What, I wondered, would a farmer standing on this spot looking out in this direction 800 years ago, be thinking? Would his mind be on food; on where he was going to find very scarce meat? Or was it perhaps that he was puzzling over the best use of his last remaining portion of Puerco irrigation water? Maybe he was pondering an extension to his room in the pueblo; an extension to make extra space for the soon-expected addition to his family? Maybe he was thinking about sex? A new woman had settled at the pueblo to whom he felt strongly attracted.

But maybe he was thinking about none of these things. Perhaps his thoughts were focused on the Great Spirits above and below; on the messages of the ancestors? What guidance was forthcoming? What voices were speaking? He was listening hard, his sensors deep and widespread.

Back in the car, in the cool, I felt grateful I was not that villager those 800 years ago. And yet, and yet. Who was I to say? I was looking with my eyes, screened by my particular life experience and modern-day values. What he saw, what he perceived was almost certainly very different. I laughed. What I saw here as bleak, harsh, unforgiving land, baked in the scorching heat of a cruel sun; to him the same land, under basically the same conditions was his haven, his little Eden, which he and his fellow villagers had shaped and adapted to meet their needs, perhaps also many of their wants.

Again, I could not help another laugh at my own expense, and perhaps his. For was not all this pondering, this reflection, mere absurd egotism and conceit? Life on this very spot, and in that valley, has been throbbing with intense vitality for at least 250 millions years—and indeed likely very much longer than that. The fossils, the dinosaur skeletons, the artifactual remnants of many, many creatures and plants, most of whose species died out many millions of years ago, they all testify to the *intensity* of that life, its mute crises, triumphs and defeats; its terrors, devastations and occasional successes. Within the span of such a clocked passage, my presence today, that villager's presence 800 years ago; both are but the blink of an eye; a solitary inch along a tortuous and perilous three-mile road already heavily travelled.

It was in this thoughtful mood that I moved further along this 28-mile Park road to view the petroglyphs (ancient writing on stone) at "Newspaper Rock," so-called. Under the overhang, there they were. Strange spidery markings; crude metaphors, symbols, abstractions of what ancient man saw round him, perhaps within him, perhaps in the heavens above? Was there serious intent here? Or was this, were the many other petroglyphs round this Park merely a bit of ancient graffiti? Perhaps simple doodling? A bit of a send-up message to baffle me and others who today are standing round and soberly puzzling? I silently looked, listened and sensed. All that I felt was the blistering mid-afternoon heat. The ancients were keeping their secret.

Back in the cool of the Chevy, it was a short run to the next turning; the Blue Mesa Trail. My first sight was not of petrified timbers, but, in the distance, shuffling in a seeming depressed state of mind, of a lone Pronghorn Antelope. It looked like it might appreciate a bit of air conditioning, some nice green grass, and a long drink of cool fresh water. But then, I admonished myself, was I not once again perhaps indulging in a little value relativism—in this case, anthropomorphic (attributing to animals human qualities/responses)? A few hundred thousand years of adaptation had surely provided this animal with a fully-equipped "survival kit?"

Up another rise, and suddenly there they were; scattered trunk-like chunks of the Petrified Forest. They looked like they'd just been sawn up into readily moveable pieces. Out of the car, into the scorching heat, closer inspection revealed the miracle here before me. Beneath the dark, rough "bark," semiprecious stones, a conglomerate of agate, jasper, amethyst, quartz of an amazing and brilliant variety—roseate, smoky, rock crystal—all throbbed with a rainbow of dazzling colours. Iron, a prominent trace element in the petrification process, produced added shades from ochre to bright crimson, yellow and brown; cobalt and chromium, sudden bright shafts of blue and green; carbon and manganese, deep sections of black.

I was alone. I closely studied several of the scattered chunks round the "field." All displayed this amazing variety of stones and rainbow hues. It was magical.

So how had these chunks got here? And how, by what extra-ordinary process had they been transformed from wood into these bright and beautiful stones? The signboards provided the answer. And briefly this was that these trees had been part of a then-tropical forest submerged some 250 million years ago. Silt with a silicone content had covered, then gradually saturated them. When, after many more millions of years, the waters had receded, and successive floods had washed away the surrounding sediment, there were the original trees. The difference was that through chemical reaction of the silicone with the tree fibres, and the enormous pressure of layered sediments—sometimes over 1000 feet deep!—wood had been transformed into these "compressed fibres", these scattered "timbers" of richly gleaming stones. As the sweat rolled, I stood silently and marvelled.

In its own quiet way, Agate Bridge, located yet further down the Park road must be one of the major wonders of the world. There it is, a petrified log, 100 feet long, suspended over a gully; the supporting sediment in this modern day still relentlessly being cut away by water and wind erosion, action which has been continuing for the past many millions of years. In fact Agate Bridge has a little man-made support. In the early 20th century, cement buttressing was provided. The Bridge has been fortunate. Were it to have been uncovered today, the Forest Authorities, in conformity with modern policy, would have "let Nature take its course."

Throughout the Park clearly delineated strata of startling colour contrasts are constantly revealed. Mainly these colours comprise hues of dusky ochre and sandy grey. In fact, these are the "Chinle Formation" deposits; those sediments which embedded the trees and much more in this Petrified Forest—before it was petrified—during the Triassic Period, some 225 million years ago.

These petrified trees may provide the most immediate and impressive remains of pre-human activity on this planet and continent, but there is more, much more. And it is even more intriguing. These exposed strata and sediment deposits have produced life-like fossilised remains of many plants, insects, animals and fish, along with an early antecedent of the dinosaur—a small, 5 foot, 50 pound specimen, known as the "Coelophysis," a creature equipped with the teeth and jaw of a chillingly efficient carnivore. All of this event and activity, this material and living presence; it is all there; all packed into these strata; all part of the deeper, wider record of the true "first principles" history of America. And it is an immensely rich history, the surface of which, literally, we have barely scratched.

In the end, after further visits along this Park road to the aptly named Jasper Forest, to Crystal Forest; after tramping the Long Logs Trail, and finally briefly visiting the Rainbow Forest Museum, I found that I had arrived at a rather startling realisation. Briefly, this land, these sites, these strata rich with life and revelation, put man in his place. In the planetary historic frame they create, man, indeed our human-kind, this very new newcomer-creature, hardly merits inclusion. What spoke loudest were the life forms of 200-plus million years ago.

It was not difficult to construct a very clear and strong image of this land at that time; of its inhabitants, its flora and fauna; of vital periods of cataclysmic change through deluge, drought, continental geologic up-lift, of sudden, massive volcanic eruption and inundation. The tracks of all these fiery and dramatic life-challenging, often life-extinguishing events are laid out clearly and sequentially in these stratified "time capsules;" in these lengthy and many-coloured sections of Chinle rock.

Back in the car, sipping on a cold Sprite, my mind struggled hard to give shape and meaning to all that my eyes had seen; to these new and awesomely powerful Phantoms which reared up from time-depths beyond even my wildest imaginings. I was, I suppose, in shock; in serious "culture shock."

In order to try to get some reasonably realistic grip on "time;" on the relation of our very "modern" period of the last 10,000 years, to the period of the Petrified Forest (250 million years ago); I constructed a mental time-scale. Using 1 mm per 10,000 years as the base unit, a simple calculation showed that the corresponding "time location" of the Petrified Forest would be about 25 metres down the road. In other words, while our modern life (10,000 years) occupies *but one mm.* on this "road from the past"; *24.999 metres* is the distance along this road one must travel to reach the days when these logs had just fallen into the water and were being covered with their first layers of sediment!

I thought about this. I measured one mm., a tiny gap between my thumb and forefinger. I then looked down the road. About 25 metres distant in the shimmering heat was a road-side sage-brush. I pondered the relationship between the two. I slowly shook my head.

I could *see* what 1 mm. and 25 metres *physically* measured. But in terms of what these *represented* in relation to *life then, and life now*, I was really no further forward. There are no even rudimentary 100,000-year—let alone 10,000 year—"hand-holds" to carry one backwards in time. Instead one is confronted with this alarmingly enormous "black hole". Even the hard-working palaeontologists and geologists; neither has managed to progress beyond error-tolerances of *several millions of years* on those few "defining" matters to which they have given attention.

But if these spirits, these Phantoms of this stark and powerful land here defied comprehension, what then of nearby Grand Canyon and its awesome 6000-feet sheer drops? There, the stratified planetary time revealed is not a mere 250 million years, but as far back as *4000 million years*! That is *16-times further back in time* than the age of this Petrified Forest; or 400 metres down the straight of this still heat-shimmering Park road!

I took a final swig of Sprite and crunched the tin. When one considers that virtually all our literature, history, science is concentrated not just in the past 2000 years, but the past 400, with huge emphasis on the past 100, how very little we know of the planet we occupy. And yet, how confidently we speak of all that we *believe* is basic, significant, of "vital importance." In fact, we have knowledge of so little, so ludicrously small a space of our planetary time, it's incredible that we have the temerity to speak *at all*!

"Robert of Fritch" (Alibates/Texas) and his fellow Southwest pre-history enthusiasts once again came to mind. It is easy to understand why they feel such passion; why they are so greatly excited by this extra-ordinary land. And yet, their measure is the *"presence of man;"* traces of his passing, his actions, his camps 10,000, perhaps 30,000-plus years ago. Certainly this kind of antiquity does place "South-west Man" some distance ahead of "Moundbuilding Man" in terms of his earliest confirmed presence.

But for me the stir of excitement here on these South-west lands goes much deeper. It derives from the land itself and the rivetting stories it has to tell; these revealed like the words from a powerfully written and brilliantly illustrated book. In a way, the Phantoms here speak to me directly, and with a force quite intimidating. And man is not needed to serve as a "timemarker;" nor as an intermediary or interpreter to give meaning and significance. No! This magnificent, fantastic land speaks very eloquently for itself!

It was late afternoon by the time I departed the Park. And it was another 100 miles or so to Flagstaff where I had booked "Super 8" accommodation. Stopping for gas at Holbrook, I also took on a cool, chocolate shake myself.

It turned out to be enough fuel for the drive. And the car was having to work far harder than me. It was another 2000 foot ascent (to nearly 7000 feet) up onto the now very High Plains. With Flagstaff still 15 miles distant, a haze started to build. I stopped at a gas station to get a cold Sprite. The haze was heavy. I took a breath. The haze was smoke! But still there was that wonderful, refreshing, sweet piney scent that had filled the morning air at Albuquerque.

When finally I pulled into the Flagstaff "Super 8," the sun was a heavy, throbbing, hot orange in the west. Two yellow, Arizona Forest Service fire-trucks were in the lot. Several grimy fire-fighters were checking their gear. I asked one where exactly the fire was. About 50 miles straight north, I was told. And was it now under control? "Nope. 12,000 acres gone and still spreading!"

After settling in, turning on the air conditioner, and making a few phone calls, I set out in search of a meal. It was by now 9 pm. I checked the main street and business section. Nothing doing. Even in the mini-fast-food strip everything was shut up tight. My stomach growled. And with good reason. It had not been fed anything approaching a square-ish meal for two days. Back at the motel I had to satisfy myself with a coffee. In the morning, I was informed, muffins and doughnuts would be available. I was planning an early start.

As night settled in, and I hovered on the brink of sleep, it was not thoughts of petrified trees, of dinosaurs and other Triassic creatures which intruded. No; it was the regular passage—one every 15 minutes—of enormously lengthy transcontinental freight trains. The Santa Fe line was about 50 yards from my window. I quickly got used to the plaintive bray of their horns.

# 47

## *Sedona Surprise*

*Prescott, Arizona*—Seven a.m., and as I step outside still there is that wonderful sweet, piney scent. I look up. Blue sky, slight smoky haze. Another fine day. And it's *cool!* The Chevy shows an external temperature of 65 degrees on its clever gauge. Bit of a drop from yesterday's 110!

Having consumed two fresh, blue-berry muffins, two cups of coffee, and tucked away two big maple doughnuts for future reference, I have packed up, paid up, and am on the South-west "scenic route" (Highway 89A) to Prescott. I am expecting an interesting drive—I've heard and read a little about the beauty of this Sedona Valley route. I quickly discover I am in for much more than I bargained for!

There is first, a gentle entry into high, bright pine forest. Behind in the distance, sharp in the morning light, is the ripple of mountain snow-caps. Then gradually, with intermittent sharp drops, the road descends. I pull off into a large road-side parking area. At the far end is a Viewing Point. I take a look. A great canyon opens up. I pull back. My stomach heaves. A sheer drop of perhaps 2500 feet, and a mile across to the equally plummeting wall on the far side. A stunning sight, its power enhanced by the sharp-slanting sun and shadow of this early morning light.

And then I note tables under the trees. People are setting out a variety of craft-works for sale. There is much exquisite jewellery, with lots of silver and turquoise; and much more. These are Navajo creations. And Navajo people from their nearby Reservation are doing the selling. I am fascinated. I quite happily could purchase the lot. But restraint is needed. It is the end of my tour. Money is running short.

And it is here that I meet Ray Joe and his sand-paintings. Superb, formalised, precise use of various bright colours. There is one of a Navajo Shaman (native priest) on his horse; both ceremonially garbed; both surrounded by beautifully etched symbols. All of these symbols, the intricate inter-relationships of one with the others, he explains. Marvellous. Navajo sacred land, he adds, is close. But the people now keep it to themselves. He goes on to explain, very simply, very clearly, very beautifully, the Navajo Creation, or Emergence belief. Enchanting. A beautiful man, gracious, dignified, not without humour; a man fully in touch with himself and at ease in his world.

I reflect. In essence, Ray Joe is the American I'm looking for; the White American I pray may one day emerge. As for the sand-painting; I want it, badly. But it is expensive. And it is fragile. Would it survive the air journey home? Too great a risk, I manage to persuade myself. I settle for a beautiful turquoise and silver butterfly pin.

After escaping this wondrous "treasure trap," and back in the car, the road now winds and twists sharply down, down, alarmingly down another 3000 feet to the cool, dappled forest shade of the canyon floor. This is the Sedona Valley. It is amazing. From High Plains and scorching heat up there, to this deep, cool green valley down here; a valley reminiscent of that wonderful green corridor of the Nantahala way back in Cherokee country of Western North Carolina.

And just like those clear bright streams in Cherokee country, here in a broad limestone cut below is an equally attractive river. I stop and speak with a Ranger who's pulled into this lay-by. The river, I learn, is Oak Creek. And the rings we see spreading in the crystal clear pool below are, I am informed, feeding trout. My amazement is complete! *Trout* in these *desert* canyons! As we are talking, an angler with lethal spinning gear appears and proceeds to trawl the pool. Back in the car and further down, another fisher with fly-tackle prepares to enter the river in his chest waders.

The road narrows; it winds and turns through this wondrously cool corridor of light and shadow. I get cabin particulars from one or two holiday-home sites. Definitely this valley is the place to stay should any future visit to this area be contemplated. Sites of pre-historic and archaeological interest are close by. And though, like Grand Canyon, the Painted Desert, the Petrified Forest, Canyon de Chelly and many more, they are all up on the scorching high ground; a cabin here in Sedona Valley would make for a comfortable base and cool retreat. I am most impressed.

Finally I come to the City of Sedona. Only 16,000 population, but clearly a well-heeled population it is. Many beautiful homes and fine shops. Nearly all buildings, commercial or residential are constructed with an eye to Indian adobe and Spanish motifs and architectural features; even the motels! Again I am impressed.

The road out of Sedona, still narrow, starts to twist and turn its way up. The heat jumps up, and the valley hardwoods, then pines, give way to desert scrub and wilting heat. And then suddenly, straight ahead, is the formidable presence of Cathedral Rock. Deeply scored and sharply stratified in bright hues of ochre and sandy gray, it looms ominously. I am vividly reminded of my Petrified Forest experience. What harrowing tales of Triassic cataclysm do *these* "story-book" strata contain? What secrets *here* have been revealed; may yet be uncovered? I wonder.

Moving on through an arid, scorched, rolling landscape, the road starts again to climb. I look ahead. In the heat haze is a distant high escarpment, up perhaps another 3500 feet. I check my map. Do I *have* to clear this mini-mountain? Is there not a route round? I look again. I spot the flash of tiny moving specks—cars, I realise—progressing with slow determination up the mountain-side. The map shows no escape . Up and over I too must go. The Chevy negotiates the switchbacks which scale the face of this precipice, it bears the heat and engine strain without complaint.

Nearing the top, another switchback, and suddenly I am into the town of Jerome. Astonishing place. Again, heavy Spanish influence evident in the houses, the buildings, all seemingly glued to the mountainside and holding on for dear life. An old mining community, it was once a very lively place, I learn. Now it is still lively. But it is artists, painters, retirees who provide the life. This I discover from an elderly man—a retired dentist from Minnesota—who is taking in the view from the look-out where I have stopped.

"Indians liked this spot. Plenty of remains been found round here," he declares. "Could have had something to do with the view." Indeed, it could. It is an awesome view. Even with the heavy haze it is possible to keep a very sharp eye on movement up to 50 miles to the East, North and South. Very valuable intelligence, whether it be of approaching tribal opponents of old, or adventuring Spaniards in their glinting armour. Those *Conquistadores*. How ever did they manage to travel such distances, in such fierce conditions, and wearing such gear? Remarkable.

Having topped the mountain ridge, at some 7000 feet, it is now a test of the Chevy's brakes and steering as it negotiates several 1000 feet of twists, turns, switchbacks in a series of sudden drops and more gradual descents. Again its performance is excellent. Down onto rolling landscape and then the flat, it is still a drive of some distance before the City of Prescott emerges from the shimmer of the now mid-day heat. I have booked at Super 8. The motel is just off the main drag. I find it without difficulty.

Booked in and refreshed by coffee and my stashed doughnuts, I check a local map. Don Gardner, a medical friend from long-ago Boston University days—I had worked there for two packed, wonderful years in the 1970s—lives and practices in Prescott. I had given him advance warning of my imminent arrival. I duly find his house, though not without difficulty. There behind bushes and scrub, on the crest of a hill, it is.

Low-lying, squat, a functional stone and stripped-pine log structure, it gives the impression of being built-in to this hill.

In fact, it is the highest property in the area—which, as I observe to Don, is entirely appropriate. Shamen and Medicine Men of earlier days, to say nothing of the Whiteman's Catholic priests, nearly always lived on the high ground. It all provided more direct communication with important healing and guiding spirits above. Quite fitting therefore that this should be the residence of the leading local modern Medicine Man. Don eyes me doubtfully.

Don and his wife Rosita, a person of Arizona origin and a fellow medic, have created here a terraced garden. They also have built a spacious pergola that affords fine distant views and catches whatever cooling breeze there may be to ease this relentless heat. Shale and gravel has been used in place of grass. Succulents and high mesa shrubs, trees and plants are all doing well. Looking round I can see that all is in keeping with this environment. Nicely done. No heavy or artificial imposition. Don and Rosita have given the land space to breathe, to be itself. Not a customary attribute of the American Whiteman.

After a cold drink and a sandwich, and touching briefly on some of the highlights of the 30 years that have rocketed past since last we met, we say our farewells, and I head back to the motel. There is much packing to be done, several phone calls to be made. I confirm my British Airways reservation. It is difficult to believe that by this time tomorrow night I shall be departing Phoenix International for the UK and home. It will not be easy.

# 48

## *Sun City Finale*

*Prescott, Arizona*—It was cool in the early hours. And still there was that wonderful piney scent. I managed my last breakfast, a no-nonsense affair, in the restaurant next door. The dining room was surprisingly full; most diners on the elderly side.

Lest I had forgotten, this was a sharp reminder. Arizona with its year-round sun and dry, hot climate is much-favoured by elderly White folk. But were they happy? Did life here amongst these magical forces and phantoms of these wondrous High Plains and Sierra Country bring refreshment, peace and happiness?

If so, it was not readily apparent; at least not amongst these early-rising diners. Conversation, mostly in loud-ringing Bronx accents, focused on health, heart attacks, funerals, and complaints about relatives and retirement home staff.

And this caused me briefly to reflect on my experiences of the past few days. It was little consolation to consider that we, our human species, were only 10,000, perhaps 100,000 years along the 150 million years time-line it had taken the lordly dinosaur to reach fully evolved maturity. We had a long way to go—should we, of course, last that long, which in this modern day of "Star Wars" sabre-rattling looks increasingly less likely.

One of the reasons I had routed this final leg of my tour through Prescott was not just to visit my friend Don. I had read much about Carlos Montezuma, the pioneering turn-of-the-century Indian doctor. Montezuma fought hard to improve not only the lot of his own Yavapai people in this his home area, but that of the Indians of Arizona and America in general. He was particularly critical of the BIA-administered Reservation system. Reservation residents, he argued, had the right to live their own lives in their own way, which included the right *not* to be forced to accept alien customs. While the "body" of Montezuma's ideas, the Society of American Indians, founded in 1911, had but a short life, the spirit of these ideas carried on. Indeed they provided the inspiration and the framework for many Indian progressive bodies that were duly to follow.

I knew the Yavapai Tribal Administration was located here at Prescott. I also knew the Yavapai, like the Absentee Shawnee, had established highly successful gaming and casino operations which funded many local Reservation programs. I was hopeful a visit might give me the chance to learn how the modern Yavapai were getting on.

I made inquiries in shops, diners, motels, at the bus station, finally at City Hall. Amongst those who in fact were aware of the existence of the Yavapai, no one seemed to know where their Administrative Offices were located. About to depart City Hall, the woman at the Information Desk signalled me back. "Not listed under Tourism, Business or Government. But I checked another catch-all category. Got it!" Well pleased with herself, she wrote out the address, and we marked it on the complimentary Prescott map supplied.

Map or no map, the Tribal Offices were still very difficult to find. There was a distinct shortage of signs as I checked one, then many another scrub-forested dirt road—and this right in the center of Prescott. Finally, turning up yet another dusty, rutted track, a sign pointed, and there in what I now recognised as standard single-storey BIA-approved building format, it was. But no plush Potawotami "clubhouse and grounds" layout this! I pulled in. There were many cars in the pot-holed parking lot.

Inside everything was light and bright. A young man at the front desk asked if he could help. I explained my interest, and that I would greatly appreciate a brief chat with a Tribal Officer on current Yavapai developments. He said he would check and disappeared. In a few minutes he returned. No, he was sorry, there was no one available to speak to me. A bit taken aback—I could see several people casually chatting in the offices behind—I repeated that I wanted only a brief word. The young man, whose name was Larry, shrugged. "You could try the end of the week. Maybe Friday. Everybody is usually back in the office. Someone might see you then." I told Larry I was departing Phoenix this evening. "Sorry," he said. "Best I can do." I found my way out much more easily.

I checked my watch. For once I was ahead of time. I was not due at Phoenix International till 7 pm. Hence I would be able to take my time covering this final 120-mile lap. And this is what I did. Taking the scenic "Southern Loop"—a sort of dog's leg instead of the straight, fast Inter State 17—proved another astonishing drive.

Having first passed through Prescott National Forest, then an expanse of high, very hot rangeland; then up over the rugged Weaver Mountain heights; then down through a tight, winding corridor with numerous vicious switch-backs, the car at last moved on to the lower, very arid "brown country", plain.

I stopped at a number of points. I put down my sensors. All that came back was silence and the throb of the heat. By midafternoon it had reached 112 degrees. Viewing Points, particularly in the Weaver Mountain heights, provided stunning panoramas of the heat-hazed plains below. And down on the plains themselves big "organ pipe" Cacti and palms started to appear. I was feeling the heat; a light breeze only enhanced its breath-catching furnace intensity. This was a challenging environment. The Yavapai, the Apache, residents from pre-historic times did well in developing the skills, the capacities to live on this land.

Just before reaching Phoenix I passed through Sun City, renowned as America's premier retirement address and playground of the elderly. I doubled back. It was, I reckoned, worth a look. In fact, in the dead heat of late afternoon I found it an eery place; like a massive, tight-packed, up-market housing estate. Up the little avenues, the cul-de-sacs, were substantial, more or less uniform Spanish-style adobe and brick-built bungalows, many with triple garages, all with tiny front gardens, and all barren of any tree or shade-giving cover.

There was no sign of life. All was very still, very silent. I was glad to thread my way back out from this residential maze and onto the main road.

In a way, this was a fitting finale for my tour of the *Phantom Trail*. Ancient man, indeed historic Indian man with family, clan and tribe, had learned to create and maintain an harmonious relationship with this hard, this powerful land. These early residents grew with this land; they gave, took, shared and flexed with this land. It was in this way that early man gradually gained his self-respect, his confidence, his sense of place within this his personal world, a world that was for *him* the font and universe of *all* people. The Yavapai, the Apache, were indeed "Chosen Peoples."

And now here in Sun City is the Whiteman, the elderly Whiteman, indeed the Whiteman at the very pinnacle of American material achievement. He lives as the Whiteman does; in brick boxes; each resting heavily on the land; each firmly fenced from the next; all uniform, all silent, all isolate. And it is this tense, this imminent lonely end, that all this material achievement, all this money—the American Whiteman's crowning measure of success—has bought for him. Despite the great heat, these were cold thoughts; thoughts about an alien people whose divorce from all that surrounds them here—indeed from all the magnificent lands of this beautiful, once-bounteous continent—could hardly have been more tellingly expressed.

By 6:30 I was in Phoenix and had returned my trusty Monte Carlo. It might not look like much, but what an excellent car it was. Not a hint of any difficulty throughout my near-cross-continent drive. Nor did it tire me. Driving was, mostly, a pleasure. It all served to confirm the benefits of spending that little bit more for a Full-Size rental car of this quality.

At Phoenix International I was checked through by 7:30. Outside the temperature was still 105 degrees. Inside, I had an hour to relax and watch the setting South-west sun, hot-orange, pink, indigo, ease down on the still-shimmering horizon. Nearly the last person to board, I was hardly in my seat than the huge engines revved, the plane lumbered down the runway gradually gaining speed, then with a final thrusting surge it was lift-off.

As the plane banked and swung round from the indigos of the west to the velvet blue of the east, it hit me that I was actually leaving, being parted from these many wondrous, magical lands; from these many spirits that had become so much a part of me.

I had set out on this tour with the aim of *stilling*, perhaps *exorcising* restive spirits; spirits raised, spirits stirred and agitated by the intense mental and emotional strain generated by the researching and writing of *Phantom Ship*. It was quite clear to me however that this had *not* been the result. Rather my tour had served simply to *confirm, broaden and strengthen* their presence. I could only hope these spirits would find comfort and solace within; that my being and theirs would find common ground; that we might share a common core.

I looked out the window at the darkening velvet, the engines whispering into the night. I had left the American land. But the Phantoms of the Trail were travelling with me. Perhaps they always would.

978-0-595-34931-9
0-595-34931-5

Printed in the United Kingdom
by Lightning Source UK Ltd.
120607UK00001B/4-27